CW00735521

Leslie Mallam

Frogs in the Well

Leslie Mallam

and

Diana Day

Sheila,

You have been such a steadfast and loving friend, over so many years. Thank you, and with love

David

15 July 2011

Librario

Published by

Librario Publishing Ltd.

ISBN: 978-1-906775-23-0

Copies can be ordered via the Internet
www.librario.com

or from:

Brough House, Milton Brodie, Kinloss
Moray IV36 2UA
Tel/Fax No 00 44 (0)1343 850 178

Printed and bound in the UK

Typeset by 3btype.com

© Leslie Mallam and Diana Day 2010

The Author has asserted her moral right to be identified as the author of this
work. This book or any part of it may not be reproduced without permission
from the author

Contents

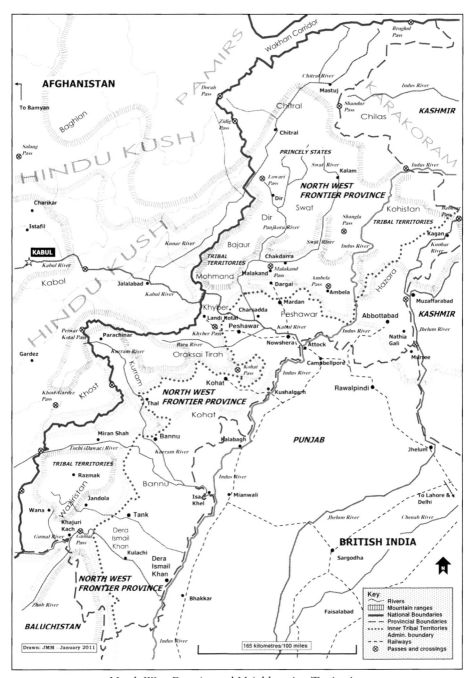

North West Frontier and Neighbouring Territories.

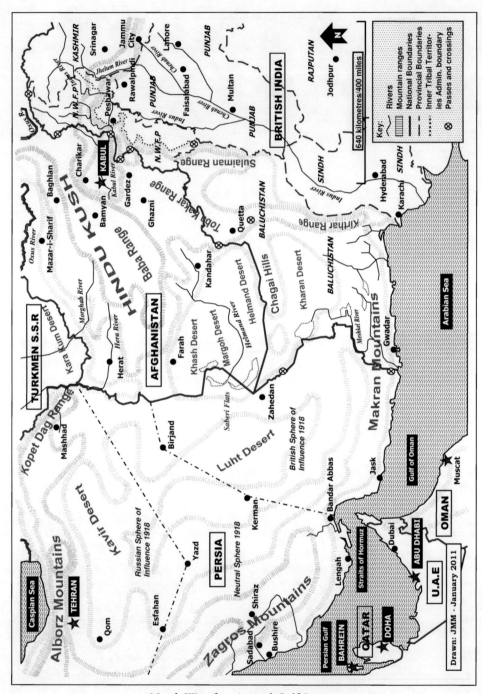

North West frontier and Gulf States.

Foreword by Dr Humayun Kahn

Col. Mallam's memoir appears at an appropriate time, because the saga it narrates deals mainly with the tribal areas of the North West Frontier of Pakistan, a subject which occupies a high priority on the international agenda today. This barren and desolate land has, throughout history, attracted special attention, because of its geo-strategic location. It has lain in the path of conquerors from Alexander the Great to the Turks, the Mongols, the Persians and the Great Moghuls. In the 19th Century, it was at the heart of the Great Game between the British and Czarist empires. In all these major events, the importance of the tribes rested more on what one might call their 'transit value'. They could hold up or facilitate the march of invading armies seeking the riches of India. They were small players in the broad sweep of history.

Today, the situation is different. These tribal areas have become the haven and the source of international terrorism. They are the focus of the entire world and their administration has become the chief concern of the country in which they are located, Pakistan. Reputedly, the headquarters of Al Qaeda are located here and Osama bin Laden is said to be hiding in the rugged mountains. Additionally, they provide the base for the Afghan Taliban fighting the US and NATO forces in Afghanistan and for the Tehrik-e-Taliban-e-Pakistan, which has let loose a fearsome wave of terrorism in Pakistan itself over the past five years or so. The tribes are now the main actors in the worldwide phenomenon of violence and the killing of innocent people, which we call terrorism.

How all this has come to pass is the subject of much ongoing research, but Col. Mallam does bring our attention to one obvious cause, which is that, over the past hundred years, no government, be it the British-Indian before 1947 or that of Pakistan ever since, has had the foresight to integrate these tribes into the framework of a nation state governed by rules and regulations. The British preferred to leave these tribal areas as a sort of 'prickly hedge' to reinforce the client buffer State of Afghanistan against potential threats to their Indian empire. Successive governments in Pakistan failed to foresee the dangers of allowing, within its borders, an area of 2,700 square kilometres inhabited by three and a half million people, to remain outside the pale of its laws and not fully within its administrative control. Little did they realise that, some day, the rest of the world would reject the argument that a part of the territory of a State was outside its authority.

Col. Mallam's memoir tells us how he tried, as a political officer on the

Frontier, to convince his superiors of the need to think ahead, and to start the process of integration through bringing a greater measure of exactitude and continuity to the system of tribal administration, and by initiating a programme of economic development which would bring to the area the benefits enjoyed by the people of the settled districts. He obviously belonged to a different breed of mandarins from those who extended British influence across the Indus to the foothills of the Tatar and Suleiman mountains. The 'Founders' like Edwardes, Nicholson, Mackeson and Warburton were firm believers in the rule of thumb style of governance which relied on the personal qualities of the political officer. Their sole objective was to prevent tribal depredations into the settled district and to win the loyalty of influential tribal Maliks. The successors of these great pioneers on the Frontier like Roos-Keppel, Cunningham and Caroe, were determined to carry on this tradition and not to take on the extra burden of reform. Mallam cut no ice with them and his ideas were rejected. His efforts were cut short by the decision of the British to leave India in 1947. Had they stayed, Mallam would probably have reached much higher rank and been able to press his case more effectively. He offered to stay on and help the new government of Pakistan in developing the tribal areas, but his good friend, Cunningham, who had returned as Governor at Jinnah's special request, said 'no thanks'.

Unfortunately, the successor government of Pakistan soon got bogged down in inertia on this score. It began well, with Jinnah withdrawing all troops from the area and the tribal elders willingly agreeing to cooperate with their fellow Muslims. However, while the new State was still finding its feet, Pakistan's national politics came face to face with its prime dilemma how to find a working relationship between East and West Pakistan. One outcome of this was to integrate all the provinces of West Pakistan into one unit and then observe parity between the two wings. West Pakistan now had one Governor and he was the agent of the President entrusted with the governance of the tribal areas. He sat in distant Lahore and the Secretaries of the provincial government who, in Peshawar, were his main support, now paid little attention to tribal affairs. To some extent, the damage was controlled by delegating more powers to Divisional Commissioners who were closer to the scene.

The crucial period when positive reforms might have been launched was between 1947 and 1967 when Pakistan enjoyed internal stability and laudable economic progress. It also had a competent civil service from which officers were specially selected for the Frontier cadre, rather like the Viceroy personally selecting entrants for the old Indian Political Service. This was the time that Mallam's ideas on reform, which had been approved by the Government of

India in early 1947, could have been operationalised. Sadly, this was not done. As Political Agent in North Waziristan and Malakand during those years, not once was I directed to promote his ideas. In fact, his five-year development plan was not even made available to field officers. There was a general directive that efforts should be made to lift these areas economically and to accelerate the process of their integration into the rest of Pakistan. A good deal of economic development did take place with roads, bridges, dams, schools, colleges and hospitals being built in the tribal areas. This was probably in excess of what Mallam had visualised, but no parallel reforms were introduced on the political or administrative front. We, the new Frontiersmen, though locals, saw ourselves as successors to the great mandarins who controlled the tribes by personal charisma.

After 1967, a general deterioration in Pakistan's internal politics and its governance was becoming evident. The loss of half the country was a direct consequence of this. Z.A. Bhutto came into power in West Pakistan after refusing to accept the results of a fair and free election which had been won by a Party from East Pakistan. He is credited with having stabilised the truncated Pakistan and given it six years of civilian rule. In fact, he destroyed many national institutions, wrecked the economy and encouraged lawlessness and disorder. One key institution he wrecked was the civil service. He introduced the concept that loyalty to the regime was the most important requirement in a civil servant, more important than competence and integrity. He inducted into service a number of Party underlings and encouraged career bureaucrats to serve his political ends. This period virtually spelt the end of a specialised Frontier cadre and led to a steady deterioration of tribal, and indeed, all other aspects of administration. He also encouraged young tribesmen to defy their traditional customs and practices and to drum up support for his Party in the tribal agencies. Political Agents connived in all kinds of malpractice and tribals fell for the many temptations offered to them. The chances of a coherent and consistent order which Mallam had advocated vanished.

The Soviet invasion of Afghanistan was the next great watershed in the history of the tribal areas. Many joined the Jihad and hundreds of mujahideen were brought from all corners of the Muslim world to fight alongside them. After the Soviet withdrawal in 1989, a large number remained, married local women and settled among the tribes. They were patronised by the Pakistan intelligence agencies and utilised to continue armed activities in Kashmir. Fired by religious zeal, these elements joined with tribal extremists to support the Taliban movement in Afghanistan. Osama bin Laden was among the Arab

Mujahideen who continued to operate in the region. After the tragic events of 11th September 2001, Pakistan cast its lot with the United States in the so-called war on terror and, after more than fifty years, the Pakistan army marched into the tribal areas as part of this war. This was the death-knell, so to speak, of the system of tribal administration, weakened as it already was, that had been so effectively run by men like Col. Mallam. The role of the Political Agent was marginalised as the army took over. In Peshawar, the Governor's authority was overshadowed by that of the Corps Commander and the tribesman quickly sensed that currying favour with the political administration no longer paid off.

The army was ill-equipped to deal with the problem and it soon had to resort to its traditional method of armed action, albeit at the request of the civilian government, following the uprising in Swat and later, in Waziristan. This action was a success in military terms, in the sense that the insurgents were dispersed and the army occupied the areas they abandoned. But it was not successful in lessening the hold of the militants on young tribesmen and the strength of the Taliban forces operating in Afghanistan from bases in Pakistan's tribal belt continued to grow. Worse still, a new phenomenon arose in the shape of the Tehrik-e-Taliban-Pakistan, which launched a massive wave of terrorism inside Pakistan. This is the situation as it prevails today. Mallam was critical of the emphasis on military action in Waziristan during the last twenty years of British rule. He would have been mortified to see the entire tribal belt, from Bajaur in the north to Waziristan in the south, as a theatre of military operations. This last happened in 1897, but then battles were fought on horses with pistols and swords. Today, the tribesmen have to face helicopter gunships, heavy artillery and F-16 fighter bombers.

Given the present conditions, it is perhaps untimely to think of enlightened reforms like Mallam did. The immediate task is to control the insurgency and, in any case, the Pakistan government is hardly a free agent. The United States and NATO are facing serious difficulties in pacifying Afghanistan and they are pressing Pakistan to expand its armed action against pro-Taliban elements. In addition, the Americans are carrying out drone attacks on Pakistan's tribal areas virtually on a daily basis. The Afghan problem and the problem of the tribes, always interlinked, are now one and the same thing. One thing is sure. Pure military force will not solve either of them. It is also clear that the international community, particularly the US, will not continue to accept Pakistan's argument that the tribal areas are not and never have been, under full government control. So it is imperative to start thinking about a permanent future for these areas, just as Mallam advocated sixty years ago.

This is not an easy task. Administration of these areas has been deteriorating for nearly four decades. No meaningful steps have been taken to bring the tribes into the mainstream of national life. Piecemeal efforts to win them over have created more problems than they have solved. The tribesmen have been given benefits without corresponding obligations. Some of them have reached high offices like Governors, Generals, Cabinet Ministers and Secretaries to Government but they have abandoned their tribal responsibilities. They virtually control the road transport business in Pakistan and have acquired vast urban properties, yet they pay no taxes. They have moved in large numbers to Karachi and abroad to the Gulf countries, yet they never invest their savings in Pakistan. They sit in the National Legislature and enact laws affecting the citizens of Pakistan, but they cannot pass laws applicable to their own area. These are but a few of the anomalies that have to be addressed. If the advice of men like Mallam had been heeded years ago, the situation today might not have been so complicated. At that time, he was right to suggest that the tribes must eventually share the benefits enjoyed by the rest of British India. These included security, justice, economic betterment, education and health care. Today, the tribesman is not entirely sure that he wants to come on a par with the citizens of Pakistan who are the victims of corruption, disorder, poverty and injustice.

Whatever the future may hold, reform has to come. Areas within a country's borders that are outside the law will no longer be tolerated. Pakistan's tribal belt is now seen as the epicentre of the greatest scourge facing the world, which is terrorism. If the Pakistan government does not tackle the problem wisely, others will do it in their own way. As Mallam consistently advised, it would be suicidal to try anything sudden and dramatic, which totally destroys the tribal ethos. The process has to be such as to carry the tribes along. Pakistan has already had a bitter experience in the case of Swat, where it decided overnight to replace the benevolent and highly efficient rule of the Wali with the traditional district administration. Swat started going downhill from that very day in March, 1969, when I personally had the distasteful task of taking over the State from Miangul Jahanzeb. Thirty years later, it finally erupted and triggered off the unrest which now grips the entire tribal region.

I am sure the reader will find Col. Mallam's memoir both informative and entertaining. Like a true Frontiersman, he writes with both wisdom and affection for a region and a people he came to love. I can still remember, as a young boy, seeing 'Mallam Sahib' walking along the Mall in Peshawar in the days when that city was renowned for its gardens, when neat hedges were the only protection the residents needed, and the streets were lined with giant laburnums, jacaranda and shisham. He seemed a mild and caring sort of person. Today, it stands ravaged by the turmoil in the neighbouring tribal belt and in Afghanistan. Later, I was to serve in many of the posts he held, in Tank, Bannu, Waziristan, Malakand. He was not remembered in the same way as the great mandarins, but had some of his dreams reached fruition, he would have ranked among the best of them.

Humayun Khan
Peshawar, 2010

Dr Humayun Khan
Foreign Secretary of Pakistan 1988–1989
Pakistan High Commissioner to the United Kingdom 1990–1992

Dr. Humayun Khan hails from Mardan District, North-West Frontier Province of Pakistan. He is the son of the late K.B. Mohd. Safdar Khan of Amazo Garhi, former Distt. & Sessions Judge, Peshawar and Begum Mumtaz Safdar, former Member of the West Pakistan Assembly. He is married to the grand daughter of the late Qazi Ataullah, former Minister in the Cabinets of Dr. Khan Sahib before partition. One of her aunts was married to Abdul Ali Khan, youngest son of Bacha Khan. Dr Humayun Khan was educated at the prestigious Bishop Cotton School in Simla, India and later at Edwardes College Peshawar and at Trinity College, Cambridge. He holds an honours degree and an MA from Cambridge University. He was called to the Bar from Lincoln's Inn, London in 1954. Later, he earned another MA and a Doctorate from the University of Southern California, Los Angeles. He joined the then Civil Service of Pakistan (CSP) in 1955 and served as Assistant Commissioner, Tank; Assistant Commissioner, Nowshera; Deputy Commissioner, Bannu; Political Agent, North Waziristan and Political Agent, Malakand.

He was Home Secretary, NWFP in the NAP-JUI Government in 1972–73, after which he moved to the Pakistan Foreign Service. He served in the country's missions in Moscow and the UNO at Geneva before he was appointed Ambassador to Bangladesh in 1979. In 1984 he became Ambassador to India and served there for four and a half years. He returned as Foreign Secretary of Pakistan in 1988 and held the post till 1989, when Benazir Bhuto made him an OSD. On the dismissal of her first Government in 1990, he was appointed High Commissioner in London. He retired from government service in 1992 but was immediately selected as Head of the Commonwealth Foundation, an inter-governmental international organisation with its headquarters in London. He held this position from 1993 to 2000, when he returned to Peshawar. He has since served on the National Finance Commission and on the Board of the National Rural Support Programme. He also works with the Pakistan Centre for Philanthropy and on a number of committees dealing with relations between the countries of South Asia. He has written extensively on Indo-Pak relations and is co-author of DIPLOMATIC DIVIDE published in India.

(Courtesy Wikipedia)

This book would never have been written in its present form, without the patient, unfailing help of my co-author, Mrs Diana Day, over many years she was inspiring, wise and constructive in her criticism. I owe her an immeasurable debt of gratitude.

I am also deeply indebted to Miss Daphne Ross Slater, who did all the initial typing. Finally I cannot fail to mention with gratitude my daughter Anne, who with remarkable energy and common sense has, together with her mother, taken an active interest in this book from start to finish.

Lieutenant Colonel The Reverend George Leslie Mallam Bar-at-Law CSI CIE
October 1978

Panorama View of Kabul in 1932. The middle ground on the left with Tents and Stands, beyond the lake, shows the Parade Ground where the King's Birthday Parade and sports were held.

Introduction by Victoria Schofield

In pre-independence India, the role of the Indian Political Officer was of paramount importance in determining Britain's ability to administer vast areas of the subcontinent with a relative handful of Europeans. Whereas the Indian Civil Service (ICS) officers were responsible for the administration of the eleven provinces of British India, the officers in the Indian Political Service (IPS) initially known as the Indian Foreign & Political Service) had a more difficult job running the administration of what were regarded as more testing 'frontier districts', aided, when necessary, by the British Army in India. They also served as representatives in the Gulf and agents of the Governor-General at the courts of the maharajahs and nawabs, rulers of the estimated 565 Princely States, whose lands covered two-fifths of India.

By far the most challenging region for a political officer was the North-West Frontier Province [now Khyber-Pakhtunkhwa] of British India. Demarcated by the Viceroy Lord Curzon in 1901 as a separate administrative area from the province of the Punjab, it was inhabited by a number of tribes, known as Pathans, according to the Indianised version of their name. In the north they spoke with a harder guttural accent and called themselves Pakhtuns; in the south they were known as Pashtuns. Sub-divided into at least twenty major and a few hundred minor tribes or khels, they clung to the tenets of a time-honoured code of behaviour – *Pashtunwali*. Whereas the British might consider many of the tenets of *Pashtunwali* as admirable – such as offering hospitality – *melmastia* – to the visitor, or the tradition of holding a *jirga* or tribal assembly to adjudicate disputes, they could not condone the importance of maintaining one's honour – *izzat* – when it invoked the need for revenge – *badal* – causing blood feuds which continued for generations. But, as British political officers found to their cost, any idea of altering the tenets of *Pashtunwali* was fiercely resisted, as was any attempt by missionaries to spread the Christian faith.

The difficulties of the IPS officer's work in the Frontier were compounded by the fact that an administrative division had also been made between what was known as 'tribal territory' (today known as Federally Administered Tribal Areas or FATA) and the settled districts, where law and order was more easily maintained. In the settled districts, the political officers, who had to be well versed in both 'Higher Arabic' and Pashtu, would be responsible for administering justice and collecting taxes, which required a thorough knowledge of law and land revenue. Like their counterparts in the ICS, their duties would often be performed on tour, with meetings generally held in the open air under a tree. Lacking any of the systems of modern communication we take for granted in the present day, a political officer might be forty or fifty miles away from the nearest British officer and therefore had to be totally self-reliant.

Since tribal territory was inhabited by a number of different major tribes, who could also be at war with each other, the British had divided this mountainous and inhospitable region, extending for approximately 1,610 miles (2,640 km) south to Baluchistan into several 'agencies'. By the early 20th century, after much trial and error, what interested the British Government in India most was keeping the area peaceful and the roads to neighbouring Afghanistan open, especially the well-travelled route through the Khyber Pass, rather than attempting to impose any administrative system on the tribes living in these borderlands. For the privilege of travelling along the roads, they were prepared to pay the tribes subsidies, but otherwise left them to govern themselves. Even so, troubles invariably arose, especially in North and South Waziristan, inhabited by the warring Mahsuds and Wazirs, whose lands bordered Balochistan and Afghanistan. Renowned for their fierce resistance to the presence of the foreigner, the *feringhee*, who – in Britain's case was also the *kafir* – the unbeliever – they also lived in constant enmity with each other.

In the late 19th and early 20th century, a few men had gained fame for their contribution to the administration of the Frontier. Their names have been recorded for posterity: Sir Herbert Edwardes after whom Edwardes College in Peshawar is named; James Abbott who gave his name to the town of Abbottabad, John Nicholson, or 'Nikolseyn' as he was affectionately known, whose monument stands on the road to Peshawar; Sir Harold Deane, after whom Deane's Hotel in Peshawar is named; the three Lawrence brothers, Sir Henry, Sir George and Lord John; Sir Evelyn Howell, author of 'Mizh', a timeless report on the Mahsud tribe; Sir Olaf Caroe, author of the highly authoritative book, *The Pathans*, and Sir George Cunningham, both Governors of the North-West Frontier Province. Among the less well known was Lieutenant Colonel Leslie Mallam.

When, aged twenty-two, Mallam arrived on the Frontier as a young subaltern with the Indian Army Cavalry, Britain was still burdened by the devastating consequences of the Great War. But, there was as yet no inkling that in thirty years Britain's authority in South Asia would be withdrawn for ever. 'I don't think we shall lose India in a hundred years,' one political officer had written to his wife in 1910. Once the war was over, what concerned Britain more was the situation in neighbouring Afghanistan, and one of the first events Mallam had to face, when posted to Waziristan in 1919 was the Third Afghan War. Bridling against Britain's long-standing control of Afghanistan's foreign affairs, the King of Afghanistan had joined together nationalist and conservative sentiment, calling on his people to fight a 'holy war' against the infidel British. Defeated by Britain's superior weaponry, the war was over in a matter of weeks but it was a sign of a new spirit of 'self-determination', which was also affecting India.

At this stage, Mallam decided to leave the Army in order to join the Indian Political Service, serving as Assistant Commissioner in Peshawar and Bannu in the 1920s. Posted to Afghanistan at the beginning of the 1930s and present when King Nadir Shah was assassinated in 1933, he witnessed the 'legacy of hate' which still existed against the British after the disastrous First and Second Afghan Wars. When serving as Political Agent in the Malakand Agency at the outbreak of World War Two, he took a particular interest in tribal customs and began to codify earlier judgments made by the tribal elders in their *jirgas*, in order to give them a rudimentary system of tribal case law. 'The result was startling,' he writes. Frequently branded as 'lawless' by British colonialists, 'the spirit of the tribe revived, with a renewed confidence in their own peculiar law and procedure.'

In a career spanning nearly three decades in the Indian Political Service, Leslie Mallam developed a special interest and love of the North-West Frontier and its inhabitants. He was therefore both a witness to a system of administration, and to the winds of political change, which were sweeping through South Asia. During and after the Second World War, Mallam served first as Chief Secretary of the North-West Frontier Province (NWFP) and then as its Planning and Development Commissioner at a time when the demand for a sovereign state of Pakistan was being hotly – and not always favourably – debated in the North-West Frontier. As Britain prepared to relinquish its authority, with an unparalleled understanding of the tribes, Mallam wrote a 'Frontier Development Plan' which showed how, with a little money and considerable foresight, the untamed region of 'tribal territory' could be developed and incorporated into a more cohesive administrative system in the new dominion of Pakistan. Previously, as he was obliged to concede, none of the 'Great Frontiersmen,' which included both Governors Cunningham and Caroe, had considered it possible to eradicate the border between 'tribal territory' and the settled districts. 'Either they regarded this as impossible without a genocidal war of subjugation or they thought it much simpler and less trouble to leave things as they were.' But Leslie Mallam thought otherwise; and, as Pakistan and the world, struggles to come to terms with the lawless 'safe haven' for terrorist activity which now exists in FATA, his proposals are as relevant today as they were then. *Frogs In The Well* is a unique portrait of Khyber-Pakhtunkwa, providing a personal insight into the life and beliefs of a 20th century British political officer. His memoirs also open a window on what might have been.

Victoria Schofield

Acknowledgements

Acknowledgements are due to:–

A. E. Lynam *The Skipper*, Broadwater Press, Welwyn, Herts, 1940
Arthur Swinson, *North West Frontier*, Hutchinson of London 1967
Flora Davidson, *Wild Frontier*
F. Yeats-Brown, *Bengal Lancer*, Camelot Press Ltd
Major General J. G. Elliott, *The Frontier*, 1839–1847
A Short History of the Royal Air Force, June 1920
Margaret Sinker, *Friend of the Frontier*, The Highway Press
Sir Winston Churchill, *Malakand Field Force*, 1897
Sir Olaf Caroe KCSI KCIE, *The Pathans*, MacMillan & Co Ltd 1965
H. Moyse-Bartlett, *The Pirates of Trucial Oman*, Macdonald & Co 1966
Sir Evelyn Howell, *MIZH*
Norval Mitchel, *Sir George Cunningham*
Sir Charles Belgrave's *"Personal Column"*
Sir Arnold Wilson, *The Persian Gulf*
Mr E. Mackay, *Report to the British School of Archaeology in Egypt*, 1925
Geoffrey Bibby, *Looking for Dilmun*, 1970
Breasted, *Ancient Times. A History of the Early World*
Ian Stephens, *Horned Moon, Pakistan, etc*
Sir Malcolm Darling, *India War Department, 1945–46*
Charles Allen, *Plain Tales from the Raj,* Andre Deutsch, 1975
Florentia Sale, *Disasters in Afghanistan,* 1841–1842
Fraser-Tytler's, *Afghanistan*
The Dragon School
Mr Gadd, PDX Services
Mrs V. Williams, Academic Typing Service
Mr P. Merry

CHAPTER I

A Young World

Pleasantest corner the world can show,
In a vale which slopes to the English sea;
Where strawberries wild in the woodland grow,
And the cherry-tree branches are bending low,
No such fruit in the South countree.

Verses written in India, Sir Alfred Lyall

My mother used to say that when she was married in December 1891, she was the seventh Mrs Mallam, and the third Mrs George Mallam in Oxford. If you belonged to the clan, you were either a solicitor or a doctor. I can remember three generations of doctors: Old Harry, Ernest and young Pat. Pat was a contemporary of mine and gave to the family its chief claim to fame by stroking the Oxford boat three years in succession. But Old Thomas, my great-grandfather, was, I suppose, the most prominent. He lived at The Shrubbery and became twice Mayor of the City.

I was born in 1895 under the shadow of Phil and Jim, the church of St Philip and St James (G.E. Street's 'new church in St Giles') was dedicated and the foundation stone laid on 8th May 1860 by Samuel Wilberforce, Bishop of Oxford. It was an important work of Gothic revival. The rood beam spanning the chancel arch was erected with a plain cross in 1896 to the memory of the same Thomas Mallam, one of the first churchwardens. There is a coloured window in the south aisle, in cruciform shape, of the Virgin Mary and St John beside the Cross. On it is written:

'In Honorem Dei et in Memoriam
Lydiae Mallam DOB Oct 14th 1869.'

She was the widow of Thomas.

The shadow of Phil and Jim fell long. It did not, however, give exactly a mind-broadening experience. The neighbourhood was select, but infected by the traditional cleavage between 'Town and Gown'. It was possible for a 'Town' family like us to grow up without any social contact with the University. We knew some of the students but not the College authorities. They dominated the City, and yet were alien to it.

My father was a taciturn man. Absorbed in his profession as a solicitor he spent a great deal of his spare time at the County Club in Holywell, or playing tennis and croquet in the Parks. For thirty-nine years running he spent the month of August in Switzerland for his summer holidays. He claimed that every one of his children, of which there were five, with myself as the only boy, had been brought under control by the age of three. My eldest sister voiced complaints against this suppression of personality, and it took me a long time to gain self-confidence. We turned for solace to an old Nurse who invariably wore black, with white collar and cuffs. She had her meals served in the nursery, including beer in a china mug. In the afternoons she took us for sedate pram walks in the Parks. Life would have been dull indeed but for a glorious month every year with Granny Rogers by the sea at Falmouth, where we rode donkeys on the sands, a first introduction to the art of equitation.

As a family we went regularly to church. My father, if he disliked the sermon, would walk out to express his disapproval. Like my great-grandfather before him he was a churchwarden, but, in his dark suit and high collar, he would simply get up silently out of his seat, which was well to the front of the church, and march past the assembled congregation to the door. In those days the churches were pretty full for Matins on a Sunday morning. When a new Vicar was appointed, these walkouts ceased, much to the relief of my mother and us all.

During this time a great deal of property was bought in North Oxford by grandmother Mary (Polly) Mallam who dominated this side of the family, but it was a plan that failed to mature. There was a crash, the property sold at a loss, and the shock killed my grandfather. Consequently, my father, the eldest son, had to pull together our finances out of the ruins. There followed a lean period avoiding bankruptcy. Over the years the firm survived, but the one responsible for the catastrophe retired to Hampstead; her name was seldom mentioned; the bad influence, the maker of tragedy.

Sister Margaret recollects, soon after my grandfather's death, being lined up in the dining room that led off the conservatory at the back of our house and being told to be especially good and quiet because we were going to see our other Granny (to us Granny meant Granny Rogers at Falmouth). "The old lady sat in a high-backed chair in the conservatory very royal and very awe-inspiring, or frightening if you like. She was immensely tall and thin, dressed in black, only relieved by a narrow white neckband, and a white band at each wrist. She had large brown eyes, and iron grey hair parted in the middle. On her head was a lovely ecru lace cap with black velvet ribbons, and her widow's weeds, consisting of a long piece of pleated black crepe that hung down her back from the bottom of the lace cap. She sat bolt upright and had black lace mittens on her hands. We were presented to her one by one. To me she always smelt strongly of stale biscuits whenever I met her, explained years later when Mother told me that it was difficult to get her to wash!"

In the good old days before the crash my sister remembers mother wearing an unusually beautiful gown when chaperoning two girls for either an Eights week or a 'Commem do'. Made of soft pale blue corded silk, it had a full skirt and low-necked tight bodice, trimmed with cream lace round the neck. The sleeves were short and full and she wore the family pearls. These same pearls were sold one by one after the property disaster, to pay for our education.

Throughout that young world the British Empire was taken for granted. I was dimly aware of this before entering the Dragon School at the age of seven. As a very small boy I had pinned to the lapel of my coat circular badges containing photographs of famous Generals in the South African War Redvers Buller, French, George White (the gallant defender of Ladysmith), Roberts, Kitchener and Baden Powell, holder of Mafeking. I was familiar with Boer place names: Magersfontein, Colenso, Kimberley, Spion Kop, Bloemfontein and with the names of Boer Generals, Cronje, de Wet, Botha and President Kruger. In my lifetime this was the first of three world-shaking wars. Barely remembered was England celebrating the Relief of Ladysmith (28th February 1900) and the deliverance of Mafeking on 17th May in the same year.

Up the Banbury Road, when I was five and a half, our family watched troops marching with Lord Roberts at their head. In Broad Street I said goodbye to a group of undergraduate volunteers. One of them, who was known to us, asked me to lift his rifle. I could scarcely get it off the ground. Darkened rooms and hushed voices announced the death of Queen Victoria on 22nd January 1901.

Within the grounds of the Dragon School there was one long hedge dividing the playing fields into two. Inside the green hollows we made forts with chosen friends, using sticks as weapons. Cedric Horton was a friend who was good at carpentry (a fact which still rankles, as I was committed to the Classics), designing ramparts and rifles. Battles were waged, but the atmosphere was pleasant and happy. Years after, my younger son said, when he joined the School, "I've seen a photo of you from way back. Why didn't you tell me you were in the First Cricket Eleven?"

As one who passed through the system, I can testify that it contained no gimmicks, no complicated contrivances, no expensive buildings or equipment, no comfort for the boys. It relied on easy personal contact between masters and boys within a framework of discipline. I was moderately well behaved, but received three of the best from the Headmaster for throwing stones into a puddle in the playground. The masters were men we could admire, they imparted a conventional education, laced with games and a good measure of common sense; they produced amazing results, both academically and in the quality of service rendered to the Empire.

The Empire itself received no conscious promotion in the system. There was no suggestion of jingoism or chauvinism. The records of distinguished Old Boys spoke for themselves and opened up vistas of worldwide service to vast uneducated Asian and African populations, eager for a taste of Western Civilisation at its best. Among my contemporaries were Jackie Smyth (Brigadier the Rt Hon Sir John Smyth VC, MC, PC, and Conservative MP for the Norwood Division of Lambeth 1950–66)[1], Ronnie Poulton of Rugger International fame, Jack Slessor (Marshal of the RAF Sir John Slessor), and J.B.S. Haldane, the Scientist and Communist.

At this stage my health was not good, and after a bad 'go' of measles, I became deaf in my right ear and had to live with only half normal hearing. My sister describes me as miserably thin and weedy, almost stunted. I only shot up when beginning to march for Kitchener's Army.

Even now I am proud to think of myself as an 'Old Dragon', as also were my uncles and my son. Between us we cover well over one hundred years. 'Skipper' Lynam was headmaster for most of my time, and we heard a lot about the voyages of his yacht the *Blue Dragon*.

About 1900, the Skipper and two boys anchored near Oban. They were invited to dinner at the one fine house on the beach. In the house party were two young lads who went to a rival preparatory school in Oxford. They had seen Dragons riding about on bicycles (a licence not permitted to any other

---

[1] The VC was won by Brig. Rt. Hon. Sir John Smyth while with the 15th Ludhiana Sikhs Indian Army, for conspicuous bravery on 18th May 1915. With a bombing party of ten men who voluntarily undertook the duty, he conveyed a supply of 96 bombs to within twenty yards of the enemies' position and over exceptionally dangerous ground after the attempts of two other parties had failed. In taking the bombs to the desired position, with the aid of two of his men (the other eight wounded or killed) he had to swim a stream, being exposed the whole time to howitzer, shrapnel, machine gun and rifle fire. (Birmingham Reference Library)

prep school at that time), and swarming up the Cherwell, unattended by masters, ragging about in punts, four-oared boats or canoes.

"Oh Mr Lynam, I've often wished I was at your school." said one.

"Well indeed," the Skipper beamed, "I wish you had been one of ours. Are you not happy at your school?"

"Oh yes, rather."

"What then made you wish to become one of us?"

"Well sir, you see, your boys are SO licentious."

Professor J.B.S. Haldane mentions in his book review: "My old teacher C.C. Lynam of Oxford was a strong radical. He used a history of England written by H.O. Arnold Forster, a Conservative Cabinet Minister. To impress his pupils with the unsoundness of Conservatism he offered a prize to the boy who could find the most mistakes in the book.".

He once marked a boy's exam paper 115% out of a maximum 100% "because it was so good", and he held strict views on holidays. "Holidays make them pleasant Remember the Commandment 'Honour thy father and thy mother that thy days may be long' I would rather put it that THEIR days may be long!"

Skipper always admitted a few girls to the School, one of whom was Naomi Haldane, later the novelist Mrs Mitcheson, sister to J.B.S. He concluded the Speech Day of 1914 by emphasizing his belief in co-education. "My staff, male and female (by the bye, I have never heard any objections to co-educating!) one and all have my heartiest thanks." His brother 'Hum', was a kind of second head, and they were ably assisted by 'Cheese' (C.G. Vassell) and 'Pug' Wallace, also by one or two lady teachers. Many of the boys (and a sprinkling of girls to sweeten the atmosphere) were the children of Oxford dons, so the scholastic standard was high. To be able to swim was a 'must', and I learned in the Cher which flowed along the far end of the school grounds. I obtained a prize of two and sixpence from Skipper when I first dived off the top board.

One of the masters, Pug Wallace, I was to meet again in France in 1916. I had landed at Marseilles from India, destined for Indian Cavalry in France, and found my way to the IC Base Depot at Rouen, where, after some delay, I was drafted to the 2nd Bengal Lancers. Before joining my regiment at the Front, I went through an intensive officers' training course in the notorious 'Bull Ring' a large circular open space of level white sand surrounded by dense pine forest, used for a last toughening up of raw Kitchener's Army battalions before they were sent into the trenches. No one was allowed to escape this discipline, not even regular Army officers like ourselves. So, unwillingly, a number of British and Indian Cavalry officers, including myself, let ourselves be lined up and shouted at by regular Army NCOs, as if we were recruits on parade for the first time. With us were a few Kitchener's Army officers, who seemed rather amused at the whole business. After we had put up with this treatment for a bit, some of our cavalry officers started being awkward and executed cavalry instead of infantry movements, with the result that the whole squad was thrown into confusion and the NCO in charge began to lose his temper. At this moment an elderly 'Temporary' officer, with two pips on his shoulders, stepped forward and calmly suggested that the regular cavalry officers should be separated from the squad, and sent to another part of the Bull Ring for more advanced training. To my amazement it was Pug. I only had time to shake him by the hand and tell him who I was before his advice was accepted, and we were ordered away. I never saw him again, but I read that he survived to live for some years after the war, and died 'in harness' in 1937. It was typical of the man that he should volunteer, at an advanced age, for active service in France.

Skipper's team worked well together. Between the years 1888 and 1919 he produced annually a Shakespeare play, his particular favourites, in which he played key parts himself, being *The Tempest* and *Macbeth*. As early as the *Macbeth* of 1897 Rosina Fillipi Dowson wrote, "I hope I shall never again miss seeing one of Mr Lynam's representations when given by his boys." I myself participated in *Twelfth Night*, being given the part of Sir Andrew Aguecheek. Because I was small, thin and retiring, it was thought appropriate that I should tackle this bawdy character.

Sir Toby Belch: "What is thy excellence in a galliard knight?"

Sir Andrew: "Faith, I can cut a caper."

Sir Toby: "And I can cut the mutton to't."

Holidays from school were filled with friends. Financially we were still in our lean period, one pearl a year from the family heirloom, so we did little entertaining. Cedric Horton, that fine maker of forts, had a great sense of fun. At home he used to tease the maids. A particular girl was very fond of him, and her voice could be heard crying out frequently:

"Master Cedric, Master Cedric, you mustn't do that," as he engaged in some new devilry. Speaking to my eldest boy's housemaster at Sherborne School years later:

"What can I do with a youngster of fourteen or fifteen in the holidays?" I asked. "There's always huntin', shootin' or fishin'", he replied.

"That's not much good to me because I'm a parson."

"Well then, I think the best thing to do with boys of that age is to bury them," was the answer.

I used to box with Bertie Eales in the basement of his house. Bertie, whose mother was Burmese, had very beautiful sisters, whom I admired immensely from afar. The eldest was quite fair, but with the high cheek bones and genuine 'hour-glass' figure of her mother's race. Unnecessary for her, the tight lacing of fashion. The other girls had blue-black hair, the colour of a blackbird's wing. Nature seemed to give them great variety and interest: all her races are perhaps intended to be mixed in the future.

Winters were spent in skating on the flooded Port Meadow. It was a huge expanse of ice, safe because only a few inches deep. We skated most of the day, buying hot drinks and roasted chestnuts from the Meadow braziers. Each summer there were expeditions to Whiteham to the great strawberry beds. To the best of my knowledge tables were set out in a private garden, and people would flock in as there were sheds or shelters for rainy days. The brilliant red cones, studded with golden pips, were ladled out by pretty girl assistants. Whiteham was on a hillside, just away from the river, quiet and peaceful. Each guest was provided with an empty wine goblet, and the fashionable thing to do, when eating these prize berries, was to squash them all up with the foot of the glass. The cream stood in a separate bowl. They have never tasted nicer than by this method.

On the subject of strawberries some of these succulent fruit probably saved the life of Jackie Smyth. He was a bit of a hero even before he won the VC in France, because he survived an illness at school from which he was reported to be dying. Rather as a condemned man may choose his last meal, he was asked by his mother if there was anything he felt like eating. He replied, 'A Strawberry Ice', and from that moment we were told his condition improved, and we next saw him at school, lying on a spinal stretcher, and receiving congratulations from all the boys and staff.

When watching the University Eights in the warm weather, we were occasionally invited onto a College barge. It seemed very exciting because we were young. As the adults of the party walked the plank onto the barge, the men wearing white flannels, and the ladies long summer dresses with shady hats, there arose in one's mind the awful anticipatory delight of seeing one of these starched gentlemen, or a beautifully dressed lady, tumbled in the muddy water of the river's edge!

One summer term my parents incurred the anger of the school authorities by taking me away to the country for about six months, as my health was not good. We stayed on a farm at Kelmscott, near Lechlade, and had a marvellous time, running wild. As a result of this break from school, however, I only won a Minor Scholarship at Malvern College, and Skipper forcefully expressed his contempt at the 'Minor' part of it.

In the year 1910 Malvern was a 'games or nothing' School, geared to the Army Class, and devoting little time to the Classics which dominated the Dragon School; a situation that is very different now. It soon dawned upon me that I was not cut out for the Army. Still thin and weedy, I was unable to excel at football or cricket. Some of my happiest memories are of old 'Smudgie', nickname for Mr Smith, the Upper Fifth Form master. He had an ingenious way of encouraging his pupils to hold their own against the rest of the school. The name of any boy pre-eminent in Latin or Greek Verse, or prose Composition, was placed on a notice board outside the door of the classroom for all to see, with the words 'Button' Hole' entered against it. The winner received a written order to give to the local florist on a Saturday morning in exchange for a button-hole posy, made up from a single large carnation or rose, surrounded by maidenhair fern, to be worn in Chapel on Sunday. This small privilege was a great boost to our morale. Smudgie was a good teacher, not afraid to show his feelings in front of the class. He used to recite poetry with tears running down his cheeks. But my progress was slow. At the end of 1913 my parents withdrew me from school and arranged for me to work at home with a coach, to prepare for the Entrance Exam to the University. I had not yet sat for this exam, at 18 years old, when on the 4th August 1914 war shook the world. I could no longer concentrate on my studies.

CHAPTER II

Tramp, Tramp, Tramp
1914–16

Let me go, with the Dead March beforehand,
to settle the score of our guilt;
No use looking back on a lost life, or crying
o'er blood that is spilt…

When, after some hesitation, England finally declared war, I wrote a poem which was published in the Falmouth Gazette.

Tramp, tramp, tramp,
Old England prepares for war;
And the world, with an answering echo,
Tramps on to fight from afar.

We fight not the German nation;
Nor desire to take innocent life;
We fight 'gainst the War God of Prussia,
The barbarous thirst for strife.

Up and rush to the battle, ye Nations,
Prove your valour, ye Britons, today
Show the world, when the Cause is a just one,
England never shall stand in the way.

This sounds a lot of bellicose nonsense now; but every war generates its own mentality. At the age of eighteen I felt young, and inexperienced, and could not see myself either as a private in the ranks or leading men into battle. So to give me time to think things over I applied for a post as assistant master at a preparatory school in Eastbourne and was accepted at once, teachers being in very short supply. Soon after journeying to Eastbourne, news arrived of a new Kitchener's Army unit in camp at Seaford, over the top of Beachy Head. It was the 13th Service Battalion, the Manchester Regiment. In an off period from teaching, I took a walk, and stumbled suddenly into the camp. It was situated below the Downs, almost at sea level, and consisted of rows of bell tents pitched on a large field. There was mud everywhere churned up by hundreds of army boots. Finding a way to the Adjutant's Office tent, I went in. "Is there a chance for a temporary Commission?" I asked. The Adjutant sent me post haste to the Colonel, the Colonel to the Brigadier. In ten days I had resigned my job, and picked up a uniform from a tailor, having received a letter from the War Office to say that I was accepted as a temporary Second Lieutenant.

The Regiment was still under canvas. It was early December 1914, cold, wet, and windy, but no one seemed to mind the life was new and exciting. Although I could not boast of the remotest connection with Manchester or the North Country, I was welcomed, made to feel at home, and, as officers were scarce, allotted a platoon at once. The platoon that I kept through a year of intense activity, culminating in Divisional training at Aldershot, was made up from an assortment of cotton spinners and miners mostly from Wigan and Oldham, and a few intellectuals with university degrees. When I took over they had no uniforms and no rifles. Dressed in a variety of civilian coats and caps, and using sticks cut from the hedgerows as firearms not even as well-shaped as our schoolboy efforts they were an untidy looking rabble on parade. But what they lacked in smartness they more than made up for in enthusiasm. Every man was a volunteer, and eager to learn the arts of war. They were in it to win in the shortest possible time.

With mechanical transport almost non-existent, we marched everywhere, and physical fitness was the first objective. On the parade ground, and later in long route marches and skirmishing on the downs near Beachy Head, we steadily built up a high physical standard through all ranks, which proved invaluable later on. When eventually uniforms and rifles made their appearance, we thought nothing of marching 15 miles a day with full pack, rifle and weights in the front pouches to serve for ammunition. In January we moved to Eastbourne and in the following May to Aldershot to complete our training for the trenches. At the end of my first nine months in the Army, I measured myself and to my astonishment found that I had grown five inches. As part of our Divisional training, we were required to dig trenches on the third line of the defence of London, in the vicinity of Maidstone. Here the officers were on several occasions invited to drinks by a wealthy race-horse owner who lived in a magnificent house nearby. The billiard room walls were covered with racing trophies, mostly horseshoes, highly polished, and inscribed with the name of a winning horse. By this time we had perfected our marching technique, including periodical rests by the roadside, during which tired infantrymen, reclining full length on the grass verge, propped up by their packs, would be sustained by regimental comics with coarse songs and quips, until a long stretch of roadside humanity would be convulsed with laughter.

> "Wash me in the water that you washed your dirty daughter,
> And I shall be whiter than the whitewash on the wall."

I kept a notebook containing the name and address of every man in my platoon, often with some confidential note about his home affairs, and I can say I knew everyone personally. We were proud to possess the best marksman in the Regiment an exceptionally pleasant fellow to deal with – but unfortunately an 'old lag' with a criminal record (nothing more serious than petty theft), who could never be relied on to turn up for parades. He was almost taken for granted as a hopeless case, incorrigible and to some extent the joke of the rest. Older than average, he was broad-shouldered and stocky, with a smiling handsome face. No correction ever seemed to have any appreciable effect; he was invariably good tempered in spite of confinement in barracks.

In due course the Colonel published a notice giving names of all officers who would proceed to the front. Mine was among them. I purchased a revolver, and prepared myself for the journey across Channel, and the ultimate test of war. Had I gone then, it is almost certain I should never have returned. In the autumn of 1915, casualties in France were reaching their peak. However Fate, in the form of a Divisional Order (issued only three days before the Regiment left), intervened to remove me from the immediate prospect of active service. It required all subalterns under a certain age I think 21 to leave the Division at once and report to a Base Depot at Lichfield. When I saw the order I was shocked and angry. It meant my platoon would cross the Channel without an officer. The intention was that the Division, consisting entirely of raw Kitchener's Army formations, would be stiffened on arrival in France by an equivalent number of commanders with experience in trench warfare. There was of course some sense in this; but I hated the idea of my platoon going into battle under the aegis of a stranger. Having been in the Regiment longer than most I felt let down. The CO and others were much too busy to listen to such a pipsqueak. The general view was 'There's a war on; you must obey orders.' The only person from whom I received comfort was the Quartermaster, an elderly Captain commissioned from the ranks, who talked to me like a father. "This may be a blessing in disguise," he said. "I'm sure the war is going to last a long time. You'll have plenty of opportunity for active service later." I never saw any of my old comrades again, but I know they suffered fearful casualties in France.

The Depot at Lichfield consisted of three or four hundred officers and about a hundred men. There was little for us to do but attend meals in the Mess. As you went in you passed a huge notice board full of names. If yours was on the list you would be despatched in a day or two to join one of the many regiments which had suffered severe officer losses; we could only regard ourselves as cannon fodder. Finding the situation so distasteful, I determined to take matters into my own hands. Kitchener's army was a gloriously successful means of focusing and harnessing the patriotism of youth in wartime, but it was inevitably an amateur business. Having been rejected as an amateur, I now wanted to face the test as a professional, and the prospect of studying the art of war tactically and strategically was exhilarating.

I decided to sit for the Sandhurst exam and luck was on my side. One of my colleagues, with whom I was friendly, was an army coach in peacetime. He took me in hand, and rubbed up half-forgotten Latin, Greek, Mathematics and History in our spare time.

Another piece of good fortune occurred in that the second in command, a Major Allen, took a particular interest in my case. He was one of the 'Old Contemptibles', and had lost a leg, amputated above the knee, in France. When a man loses a limb, or an eye for that matter, the shock often intensifies a most attractive side to his character. One of my earliest and best friends in India, D.T. Long, who was with me at Wellington Cadet College in the Nilgiri Hills, lost a leg after the war. Posted with his regiment in the Central Provinces, he acquired a motor cycle, and being young and lively, drove headlong about the station. One evening, after a late Guest Night at the Mess, he was speeding to his bungalow when he started to overtake a long line of bullock carts, plodding slowly through the darkness. Although most of the drivers were asleep, the carts kept well to the left of the road leaving plenty of room, except for one near the front of the line. These bullocks had edged to the centre, and worse still, the beam which acts as a brake behind the wheels was thrusting out. DT missed the cart, but the beam sliced his leg clean off. He was thrown into a ditch on the side of the highway cycle and all. If one of the guests returning from the Mess had not seen him and gone to his aid he would have bled to death. Years later I met him in England. Forced to retire from the Army, he was making his way in civil life, as ebullient and lively as ever, giving hope and courage to all around. No one whom I ever met, however, had such a decisive influence on my career as the cheerful Major Allen. He invited me into his office, where he sat at a table, propping up his peg-leg on a box.

"Why do you want to join the Regular Army?" he asked.

I described my experience with the Manchesters.

"Have you ever thought of the Indian Army as your first choice?"

"For years I've wanted to go to India," I answered. "Service in the civil administration has always had a great attraction. It never crossed my mind to apply for the Indian Army operating so far from the main front."

He then told me something of his own history. He had served in the British Army in India and knew many personnel in Indian regiments who were on active service both in Mesopotamia and France. He added: "This is the time for you to think ahead and plan your future, not only during the war but after. You will probably see service in one of the main theatres, and when the war ends if you do not wish to stay in the army, you will find openings in the Civil Administration in India a career to last you a lifetime."

His words were in strange contrast to the prevailing outlook in the depot, where most could see little beyond the next few weeks, the tumult of battle and extinction. I declared my preference for the Indian Army, and a few weeks later in November 1915 sat for the Sandhurst exam. To my surprise, I passed third on the list, and before the end of the year was sent home to Oxford to await a ship to India.

It was March 1916 before I finally left England, and in the meantime was required to pass a medical examination. This caused me some anxiety, because the deafness in my right ear, as the result of measles, had intensified. If this was discovered it might disqualify me. When I stood stark naked before the doctor my heart sank, because he seemed such a thorough sort of chap, not the kind to overlook anything. He was quite satisfied with my general health and started to test my sight and hearing. I wore glasses occasionally for long sight, but this did not worry him. To try out my hearing he placed a tiny wristwatch in the palm of one hand and closed it, then told me to shut my eyes. He moved both hands (one with the watch and one without) round my head and asked me to point to the place where I could hear it tick. When the watch was near my right ear of course it was not audible, but I made a guess or two and hoped that they were not too far out. After a bit his suspicions were apparently aroused. He told me to open my eyes, putting both hands behind his back. Looking at me rather queerly he said: "Close your eyes again." I then felt his fingers brush my right ear very lightly and he said at once, "Where is the watch?"

As I could not hear a thing, I was foxed. Making up my mind in a flash, I replied, "I can't hear it."

To my surprise he laughed and, telling me to open my eyes, showed me both his hands, empty. "I just wanted to find out if you were telling lies," he said. "You'll do."

I joined a party of sixty Indian Army Cadets. We were a bit of a mystery in a war-conscious world. In civilian clothes we crossed the Channel, and got into a French train for Marseilles. In the middle of the night the train stopped a few minutes at Amiens, and I put my head out of the carriage window. There were some British troops on the platform. "Where are you going?" one of them asked.

"India," I replied.

"You're going the wrong way, he said." I could understand his feelings when in a little while the train moved off, and I saw star shells, and flashes of the big guns lighting up the dark sky over the Front, about twenty miles away.

At Marseilles we embarked on the P & O *SS Khyber*. I have tender memories of this wonderful old tub, which struggled so hard under the privations of war to provide the semblance of a peacetime 'passage to India'. There were a few intrepid ladies on board, and a 4.7 inch Naval gun at the stern. One of the first things we had to learn was gun drill, so that we could fire at any submarine that might attack us. We were divided into watches. All went on duty in turn day and night, the watch being supplied with rifles and ordered to shoot at any periscope showing. We dodged U-boats in the Mediterranean and passed through the Suez Canal.

CHAPTER III

India, France and Palestine
1916–18

Charley it's time that we were away,
Well I know you will come with me,
We must be tossing in Biscay's Bay.
Cross the desert, and steam away
Down the Gulf to the Indian Sea.

Since the destruction of the famous German sea-raider, the *Emden*, off the Cocos Islands by the Australian Navy on 9th November 1914, the Indian Ocean had become comparatively safe for shipping, and we had an uneventful voyage to Bombay.

"You'll forget your load of sorrow, coming home,
It will wait until the morrow, coming home,
All the way ..."

chorused the ladies to the saloon piano, on the long evenings when the sun had sunk into the sea with a green flash of fire. I responded with:

"Pale hands I loved beside the Shalimar,
Where are you now?
Where are ... you now?"

As soon as we set foot on Indian soil we were assaulted by heat and flies, and by many strange noises and smells. The composite odour of an Asian city is outrageous sweat mingled with bile, heated over a charcoal brazier. The first impact on the western nose seems overwhelming. The sudden transition from the close orderliness of a British ship to the streets of Bombay introduced you all at once to a hot steamy climate, a melee of brown skins in a variety of clothing or almost none, rickshaws, bullock carts, horse-drawn vehicles of all descriptions, and sacred cows. The main life of the busy port seemed concentrated in the railway station the high roof covering a vast area of platform echoed to the hiss of steam from numerous engines preparing to draw trains over the far-reaching network of Indian Railways. Men, women, and children jostled one another for seats in carriages, already packed to the roof with sweating humanity. Vendors of chapattis, sweetmeats, and strange foods pushed trolleys up and down the platform: "*Hindu paaaani, Musalman chaaaar.*'"

In the midst of the confusion, pungent aromas, and unintelligible shouting, a calm figure could be seen here and there clad in a smart black knee length coat, tight fitting from the neck, below which gleamed white cotton jodhpurs and black shoes: the Bombay business man, clutching an umbrella and a black briefcase. If he was a Parsi, as many were, he would be wearing a chocolate coloured hat of stiff material without a brim, slanting slightly backwards from the top of the forehead. In India great importance was attached to headgear. Apart from the Parsi hat, and later the white Gandhi cap (which came into fashion about the time of Gandhi's Salt march in 1930), almost all classes wore a turban or *pagri* consisting of several yards of narrow muslin or cotton cloth wound round a fitted cap on the head. The way in which the pagri was wound indicated the racial or religious group of the wearer. The first duty of a raw young British Officer, newly appointed to an Indian regiment (particularly a Punjabi one made up of several different classes in separate platoons or companies) was to recognise and distinguish Dogras, Rajputs, Sikhs, Pathans and Punjabi Musalmans. The facial distinctions alone are to Western eyes so slight as to make recognition difficult even after years of experience. But once you had learned the characteristic fold of the pagri adopted by each genus, every man of which dressed alike, there was no problem in differentiating one from another.

A shrill whistle, bursts of steam, and our train began to move. The war in Europe seemed a long way away.

In May 1916 summer was getting under way, and the journey southwards to the Madras Presidency was hot and uncomfortable. Banned from drinking alcohol during the day, for fear of heat stroke, we were also forbidden to imbibe the wayside beverages which might contain typhoid germs. There was a limited amount of drinking water on the train, and a large slab of ice, wrapped in sacking, was placed inside a tin tub in each compartment, to cool the air. Our destination was Wellington, between Cotacamund and Coonoor in the Nilgiri Hills. At Mettapuliam, a little station at the foot of the hills, we changed trains on to a tiny 'rack' railway which took us up steep gradients, through thick jungle, into cool clean air at about 5,000 feet. Many of these railways can be found in Europe, especially Switzerland. However, the most well known in Great Britain is the Snowdon Mountain Railway, Llanberis, Caernarvonshire, the gauge of which is 2ft 7ins. Four of the engines running on the line were supplied for the opening in 1896 by the Swiss Locomotive and Machine Works, Winterthur. The Abt system is the method used: a cogged wheel beneath the loco engages with a toothed rail in the centre of the track.[1]

The following six months were spent in intensive training, as it was understood, 1916 fashion. No Cadet College in India could be expected to keep abreast of the technological changes produced by the battles in France. Trench warfare had made the fighting static and driven it underground. It was becoming evident that the deadlock could not be broken by surface attacks launched by waves of unprotected infantry the cost in lives was far too high. The first engagement in which tanks were used effectively, the battle of Cambrai in late November and early December 1917, was still far ahead. While the West was thinking of war in mechanical terms, India was still treating cavalry as the shock weapon, and infantry skirmishing and attack, supported by artillery, as the decisive factor in overcoming resistance. Europe was faced with a Great War. India's experience was limited to small wars.

One of our most able lecturers was a Colonel Cloete of South African origin. Of middle height, lean, spare, and possessed of a vigorous intellect, he would enter the classroom briskly, and announce, "Small wars, gentlemen, small wars." Even in 1916 the tactics of small wars were not to be despised. I was to discover later in Palestine and on the borders of Iran that the day of the horse was not yet over.

The Cadet College at Wellington covered a considerable area of open rolling downs, dominated by the highest range of the Nilgiris round Ootacamund. Barracks formed the main buildings, constructed originally for British troops, to which had been added an Officers' Mess, lecture rooms, riding school and bungalows for the staff, several of whom had their wives and families with them. The buildings were surrounded by tennis courts, and sports grounds leading down to a small lake, beyond which stood an Indian village. At a lower level still, but within walking distance, lay Coonoor which owned some European-style bungalows and a golf course. In fact the Nilgiris, with a delightfully temperate climate, was a vast hill station for those seeking a refuge from the stifling heat of the plains. English foxhounds had been imported for hunting jackal, and the hunt seemed to flourish in spite of war. At lower levels stretched huge tracts of jungle containing, we were told, tiger, panther and elephant, as well as monkeys and a variety of other wild life. We made good

---

[1] Information supplied by the Railway Museum, York. (The new National Railway Museum, York, opened to the public during 1975.)

use of this terrain for military exercises, map-reading, etc. and there were craggy uplands such as 'Lamb's Rock' and 'Dodabetta' which demanded some serious climbing, and offered the reward of a magnificent vista of the plains.

The contingent of cadets from England was strengthened by some older temporary officers who wished to make a career of the Indian Army. These men had some experience of the country and a knowledge of Hindustani, which gave them an advantage over us. Their presence was an incentive and introduced an element of realism. They were exceptionally pleasant fellows, several later rose to high rank.

Of the many friends I made during the course I can remember only two: D.T. Long my room mate and delightful companion, whose ambitions were cut short by the loss of his leg, as already mentioned. The second was C.E.L. Harris an outstanding cadet, who was promoted to Sergeant during the course. He and I joined the same regiment in France, the 2nd Bengal Lancers, and he thereafter had a distinguished career in the Indian Army. In the autumn of 1945, just after the end of the Second World War, Harris and I found ourselves returning to the East on the same troopship. Many years previously I had left the army and joined the Indian Political Service, but I retained the honorary rank of Lieutenant Colonel. Harris was the most senior commander on the ship, with, I believe, the rank of Major General. During the voyage we paced the deck for hours, while the sun descended beyond the horizon and night fell swiftly, discussing the impending transfer of power in India, and our own future on retirement. On the latter point our views coincided. "Do you think," I asked, "it would be too late at the age of 50–55 to get ordained to the Ministry of the Church of England?".

"Not a bit," he replied. "With our experience we would have a lot to give to the Church, including twenty active years."

"Would you prefer full-scale ordination to working, say, as a lay reader?"

"Nothing less than ordination would satisfy me," he answered. In the event, we both went to the same theological College, Ridley Hall, Cambridge, but as he retired about eighteen months before me, he had just left when I arrived.

As I look at the two official photographs of cadets and staff taken at Wellington in 1916 and now hanging in my study, I find I can recognize every face in my own platoon. The larger group of the whole College is different: there are many strange faces. One I remember well is that of the Riding Master. He was a tall good-looking man, rather on the heavy side for a cavalryman, with a fine voice and an effective vocabulary aimed at the rider and never at the horse. The man had to answer for the waywardness of the animal, however perverse. We got used to being the target of a string of names – "Sack of potatoes, Dummy, Father's despair". "If you don't find that stirrup quickly, you'll damage your prospects,'" he roared. And when you fell off, "Who gave you leave to dismount?" The lesson always ended with a pat on the horse's neck. "Make much of your horses one, one-two." I had thrown my leg over a mount before, but knew next to nothing about the art of horsemanship. This instruction gave me the feeling that I could, with further training, do well as a rider, and made me wish to enter a Cavalry regiment. However as the war appeared to be an infantry one, I suppressed the desire and applied for the 27th Punjabis.

Wellington specialised in another popular sport: hockey. After the war I often played at the military station, and even at the British Legation, Kabul. But the study of Hindustani (or Urdu) was the one point at which the course brought us into personal contact with India. At once I appreciated the value of a classical education, teaching grammar in a logical form, applicable *mutatis mutandis* to most languages. We first had to master reading and writing Arabic characters, Hindustani being an amalgam of Persian, Arabic and Hindi, thought up by the Moghul Emperors as a means of communication between rulers and ruled, and the varied races of their empire. Like Arabic and Persian it is written from right to left, the same letters inscribed differently depending on whether they are initial, medial, or final. Toiling through the grammar we memorised a vocabulary, strung sentences together and tried to read Indian newspapers which was rather hard work until it was realised that without it there would be no communication with one's troops. When the time came to pass out in November, I won the prize for tactics – a lovely compass floating in oil (which was lost later in the Jordan Valley) and came second in Hindustani.

As the 27th Punjabis were in Mesopotamia, it was necessary to report to the depot regiment, 28th Punjabis, stationed in Bannu on the North West Frontier, and await orders. An interminable journey by train across dry dusty plains, broken only by a short passage across the Indus by steamer from Mari Indus to Kalabagh, ended at last at the foot of a long line of barren hills against which the lowlands seemed to hurl themselves, like the sea on a rocky coast. My arrival in Bannu coincided with the capture of a notorious outlaw, who had led many gang raids from tribal territory into British India. He was publicly hung, his body dangling from the main gateway of the walled city. The town was only a mile or two from the frontier (which ran roughly north and south along the base of the hills) and on the right bank of the Kurram river whose waters were used to irrigate a considerable area, forming a green oasis in the desert plain between the highlands and the Indus. The military cantonment, with an old Sikh fort in its centre, included a grass polo ground and even a 9–hole golf course.

The OC commanding Bannu Bridge was Brigadier Bruce, later of Everest fame, a truly remarkable man. He had a favourite trick of ordering all officers to meet him at the top of a nearby hill, which might be anything up to 1,000 ft. When we arrived breathless and sweating, we would find the expert on mountain warfare already seated on a rock, stripped to the waist. His agility was more remarkable because he had a clubfoot. Loving a rowdy guest night in the Mess, he used to show off his tremendous physical strength by lying on the floor and getting the biggest of us to jump on his chest. Occasionally, he used to take bets as to whether it was possible to get round the room on the walls, without touching the ground, clinging to picture rails and ornaments. He won every time.

My twenty-first birthday arrived, but I had no chance to celebrate. That evening, however, I was invited by the Brigadier and his wife to a party at their home, at which he gave a talk, with magnificent lantern slides, on mountain climbing in the vicinity of Everest.

I had been in Bannu a matter of weeks when a circular came, addressed to all commissioned with me from Wellington Cadet College, asking if we would volunteer for Indian Cavalry in France. I sent in my application at once, as did several others. We had to pass a simple riding test, and soon were sailing for Europe. A troopship was leaving Bombay, 'bound for old Blighty's shore ...'

Changing ships at Alexandria I joined a group on leave for 48 hours to visit Cairo. There were no tourists so our small party brought a little welcome business to the unemployed Egyptian guides, camel drivers, donkey and pony men who flocked round us. We stayed at an almost empty Shepherd's Hotel, visited the Pyramids, the Sphinx, Memphis, and the many mosques of the capital. To me the highlight of all was the Museum. I must have visited it alone. It was like entering a strange world. After feasting my eyes on the wonders of the ground floor, I was drawn instinctively up a broad flight of stone steps to the floor above. Pushing open a swing door, I entered a long room full of glass cases, all about the same size, each supported by four wooden legs. The chamber contained nothing but the embalmed bodies of the Pharaohs of Egypt. (Shortly afterwards the Government moved the cases to 'a private' part of the Museum, on the grounds it was dishonouring their ancient rulers to expose them to public view.) I looked round for an attendant. There was none in sight. Alone! Alone with the Pharaohs of, Egypt! The names on the coffins meant little, but one was familiar Rameses II, the reputed Pharaoh of Moses and the Israelites in bondage, whose exploits are described in the Book of Exodus.' There he lay, with his hands folded across his breast, curiously humble in death, though in life he had been one of the most powerful rulers in the history of Egypt. I believe he was well over ninety when he died (as opposed to later sovereigns who perished young; probably owing to the habit of brother marrying sister) Rameses looked an extremely old man, the most prominent feature being a pronounced aquiline nose, which gave him a touch of European aristocracy. As I stood by his side, I reflected that in space only a few inches, including the thickness of the plate glass, separated me from this great man, but in time, over three thousand years!

A troop ship, the *Minnetonka*[2] took us from Alexandria to Marseilles in January 1917. Crammed with troops, mostly Gurkhas, but including a large Egyptian Labour Corps, we were harried by enemy submarines all the way. Fortunately for us, the weather was so stormy that no craft could operate efficiently – even so, we were forced to take refuge in Messina for some days, slipping out again at dead of night in a gale. Soon after reaching our destination, I got myself included in a draft taking Gurkhas to the base depot at Rouen. Although my orders were to return to the port, after handing over, it was possible in wartime to get orders modified. At Rouen I discovered an Indian Cavalry Base Depot to which all officer reinforcements from Marseilles would eventually have to come. I saw the commandant, whose name was Hammersley-Smith. He insisted on my returning to Marseilles. I argued, and went on arguing, until finally he allowed me to doss down in a corner of a tent, filled to capacity already. One of the officers returned in the middle of the night to find me occupying his straw mattress on the wet floor boards, and raised hell. Somehow I managed to stay on. It was a cold business sleeping under canvas that January, and wading about almost knee deep in mud. Gradually I got absorbed into the training scheme, which was run very efficiently by British Cavalry Officers and NCOs. Later we were inspected. I was accepted for the 2nd Bengal Lancers, and joined them at a village called Athies near Peronne, on the Somme. Here we were close to the Front Line. The whole area for miles round had been devastated during the agony of the great battle a few months earlier. The only accommodation available was in cellars below ground. Many of the horses were shivering under rough shelters, rigged against crumbling walls. The inhabitants had long since deserted their homes. It was a strange ghostly world we lived in, especially at night, when the

---

2   The *Minnetonka* was sunk by enemy action the next voyage.

grotesque shapes of half-ruined buildings were lit by flashes of the guns. Soon my squadron was detailed for a spell in the trenches. We mounted at dusk and picked our way through hollow remains of villages until, in pitch dark, we reached the rear communications. Here the squadron dismounted and, leaving one man to four horses, the rest filed on foot into a trench which led to the Front. I was left in charge of the horses. No sooner had the others disappeared than a staff officer came up. "A barrage is opening up behind us," he warned.

"Can you wait to get the horses clear, otherwise the noise will stampede them?" I asked anxiously.

He replied with a gesture of impotence. Next moment all hell broke loose. The animals were uncontrollable; most of them galloped away, almost immediately becoming entangled in barbed wire. The only thing to do was to keep the men together, and when the guns stopped firing, organise a search. We found some of the horses, but had to abandon the remainder, and spent the rest of the night getting back to billets near Peronne a tragic and difficult journey through unfamiliar country in the dark.

I went into the trenches several times after that in a part of the line near St Quentin, where no man's land was about fourteen hundred yards wide. It was late in 1917, when the Germans were planning an offensive in this sector, which materialised the next Spring. Headquarters were anxious for any news they could get of activity in or behind the lines, sending us on patrol into no man's land at night, with orders to inspect the German wire at various points. I well remember the first night we went 'over the top'. It was a full moon in September. Captain Ranking was in charge, and I was his assistant. He was a fine soldier with a cool head, and the Indian ranks showed no signs of nervousness. Perhaps they remembered raids in their own country, creeping, making use of the terrain, under a warmer moon. All had been issued with Mills bombs in addition to rifles and ammunition. Most carried the bombs in their hands or pockets, but I caught one or two with them hanging from their uniform buttons by the ring of the safety pin. Any sudden jerk could have easily pulled out the pin and detonated it.

When we came to the 'Bumps', a steep grassy slope facing the German trenches, with a line of old disused dug-outs at the foot (the scene of many violent clashes with German patrols), we sat on our backsides and slid. I had my revolver in my hand, ready cocked. Fortunately there were no enemy 'crouching in the shadows'. We moved on towards the wire, making for points marked on a sketch map. A tremendous noise was going on, apparently the loading or unloading of heavy crates. Now and again they opened up with a machine gun, sweeping their front in a wide arc and scattering bullets all round us. We felt like a lot of sitting ducks in the pale moonlight. Suddenly a formidable artillery barrage opened up from the rear. Big shells thudded into the enemy trenches just ahead. This frightened me. The hair stood up all down my back. One felt an awful sense of isolation alone in space between two unfriendly worlds. Eventually we crept back to our own lines, where a welcoming cup of coffee, laced with rum, awaited us.

Ever since I had arrived at our mess in the cellar at Athies there had been talk of plans for a big battle in which tanks and cavalry would play a leading part. The idea was to launch a determined attack on the German fortifications near Cambrai. This was to be preceded by an intimidating bombardment. As soon as it lifted tanks would go in, drop bridges over the trenches and clear away barbed wire on a narrow front. The cavalry would then gallop through the gap, surprising the enemy in the rear. Waves of infantry would follow to consolidate any ground gained. "At last we will be going through the 'G in gap', and trench warfare will be finished," said everyone. "After this, battles will be fought in the open and it will be a cavalry war." We had no notion when this might happen. Excitement grew more intense. Finally, told to complete our preparations, we were ready to go in a matter of days or even hours. Maps were brought out and pored over, periods spent in meetings and discussions. In the midst of the briefing I was summoned before the CO and told that, with a number of others from our division, I would have to attend a Hotchkiss gun course at Etaples immediately. Once again it was a question of weeding out the youngest and most inexperienced officers. Back we went in lorries to the nearest rail-head, twenty or thirty of us on the verge of mutiny.

In the strangely peaceful surroundings of Etaples we tried to concentrate on the intricacies of the Hotchkiss, and its tactical use by cavalry, while all the time our thoughts were with our comrades in the great battle of Cambrai perhaps the most decisive of the whole war.

News began to trickle in that all had not gone well. Our second-in-command, Major Knowles, was evacuated to a hospital near Le Touquet, wounded in the shoulder. I went to see him. Lying in bed, his face was grave. "The CO is dead," he said. "We attacked through a gap in the Hindenburgh line in the vicinity of Villers Guislain. A track had been laid across the deep trench system by 2nd Lieutenant Peck with a working party, following an assault by tanks and infantry. The regiment charged on the right of the Inniskilling Dragoons, but we got held up by machine gun fire and took shelter in a sunken road called Kildare Lane. Here Colonel Turner was killed. Also

Lieutenant Broadway. Most of the men and horses spent the day there, but thanks to the gallantry of Lance Daffadar Gobind Singh, who carried messages under fire to HQ (for which later he received the VC) the rest of the regiment and all unwounded horses were got out under cover of darkness."

After a pause: "The death of his father will be a great shock to young Turner. Isn't he a friend of yours?"

"Yes," I rejoined, "but he has a strong will of his own."

"I want you to do your best to steady him."

"I will certainly do what I can, sir," I answered, "but I cannot be sure of complete success."

Major Knowles' description of the cavalry charge emphasised the conclusion which was becoming clear: the machine gun would soon eliminate the horse from modern warfare.

Shortly after this, our cavalry division was ordered to Egypt and Palestine. We were taken out of the front line and began marching south, billeting men and horses in French villages. I was given ten days home leave. In Golders Green, where my father and mother were living temporarily, I walked along the road in uniform, pack on back, and came across my mother standing in a food queue. She nearly fainted when she saw me: a telegram warning her of my arrival had not turned up. The other women in the queue allowed her to go straight to the top and into the shop to buy food for the homecoming.

Back in France the trek continued southwards to the Mediterranean and I embarked at Taranto in Italy with an advance party of men and horses en route for Port Said. We made a camp at Qassassin near the Canal, in readiness for the Regiment and the rest of the cavalry division, to join Allenby's Army in Palestine.

In peacetime ships travelling east entered the Canal at Port Said, a busy bustling harbour, where most passengers would land for a first taste of oriental colour. The narrow confines of the canal are a striking contrast to the open seas, and the sun, reflected by wide stretches of sand and distant arid mountains, takes on a new power, which intensifies as you travel towards the tropics. The journey through (at a speed of dead slow) took several hours and time was often spent tied up waiting for a ship to pass from the opposite direction. Vessels travelling by night used powerful search-lights, which combined with a full moon, a passing caravan of camels, and the limitless desert produced a delightful sense of the romantic. The war gave me a 'camel's eye' view of the Canal, when the regiment moved from a temporary camp at Tel el Kebir to Kantara to entrain for Gaza. I had been left behind with a small party to clear up. The job took longer than expected it was dusk by the time we started. Without a regular road it was not easy to find the way, but, with the aid of my prize compass we kept to the general direction. Suddenly the semi-darkness ahead was pierced by a dazzling shaft of light, (as bright as the light which blinded St Paul on the Damascus road) and the outline of a huge ship followed, seeming to glide silently over the sand. We had reached the Canal, and safety.

Tel el Kebir was interesting in that, under Sir Garnet Wolseley in 1882, the 2nd Lancers were engaged in quelling the revolt of Araby Pasha, who was defeated there in a decisive action. The regiment took an important part in this battle, and afterwards marched on Cairo, which surrendered to the British without resistance. (While at Qassassin I visited the old fortifications just mounds of sand in the desert.) Later reflection proved that Araby Pasha, so far from being a mutineer and bloodthirsty fanatic, was in fact the national spirit of an Egypt becoming, for the first time in modern history, articulate.

In due course the regiment, the cavalry brigade and Indian cavalry division from France assembled on the Canal, and then entrained, horses and all, for the journey across the desert to El Arish, where a temporary camp was made on the sand, under palm trees, close to the sea a lovely spot. After 'stables' (the grooming of mounts) we put a snaffle in the horses' mouths, threw loose blankets over their backs, secured them with long girth straps and jumped on no saddle. Down to the sea we went in droves, animals and men bathing almost simultaneously, laughing and splashing. It was early spring, the water was pleasantly warm, the weather perfect a great contrast to winter war conditions in France.

The long march northwards to join Allenby's Army in the Jordan Valley then began. We found ourselves riding through long grass and wild flowers hock-high over rolling downs between Gaza and Jerusalem. I turned in my saddle to see line after line of mounted men extended on a troop frontage stretching to the far horizon. It was a wonderful sight. Arriving at Jaffa, horses were picketed in the orange groves, whose trees screened us effectively from Turkish aeroplanes. Travelling by night we turned eastwards and struck the mountain road for Jerusalem. A perfect moon shone on the ancient battlemented walls of the Holy City. Within, the inhabitants (only recently freed from Turkish rule) slept securely, as the long column of mounted men wound its way past the Jaffa Gate, across the Brook Kidron, and round the shoulder of the Mount of Olives to Bethany. We looked like an invading army from the remote past. A forest of lance points reflected the silver light of the moon. The dim figures of Indian cavalrymen astride their horses, seemed strangely fierce and outlandish with their pagris and beards, while the old walls and the older hills echoed the sound of hooves as regiment after regiment clattered by on the hard road.

> 'The Assyrian came down like a wolf on the fold,
> And his cohorts were gleaming in purple and gold,
> And the sheen of their spears was like stars on the sea
> When the blue wave rolls nightly on deep Gallilee...[3]

All that night we rode downwards towards Jericho, finding ourselves at dawn in a narrow define, where a half-ruined building stood close to the track, Talaat-ed-Dum, or the 'Good Samaritan' Inn. Halting, and tethering the horses, we settled down for a bit of sleep. Only dimly aware of the biblical associations of the place, we spent a hot and uncomfortable day, plagued with flies. It was a relief when darkness came, and we could complete the descent into the Jordan Valley.

The narrow hill path was dusty and precipitous. I rode at the rear with the second in command, enveloped in haze. A British Yeomanry regiment and strings of camels, coming in the opposite direction, added their quota of dust, until all were cloaked in impenetrable gloom. Word was passed that some camels had fallen into a ravine to our right. A concertina movement began. One moment we lost touch with the horses ahead and galloped madly to catch up, the next coming up hard against their backsides. A tiny light appeared below. I was told to halt and investigate. Climbing down thirty or forty feet I found a horse with its neck broken and a sowar lying near with an injured back. He had used a small torch to signal for help. Against the night sky, I could see that the regiment had passed over a narrow bridge spanning a side gorge, a bridge without parapet or guard. Contacting a first aid team with a stretcher, I handed the casualty over to an ambulance unit.

Down in the Wadi once more to salvage equipment, I heard a noise above. A double limbered artillery wagon, with a team of four horses and rows of men sitting on both limbers, was approaching at a fast trot. "The bridge is dangerous," I shouted to the sergeant riding in front. He took no notice, as he was probably half asleep. The transport swept onto the bridge. Almost immediately a wheel went over the edge, pulling the animals back on their haunches. One fell over, and with the rider still on its back, hung suspended by the traces. "My horse" the poor man yelled, and throwing up his arms, dropped

---

[3] Lord Byron, *Hebrew Melodies*.

into the ravine. As it turned out he crashed down onto the dead horse, which broke his fall, and managed to crawl away before the wagon abandoned by the artillerymen tipped over, dragging all four struggling animals into the depths.

We bivouacked near Jericho, 1,300 feet below sea level, and in May with no tents and practically no shade, experienced some of the hardships of desert life. The Turks were holding the line of the Jordan, but our mounted patrols penetrated into the arid gorges round the Mountain of Temptation. In the course of one of these patrols, young Turner remarked: "I am told that there is a rope across the river about half a mile downstream from the Ghoranieh Bridge, and I want to swim down to find out if it is true as the information might be of use to 'Intelligence'. Will you join me?" Mindful of my promise after his father's death to stick to him, I agreed. We dismounted at the boat bridge, guarded on the opposite side by a small 'bridgehead', stripped and handed our gear to our orderlies telling them to take it downstream to the point where we believed the rope was secured. We then plunged in. A strong current took us round corner after corner. Where was the rope? Steep brush-wood covered the verges. It was impossible to climb out. Revelling in the deliciously cool water, neither of us gave a thought to the Turks, supposedly holding the left shore. At last the rope hove in sight, slung from one bank to the other and half-submerged. We clung to it and pulled ourselves to safety, but no sooner was an arm put out of the water than it was black with mosquitoes. We shouted for our clothes. There was no reply. Out we got, covering ourselves with leaves, to keep the marauding insects at bay, and waited anxiously for the patrol to turn up. We had travelled much further than expected, and were overtaken by darkness before we got back to camp.

During this period the Desert Corps, to which we belonged, was not called upon to do any serious fighting. Allenby was mustering his forces for the great advance northwards, which was to sweep the Turks and Germans out of Palestine and Syria. A severe reduction of officers on the strength of the regiment was ordered, to comply with transport restrictions, and in August 1918 I accepted the post of Adjutant in a new Indian Cavalry regiment, the 44th, which was being formed at Chaman near Quetta, as part of a Cavalry Division about to advance through Southern Persia. Here the great news of the Armistice reached us. The wide open spaces of Baluchistan made it seem a bit unrealistic, perhaps because we knew that although the war was ended we had to soldier on.

CHAPTER IV

Base Depot Allahabad
1918–19

What far-reaching Nemesis steered him
From his home by the cool of the sea?
When he left the fair country that reared him,
When he left her, his mother, for thee ...'

Once the ink on the Armistice was dry, the plan to advance into Southern Persia was abandoned. The cavalry division at Chaman broke up. All ranks returned to their normal stations, and I joined the 2nd Lancers Base Depot at Allahabad.

The 2nd Lancers enjoyed a justifiable reputation for efficiency both in war and peace. One key to its success was, I believe, the weekly Durbar. The Indian officers had just as much say in practice much more than the British in these functions, because they were in touch with the men. They knew where the shoe pinched. The CO, or in his absence the second in command, was Chairman. Before the Silladar system[1] was abolished, time would be taken up with affairs of the Regimental stud farm and the supply of remounts, but in the end the discussion would always come round to what was in the best interests of the Regiment. I was very impressed with these Durbars. They seemed to entrench the dignity and importance of the Indian Officers.

It was here in peacetime, through such institutions as well as through discipline and training, that the Indian Army was forged. No army is a mere machine, though in some the rules are far more rigid than others. In India, to win the allegiance, even the devotion of young men from remote villages in the foothills of the Himalayas or the plains of the Punjab, involved, for one fresh from the parade grounds of Sandhurst, a delicate exercise in human relationships. The Indian Army, volunteers throughout, will always rank as one of the greatest triumphs of the British Empire. What made the martial youth of India follow alien leaders overseas to fight a bloody war in France for a cause so dimly understood? I offer two pictures which stick in my memory.

---

[1] The Silladar System: a system of regimental self-sufficiency in horses. Originally, each recruit brought his own horse. Later, instead of a horse, he brought money in exchange for which he received a mount from the Regimental Stud Farm.

First is a small outpost of half a dozen dismounted sowars (troopers) of the 2nd Lancers occupying a shallow trench in advance of the frontline. It is midnight in the winter of 1917–18. Snow has been falling, but the moon rides clear of fleecy clouds. A bitter cold has settled over the tumbled waste of icy trenches, now as white as the soil around them; two of the sowars crouch over a Hotchkiss gun, and the rest hold their rifles in readiness. The dark faces look pale, almost green, in the frosty air, beards are flecked with snow, black eyes gleam in the reflected light of the moon. How lonely they look in the silence that has temporarily fallen over the opposing battle lines. On the surface the picture is one of alertness and intense concentration, but behind it lies an almost unbelievable story of romance, heroism, sacrifice, trust and devotion to duty transcending all bounds of class, creed or colour.

The second picture corrects any impression that the Indian soldier was out of place in a strange environment. It is the spring of 1918 and the Regiment, having been withdrawn from the Western front, is marching southwards to join Allenby's army in Palestine. At the end of each day the problem was to find billets in French villages for the men, and some kind of shelter for the horses. The squadrons dispersed to different areas, and French homes opened their doors surprisingly quickly to Indian troops. Before I became experienced I worried over the horses, particularly if it was wet. Tethered to trees or railings, they had to be left in the street. "No problem," smiled the Squadron commander. "Before nightfall, I guarantee every horse will be under cover." Invariably he was right. When I went round the billets in the evening the roads would be clear; and inside the house Ram Das would be sitting in a comfortable chair in front of the kitchen fire, chatting in broken French to Monsieur and Madame, with a couple of children on his knee an honoured guest and, an hour or two later, one of the family.

But to return to the Durbars,[2] an armchair is set for the Colonel, with a low table before it. By his side are chairs for the Adjutant, Second in Command, the Rissaldar Major and Woordie Major. At right angles are two benches on which the remaining British and Indian officers sit in any order, intermingled. At the fourth side of the square, opposite the Commandant's table are marshalled the persons to come before him. All round, the men of the regiment are sitting or standing; spectators to our way of thinking, but something more in their own estimation, for they are there as important members of the regiment. That they do not exercise any authority is

---

[2] Amended extract from *Bengal Lancer* by F. Yeats-Brown (The Camelot Press Limited).

immaterial. Durbar is a testing time for the Commandant. If he has not the wit and personality to rule, his deficiencies are soon apparent.

The Indian officers rise, in turn, to present their recruits, who are generally related to men already serving, or from the villages of those men.

The regimental accounts are read by the Accounts clerk Daffadar Ganesh Das in Hindustani. Everyone looks particularly interested when the balance remaining in the fund is announced in lakhs of rupees. This fund is so large because it was built up in the days when the regiment ran its own affairs under the before-mentioned Silladar system. A lakh of rupees seems to be so enormous to a sowar receiving about 30 rupees a month, as it does to a British officer just able to make both ends meet.

There may be some defaulters. One of the men has allowed his horse to become rope-galled. A small offence apparently, but the point is that the horse cannot be ridden until the sore is healed, and the Colonel is always very severe in cases of injury to a horse. He has summary powers of discipline and the offender is unlikely to get away without a period of confined to barracks 'C B', loss of leave, or even a fine.

There are always questions about animals, who number 500, and whose affairs are complex in the extreme, particularly goats. Sometimes the Colonel has found that there are too many goats being kept in the family lines and he suspects that the goats are being fed on part of the horses' grain ration. The numbers of the herd have to be drastically reduced. This is not a popular move because of the milk which is valuable for an Indian family. "But Colonel Sahib," the cry would come, "what are the Baba log to drink?'

I shared a bungalow at Allahabad with three others in a 'chummery', one of whom (I believe Dick Ambler) kept a tame hyena. Chaos reigned at night, when this animal was allowed loose. It had a nasty habit of racing round the verandah where we slept, and jumping suddenly onto the beds. Imagine one's tranquil dreams being disturbed by a shaggy head thrust into the sheets, and an equally unpleasant odour filling the air. "*Jehennam ko jao you lousy banchute,*" the unhappy sufferer would rage, giving a shove to the heavy forequarters, "*apne Sahib ko takllf dedo!*" lousy rascal annoy your own master.) I attended Regular stables; a formal affair in an Indian cavalry regiment but very enjoyable. Animal welfare was an understandably urgent subject. Stables included grooming, but many other things as well. If a horse were ill or injured it would receive attention from the Veterinary officer. Injury and disease could be prevented, however, by constant care. Every part of the animal came under inspection in the course of grooming, and with a little experience it was

2nd (Bengal) Lancers. Gardner's Horse circa 1914 Sabreur 1970

possible to spot signs of saddle sore, strained tendons or a loose shoe. Lameness would be noticed at once, and a report made if a horse was off its feed. A clumsy mover would be led out and its action at the trot carefully noted. With practice it was possible to tell at once from the drop of the head or the hindquarter whether the horse was lame, and if so in which leg.

About three afternoons a week the regimental 'drag', a four-wheeler drawn by two pairs of horses, took us to the station polo ground. Our mounted gymkhana every Thursday morning attracted the whole British and a large section of the Indian community, and was a big social occasion. The main events were tent-pegging, lemon-slicing with a cutlass, being careful not to sever the ear of your charger and acrobatics on horseback.

Once or twice a week we went pig-sticking in the drag, leaving before dawn and returning late in the evening.

Those early dawns were magnificent. A haze of charcoal smoke lay over the town muting the colours of sunrise to soft pinks and ochres, somehow giving an impression of heat during the so-called cold weather. Even one set of hooves threw up a considerable amount of dust and this, in the semi-dark, muffled the barking of pie dogs and shouts from the populace attending to their cooking fires, from which rose an indescribable smell of sweetness and ordures.

The object of pig-sticking was to chase and kill wild boar (food for untouchables only) in its own country. The hunter was mounted with a spear in his hand. No firearms or dogs were allowed. The spear was diamond shaped, with a lump of metal attached to the butt end, to give momentum to the thrust. A *shikari* was employed who lived in the region and sent back information of the movement of sounders (herds) at regular intervals, and also engaged beaters on the day fixed. The evening before, horses were despatched to spend the night with their *syces* at the assembly point which might be at least twenty miles away. With them went the regimental camel, its *yak-dans* well-stocked with curry puffs and bottles of beer and boiled water, packed in ice.

Soon after sunrise the beaters extend out into a long line and the hunt starts. The spears are dispersed behind in groups of four, all moving forward over level open country at a steady walk. Suddenly there is a commotion. The nearest group of four spears advances quickly through the beaters. A sounder led by a huge boar is on the run and travelling fast. The hunt is on. The rules come into operation at this point. The boar already belongs to the four spears on its tail. No other member of the sounder is ever chased. At full gallop go the four; one will be closer than the other three. He must be allowed to stay providing he can hold his position immediately on the line. No riding-off, as in polo, is permitted. The terrific pace over unknown and treacherous country is a real test of a good horse and rider. The swiftness with which a boar can move is remarkable, but this cunning animal does not rely entirely on velocity. He has many tricks up his sleeve, by far the most disconcerting being his capacity to jink. Performed at high speed by digging his forefeet, and his snout between them, hard into the ground, he allows his hindquarters to skid to right or left. Almost without stopping he is off at right angles as fast as ever. No horse can compete with a turn like this. Some try to do so, cross their forefeet and come down hard. The jink gives one of the other three spears a chance to get on the line. The first to draw blood was entitled to the prize. Once the boar was wounded it became dangerous and the quartet were under an obligation to kill it as quickly as possible a difficult business, as only the bravest horse could be persuaded to close in.

What a wonderful fighter a boar is! Choosing the most inaccessible site, he stands at bay. On the other hand some horses take an intelligent part in the hunt. On one occasion I charged a wounded boar and only discovered, when my spear thrust had gone home, that he was close to the edge of a deep *nullah*, the lip of which curved round him in a semicircle. Pulled up sharp to avoid falling in the ditch, my horse could not move forward without stepping into space, nor could it turn since I could not withdraw my weapon. The boar was quick to take advantage of the situation and began to move behind the horse to the near side where we were both defenceless. At that moment I felt my horse heave under me as he let out a tremendous kick with both hind legs, which caught the boar under the chin and sent him reeling back half stunned. There was enough time to disengage my spear and retire to a less perilous position from which to finish him off.

I afterwards experienced a different technique near Jhelum, in the Central Provinces, where a level plain is dotted with isolated scrub covered hills about 100 ft. high, which harbour pig. Here spears do not follow beaters but station themselves dismounted round, and at some distance from, the hills, which are swept in the usual manner. In addition flag-men are posted along the tops to signal the position and movement of the sounders which are not hunted until they are clear of the hill. I recall one chase ending with clothes torn, riding boots slashed, and the horse covered with gore from head to foot after charging through thick thorn bushes in close pursuit of a boar.

> 'Over the valley, over the level,
> Through the dark jungle, ride like the devil,
> There's a nullah in front and the boar as well,
> Sit down. Sit down in your saddles and ride like hell.'

So goes the chorus of the old pig-sticking song. I sent home a fine head which I won with a first spear near Pahooj (CP) on 14th April 1920. It is still in excellent condition after fifty-five years, and hangs in the hall, presenting a fearsome appearance with tusks bared. The boys of Eckington Parish particularly the choir boys knew it well, and the family looks upon it as a household god.

Later with the 27th Light Cavalry at Dera Ismail Khan we tried our hand at pigsticking in a rough and ready fashion. A few sounders were known to be lurking in the reeds close to the Indus, but we never hunted them in the methodical well-organised manner of the 2nd Lancers. We had no beaters. Mills bombs were thrown into the rushes to frighten out the pig.

Once Major Durham, commanding 'D' Squadron, saw some spears stand hesitating round a large clump. "Why the hell aren't you getting on with the job?" he yelled. To give an example of what he meant he dismounted and, spear at the ready, advanced into the reeds, followed closely by his orderly. Almost immediately the boar charged him, and Durham, pressing the butt into the ground, knelt on it and presented the point to the target. This was the orthodox defence for a dismounted man, but the great weight of the beast and the ferocity of its attack carried it up the shaft of the spear until it struck the Major on the chest and laid him on his back. White tusks were about to gore Durham's stomach when the orderly, with great courage, threw himself on top of his master, and received the slashing wounds on his own back. Another officer then shot the boar with a pistol. After some weeks in hospital the man eventually recovered and, I think, won a medal for gallantry. It was an example of the devotion of many Indian orderlies to the commanders they served.

Give a man the wide open jungle plains of India, a good horse between his knees, a spear in his right hand, a wild boar to chase, and he feels a direct link with his primitive ancestors, hunting innocently for food and survival. Needless to say the military authorities encouraged pig-sticking as it was excellent training for a cavalry officer. Just as I was beginning to savour some of the pleasures of peacetime soldiering, in September 1919 came orders posting me to the 27th Light Cavalry at Dera Ismail Khan (DIK), then part of the Waziristan Field Force engaged in the 3rd Afghan War. DIK was a sizeable military cantonment sheltering among palm trees on the right bank of the Indus, about forty miles from the hills. It was in these hills, close to the border of Afghanistan, that severe fighting was taking place.

On the long grimy train journey across northern India, I began to examine my feelings about the life I had chosen in the army. Hitherto there had been a good deal of variety, if little distinction, about my service record. Having been saved fortunately from the worst grimness of war, I had seen enough to know that I hated it. At heart I was a man of peace. The brief experience of living in a cantonment, enlivened by all the advantages of belonging to a first-class

Cavalry Regiment, was enjoyable. But I shrank from the idea of turning it into a life's work. I arrived at the conclusion that the Army was not my métier: some suitable civil employment must be found as soon as possible. The train stopped at Darya Khan, a small railway station east of the Indus. At sunrise on a perfect autumn morning I loaded a *bistera* (that perfect bed-roll of green waterproof canvas, with compartments for pillows and blankets) and two suitcases onto a tonga, and drove to the river bank. Here, to my surprise, I was told that the only way to cross to DIK a distance of six to eight miles as the crow flies was by a small open sailing boat. *"Kitne pice?"* I asked. A long session of haggling ensued in which the poor man groaned over the number of mouths he had to feed, undoubtedly true. Finally *"Tik hai Sahib"* the boatman agreed cheerfully as we embarked in the frail craft.

Caesar burnt his boats at the Rubicon, and I had a special feeling about this crossing. In summer when the snows of the distant Himalayas are melting, the river bed is covered by a single stretch of water, but by mid-September the great Shyok and Kailas glaciers, the main sources of the Indus many hundreds of miles upstream, begin to release less water, and sandbanks appeared in the river bed. These sandbanks make over-stream navigation extremely difficult and reduce the flow of traffic to a few trips a week by experienced steersmen. The journey took at least seven hours. By the end of October the flow dwindled to two or three main channels, across which temporary boat bridges were thrown, and a rough motorway laid over dry stretches of sand. A car or lorry could then be driven from one side to the other.

The two boatmen loaded my luggage, and I sat down in the stern. The sail was hoisted. We steered towards a low sandbank in the middle distance across an open stretch of water. A strong wind was blowing down the great expanse of riverbed, and the helmsman began to handle his little craft with great dexterity. It was necessary to change direction frequently to avoid running aground, or being swept downstream by the strong current. Sometimes one or both of the men would jump into shallow water and start dragging the boat upriver with a rope, but they used their sail to good effect whenever the width of a channel permitted. The dry bed was almost completely devoid of vegetation; the grey water and paler grey sandbanks, formed by white silt carried down from high altitudes, reflected the glare of the sun the only relief to the eye were a few tufts of coarse grass here and there. The sun shone brightly and pitilessly through a light haze, and without any shelter but my topee the heat was appalling. There was plenty of time to take stock of the situation and meditate on my future. No sound but the wind in the stays and a dull scrunch if we ran onto the shore. The Indus represents one of the largest natural barriers in the whole sub-continent, south of the Himalayas. When the river is traversed from East to West it is like entering a new world, with a people inclined more towards Central Asia than India; the contrast is noticeable in physique and character. In appearance and outlook a Pathan is much more like an European; his language, Pushtoo, more closely related to Persian than to Hindi. In the history of British relations on the North West Frontier it is possible to see failure to make full allowance for this difference; there might have been less conflict of interest between the Government of India and the Pathan tribes if the former had conducted business less on the assumption that the tribes owed a moral allegiance to India and more on a recognition of their traditional inclination to look the other way.

The Amir of Afghanistan was prohibited by treaty from having any relations with foreign powers except through the Government of India. If his request to be released from this prohibition and for his country to be given full independence in return for maintenance of a neutral position during the whole of the First World War a reasonable request by any standards had been accepted, the Third Afghan War might never have occurred. As it was, the abruptness with which the Viceroy, Lord Chelmsford, brushed aside this proposal sparked off a crisis in Afghanistan. The Amir, Habibullah Khan, who had been friendly to Britain throughout the war, was assassinated, and his successor Amanullah Khan embarked on the foolish project of invading India. His futile thrust in May 1919, against the British fortifications in the Khyber, was easily repulsed, but the much more dangerous attack by the Afghan General Nadir Khan (whom I was to know later as King of Afghanistan) versus British outposts on the borders of Waziristan was only thrown back after very severe fighting.

These actions brought hostilities to a rapid conclusion, and a treaty was signed on 8th August 1919 in which the British Government generously, but belatedly, recognised Afghanistan's complete independence. The treaty brought an international war to an end, but it did not stop the fighting. The turbulent tribes of Waziristan Wazirs and Mahsuds had seen with their own eyes an Afghan general come within an ace of invading India. The sight was intoxicating. It drove them to exploit the imagined weakness of the Indian Government in conceding independence under threat of invasion, and they were encouraged by the withdrawal at this very moment of the militia garrisons from posts in their country. Tribal raids into the administered districts of DIK and Bannu increased alarmingly and it was decided to send an expeditionary force into

Waziristan to occupy strategic points, build roads and forts, and compel the tribesmen to abandon their forays into British India.

Personally I was an extremely reluctant traveller to this engagement. I would not have minded if the current of the great river had swept us down to the sea: I was war-weary, and had nothing but the remotest interest in the causes of the present conflict. It was impossible to see in the chronic turbulence of the North West Frontier any opening for myself in the Civil administration. And yet, as the day wore on, as the haze lifted, the broad river, the desolate scenery, the dim outline of bare jagged mountains in the direction of Waziristan, and away to the south-west, the towering crest of the Takht-i-Suleiman (throne of Solomon) 11,000 ft. above sea level, had a beauty which I was beginning to comprehend. When I stepped ashore, my mind was calmer; I determined to make the best of whatever fate had in store.

CHAPTER V

North West Frontier –
Indian Political Service
1919–20

Let him cry, as thy blue devils seize him,
O Stepmother, careless as Fate,
He may strive from thy bonds to release him,
Thou hast passed him his sentence Too Late.

Horses, mules, camels, goats and lorries churned up more and more dust, which spread like a parched blanket over the town. Numerous wells, equipped with Persian wheels, and driven by blindfold oxen, poured water into narrow channels leading to patches of garden. Beyond the reach of the precious fluid all was desert.

One's ear had to get used to the continuous creaking and groaning of un-oiled wooden wheels. The chain of earthenware cups went down empty and came up full. It was a continuous process. At the critical moment they discharged into a trough which sloped away from the well mouth. "Tonk Tonk" chanted the coppersmith bird and "Brain-fever! Brain-fever!" sounded mockingly from every tree.

Most of the bungalow gardens in Dera Ismail Khan cantonment had their own wells, providing life for tall eucalyptus, palms, oleander and hibiscus. What colour blazed from beds of blood-red canna lilies!

The main body of the Waziristan Field Force was operating in hills west of the Administrative border, and had already encountered strong resistance from tribesmen, who were well-armed and stylists in mountain warfare. As cavalry could not move freely in enclosed and rocky country, the 27th were used to guard and patrol the lines of communication, and to assist Frontier Constabulary in the protection of the Derajat. There were valuable lorry and camel convoys moving between the base at DIK and the high lands – a distance of forty-odd miles. "A squadron of the 27th has surprised a gang of Mahsuds, charged them with the lance and inflicted heavy casualties," I was told on arrival. In spite of rough-seeming ways I came to realise that this regiment was perfectly suited to the hard life of dawn to dusk patrolling over desert with an enemy never far away.

There were no frills and no nonsense. The horses were fine, all of them 'Walers' from Australia. I was in 'D' Squadron consisting entirely of black horses. We made a grand show on parade. Colonel Abbaye was a rare old fire-eater, eager for a scrap at any time. Dropping in for a drink at the little station club in the evenings, we often found the CO and Handyside, the famous super-intendent of police, with their heads close together, hatching a plot of some kind. Handyside made a great reputation for himself throughout the whole length of the Frontier as a daring and implacable hunter of tribal raiders. The tribesmen admired him as much as we did, and when we saw those two heads the red and the dark together in the club we knew that we were in for it. Sure enough, we would be wakened in the middle of the night a day or two later and told to march at once to a nearby village, where Handyside, with a small force of constabulary, was besieged by a large gang.[1]

The colonel had invented a special harness to enable a pack-horse to carry a mortar and ammunition. Our main job on arrival at the scene was to get the mortar into action. That usually did the trick. After a few shell bursts near them the raiders would melt into the hills, using the cover of every bush and rock. We tried to cut off their retreat but they were too clever for us, using deep nullahs and country difficult for a horse to traverse.

Colonel Abbaye was far from satisfied with these rather inconclusive skirmishes. He wanted something much more spectacular in the way of a fight, and so he would lead the regiment out of DIK on a sort of 'tour de force' lasting two or three days. We would spend a few nights in a fortified rest house close to the hills. During the day some of the passes would be approached leading to the plain. One of these was the Chaudwan Zam (River), which

---

[1] 'The Frontier Constabulary numbered in their ranks many remarkable characters, none more famous than Eric Charles Handyside who was their Commandant for five years from 1921. He was killed leading an attack on a village house occupied by a raiding gang, and as a tribute to his fearlessness, tenacity, and almost quixotic bravery, which gained for him the name of Kishn Sani Mackeson the Second[2] an arch was erected over the road at the summit of the Kohat Pass. It stands there to this day. The body of this gallant man, however, riddled with gunshot wounds was buried at Peshawar, on 12th April 1926. He was forty-four years old, and died with his boots on. *The Frontier 1839–1947* by Major General J.G. Elliott.

[2] Mackeson the First was one of the Great Frontier administrators in the early days of British rule. A memorial and public gardens in Peshawar Cantonment testify to his exploits George Leslie Mallam.

emerges through a ravine with a steep rocky hill on either side. One squadron was detailed to ride to the top of each hill and hold it. The rest of the regiment searched for hostile tribesmen below. It was no easy task for a horse with a rider on its back to scramble up those escarpments: very often the men would dismount, presenting a large slow-moving target. I never heard of any other cavalry regiment manoeuvering in that area as we did. It was almost like going down on your knees and begging the tribesmen to come out for a scrap. They didn't take us on however, apart from spasmodic shots at the hill pickets.

Several times the CO asked me to act as adjutant, and on many occasions I crossed the shallow stony bed of the Chaudwan Zam at full gallop nothing less would satisfy our mettlesome commander with a message to a squadron on the far bank. He was a keen fisherman and once his patrols had reached the hilltops safely, he would dismount, take out his rod, and begin casting for mahseer with a spoon bait. "What methods of chivalry were these that allowed such goings on in a war only a year from the Armistice?" I wondered. Could a sniper have got through the cordon though, it would have been part of the game to have a shot at the gallant fisherman, and best of all, wing him while gaffing his catch.

On the whole, I think we did a good job by showing the tribesmen that we were ready for anything and very far from being asleep. That kept them from raiding our lines of communication.

When we weren't out searching for the enemy the regiment assembled for routine daily parades. At the end of each session the Colonel would order the bugle to sound 'Officers' and all British and Indian officers were expected to gallop up to him and salute. Then came the order 'Cross your stirrups', and the CO led the way over the obstacle course. When we came to the straight line of jumps it was usually a case of 'Fold your arms'. This was often a bit too much for some of the more senior Indian commanders, but there was no sympathy for anyone who fell off. When we had done this every day for some weeks, we all acquired a stronger seat and a better sense of balance.

Of my personal falls one stands out in my memory. I joined a boar hunt one day across the Jumna river from Delhi. The pig took cover in isolated groups of thick tall bulrushes. It was difficult to drive them out. Once the animal left cover he would be in another before he could be brought to bay. The day's hunting was nearly over, when I found myself on the tail of a boar, with just time to spear him before he reached the next hiding-place. We were going all out, and I was reaching forward with the spear, when my horse put his foot into a hole and came down. I skidded along the ground on my shoulders and looked round to see my mount on his back, legs in the air, approaching fast. The horse recovered first, swam the river, and was afterwards seen trotting riderless through the streets of Delhi. I recovered him later. Neither of us was much the worse for our adventure; still, falling with a spear in your hand can be tricky the weight on the butt throws the point upwards!

During the winter of 1919–20 we were detailed for protracted periods of convoy duty, involving long dusty marches between DIK and Tank, a small military cantonment close to the hills, where we encamped for some weeks. Early every morning we moved out to occupy positions commanding the road between Tank and the highlands a vital route for the WEF. With our field glasses we watched the lorry and camel convoys in two roughly parallel streams threading their way up and down the winding road, and searched the bare escarpments on either side for the tiny movement that might give away a crouching sniper. It was then I felt for the first time the lure and it was a definite magnetic attraction of these savage Frontier hills, rising steeply before me. I desired to penetrate their mysterious depths once the war was over. The air was cold and clear, like stream water, fed from the melting snows. Behind, barren stony ground sloped down to the oasis of Tank, its fortified mud walls surrounded by palm groves and fields of young corn, forming a splash of green in the limitless grey plain. To right and left the long mountain inclines fell away into the distance and the waterless plain swept up to meet them. Along the foot of the hills runs the administrative border. This was the North West Frontier its wild dramatic scenery hiding a convulsion of primitive savagery, hostile and dangerous.

After two months of the fiercest fighting known in these parts, British and Indian troops, supported by the RAF,[3] overcame resistance and secured control of Waziristan. At long last there was peace, and at the end of January 1920 the 27th moved back to DIK.

In those days a postwar madness seized most of the Officers' Messes on the Frontier. A Guest Night was the signal for a rough house. Some guests would arrive dressed in smart regimentals. I could not afford the expense of a 2nd Lancers mess dress at this time, so I stuck to khaki. As soon as a visitor had

---

[3] On the 24th May 1919, Lieutenant R. Halley, in a super Handley Page, had bombed Kabul and helped to produce a desire for peace. (Subsequently in operations against tribes in Waziristan, aircraft were supplied to an increasing extent, particularly Bristol fighters and SE2Cs, although little bombing was done, in order to give the tribesmen the least possible cause for resentment.) From, June 1920. From *A Short History of the Royal Air Force,* June 1920

a drink in his hand he would be tackled low and sent flying, his shirt front and uniform splashed and torn. No one minded even when the rowdiness increased during the evening's festivities until most of the furniture collapsed around one's ears. It was a form of letting off steam, the intense relief at the cessation of five years of unending conflict.

On one of these boisterous nights we formed a rugger scrum in our ante-room, in the middle of which Handyside stood up, well primed, and shouting incoherently, caught hold of the next man to him, which happened to be me. He was immensely powerful. I was very light. He lifted me easily and threw me bodily into the fireplace where a collection of logs was burning merrily. I regarded this treatment, in the light of Handyside's reputation, as an honour.

In the spring of 1920 the 27th moved to Lahore. In the course of the last six months' military service much of my old antipathy to the Frontier had worn off. I realised that Pathans, though admittedly warlike, turbulent, even to our standards criminally inclined, nevertheless possessed many qualities, which made them both lovable and demonstrably superior to the more servile masses of India proper. Above all, the Pathan was a man, with a physique equal to, if not finer, than the average European. He might be dressed in rags but he strode about the station platforms like a god. He allowed no man his better not even a British officer of senior rank. As a good Muslim he had the utmost contempt for all Hindus and for all whose skin was darker than his own. There was something irresistibly attractive about these people, which was to draw me back to the Frontier for the rest of my service in India.

In Lahore, capital city of the Punjab in northern India, cantonment life was formal. A young unmarried British officer in a cavalry regiment was under strict discipline. For instance, if he was ever seen in the Ladies' Drawing Room in the Gymkhana Club he was 'on the mat'. It was permissible to spend one's time training polo ponies or racehorses (the 27th was a 'racing' regiment) or in the club to prop up the bar in male company, but the presence of the fair sex, and above all that most unmanly of places their 'Room', was out of bounds. All this seems absurd now. I did not resent it, perhaps because the 'fishing fleets' from England had not yet begun to arrive. There were few unwed English girls around.

With no interest in racing, and only a mild one in polo, I discovered a fine black troop horse that was known to be a good jumper and began to train him for shows. Owing to the peculiar conformation of his body, the saddle was apt to slip back and turn underneath him – disconcerting for the rider. I anchored the saddle with a breast-strap, and we made good progress. His name was

'Coalheaver'. After Coalheaver and I had won a number of local jumping competitions and were ready to compete in the All India Horse Show in Lahore in the early summer, I was suddenly ordered to Amritsar with a squadron for duty in support of the civil power. I was promised leave for the Show, but for some reason never got it.

My short period of special duty introduced me to the political situation. Exactly a year before, Brigadier General Rex Dyer had fired on a mob in the Jallianwala Bagh and killed over three hundred unarmed civilians. This drastic action had effectually quelled a revolt, but it had shocked India and the Home Government as well, and ended General Dyer's career in disgrace. The consensus of opinion in our mess was in his favour for taking strong and effective action in a crisis, but against him for allowing his men to continue firing after the main object had been achieved: the restoration of civil order. Moreover Dyer severely damaged his own case by intemperate remarks before the Hunter Commission, which enquired into the affair. The net result was to place the military, which was called upon to act in aid of the civil power, in an uncertain and hazardous position. Fortunately the Amritsar which I saw, a year after these events, was quiet and orderly. My instructions were to remain in the cantonment next to the town, where quarters were provided, to show my squadron occasionally to the populace, but not to do anything provocative unless called upon. I wanted to visit the famous Sikh temple (whose copper roof, covered with gold leaf, smouldered in the heat) and, the Jallianwala Bagh itself, where the high surrounding walls and enclosed space had caused such havoc in the shooting, but it seemed more sensible as I was in uniform to leave these controversial places severely alone.

A study of the Punjab revolt in 1919, so drastically suppressed, revealed its close connection with the 3rd Afghan War. It appears that the intention of a group of Indian revolutionaries in Kabul was that the rising in the Punjab should take place simultaneously with Amanullah's invasion of India. But the timing went wrong, and when Afghan troops began to attack British positions at the western end of the Khyber Pass on 5th May, the situation in the Punjab had already been brought under control.

The 3rd Afghan War had two consequences from which most British officials in India (particularly those serving on the Frontier), and the people of India generally, were to suffer for the remaining period of the Raj: firstly, the Government of India was driven into an unproductive and vastly expensive occupation of Waziristan, and secondly, the war and the suppression of the Amritsar insurrection together poisoned political relations between the two countries and led to successive waves of revolutionary anti-British agitation, until finally India and Pakistan achieved their own independence.

For myself, I had these hostilities to thank for an introduction to the North West Frontier and its attractive people, and for twenty-six years of excitement and absorbing interest in the Indian Political Service, of which I began to think seriously on my return to Lahore. I spoke to Colonel Abbaye about my intention. "I'll back your application," he promised. On a visit to Delhi, I interviewed the secretary concerned with recruitment to the Service (shades of Major Allen), ascertained the qualifications required and collected all necessary information.

As its name implies, the Foreign and Political Department was divided into two main sections. The Foreign side was concerned with the staffing of posts along the border of India and beyond, from the Burma Frontier in the east to Basra on the Shatt-al-Arab in the west. Included in this category were the North West Frontier (Province and Agencies), the British Legation in Kabul, Afghanistan, consular posts in eastern and southern Persia and agencies in Arab States of the Persian Gulf. The Political side was concerned with appointments of Agents to the Governor General, Residents and Political Agents in Indian States.

Members of the 'F and P' were supposed to be handpicked by the Viceroy, then Lord Chelmsford, and regarded themselves as the elite of the Civil Service. Incidentally, among the fighting services on the Frontier, Political officers were known as 'the bloody Politicals' mainly because, with an expedition against a recalcitrant tribe, they would have the job of drawing up peace terms when the conflict was over, and were often suspected of giving away much of the hard-won gains in order to win the good will of the tribe in future. The composition of the F and P was 30% ICS and 70% Indian Army. There was no direct recruitment and no entrance examination. You were accepted or rejected with no reason given, but there were some unusual conditions: for instance, an applicant had to undertake not to get married before the age of twenty-eight so as to make him available for a remote posting. Some special qualifications in oriental languages were also required.

When I filled in my application form, I did not rate my chances very high. Colonel Abbaye had to say that he would be prepared to take me on as his Adjutant. "I have a clear conscience about this," he said, "as you have already done the job on several occasions." A serious omission, however, was my lack of a relative in the Service or in any other senior profession in the land. 'By their spots shall ye know them' Kipling might have written, and indeed my 'spots' must have been an unknown element. My application seemed to have little to commend it, except possibly passing third on the Sandhurst list in 1915.

Realising there was no one to rely on in furthering my prospects, I took to hanging about the corridors of power at the Imperial Secretariat, Delhi, making myself and my purpose known as far as possible to unapproachable staff in important looking offices. "What language qualifications are needed?" I asked.

"Higher standard Arabic" I was told in a tone of voice that implied, "That'll finish him!"

Determined to accept the challenge I bought grammar books and looked around for a munshi. Arabic is a hard language – little less difficult than Chinese and to reach the higher standard from scratch entailed considerable effort. Working hard for most of the year progress was made. All this time the 27th were very accommodating and helpful, excusing me from many parades and other duties to enable me to study.

About October, at the request of the Foreign and Political Department, I was posted to Delhi to assist at the great ceremony of the opening of the Chamber of Princes by the Duke of Connaught. This special duty only lasted ten days but it was tremendous fun. To the railway station I hurried, to superintend the laying of a red carpet. As His Highness stepped off the train, I stood behind the Political Secretary, acting as aide-de-camp. Cars must be marshalled for all important personages and I was also on duty in the great camp where all the princes were to stay. This camp was a miracle of construction and organisation   a series of palaces under canvas. Bedrooms and reception rooms were decorated in oriental style with Persian carpets and silk cushions, so as to make the noble guests feel at home. Extreme care had to be taken to see that the food was cooked in accordance with the religion and caste of each ruler. Some of them were extremely touchy gentlemen, jealous of their privileges. Their ears would be attuned to the salute on arrival ensuring that they received the correct number of guns to which they were entitled. Complaints must be quickly redressed. Feeling like a general bottle-washer I made myself as helpful as possible, knowing that I was being vetted for the F and P. One or two other young men were in the same boat.

A considerable number of mixed troops were required to line the route for the Duke's reception. On the day before we held a dress rehearsal at which the Political Secretary (Sir John Wood) impersonated the great man and I marched down the platform behind him. When we reached the steps leading to the road outside the station, the band played the National Anthem. A Royal coach and horses, outriders, and all the trappings had been specially imported from England for the occasion, but for the rehearsal a regimental brake had been substituted for the coach. Everything else, including the driver, was the real thing. With one foot on the step of the 'coach' the 'Duke' looked round on a sea of watching faces. "I'm not going on this thing alone," he announced. His eye fell on me. "Come on," he ordered. Climbing up, we sat on top of the brake from which vantage point we gained a magnificent view of the proceedings. A cavalry escort swept in front, and horse artillery guarded us behind, while our four splendid greys trotted fast along the road to Viceregal Lodge. At every junction with a side road, British or Indian troops were drawn up and presented arms. 'Long live our Gracious King,' trumpeted the band. It was a truly royal progress until we passed through the gates of the old Lodge. The driver, flanked by high close clipped hedges, forked to right and left. The cavalry escort had vanished. There was no indication of which way to take.

The driver, of course a stranger to India, called out, "Which way, Sir?"

"Left," replied Sir John, absent-mindedly, but we had not gone far before realising we were headed for the tradesmen's entrance at the back of the house! There was nothing for it but to turn in the narrow approach and regain the fork. This was a difficult operation with four horses. Eventually we appeared before the imposing front door, where all the posse, mounted and dismounted, together with the Viceroy's Bodyguard in red and gold, and a brass band, were waiting in strained silence. At the top of a broad flight of steps stood the Viceroy, Lord Chelmsford, fuming with rage.

Sir John, obviously embarrassed, hastened to get off the 'coach' and make his apologies. No sooner did his foot touch the ground, however, than the band struck up the National Anthem and everyone froze to attention. I felt glad not to be in Sir John's shoes. "Where on earth have you been?" demanded the angry Viceroy, as, with red faces, we crept up the steps to present ourselves.

All went off well on the actual day. The old Duke of Connaught, looking magnificent in a light blue silk cloak glistening with insignia, duly opened the Chamber of Princes. On duty as an usher, I handed the potentates to their seats. Most of them were covered with superb emeralds, diamonds, and pigeon's blood rubies. When the ceremony terminated another usher and I righted all the seats to see if any jewels had dropped off and been left behind. There was none.

At this time Lord Chelmsford gave a great ball to which all the Indian Princes and important British officials and their wives were invited. The Viceregal ballroom was brilliantly lit, and glittered with the fantastic sight of numerous Native Royalty outvying one another in the splendour of their dress, in the size, quantity and effulgence of their gems one seemed to be weighed down by ropes of huge pearls.

As janitors at the doorways, stood the Viceroy's Bodyguard in crimson and gold with lances at the ready; and among the military dress uniforms were the tail coats and kerseymeres of the civilians, with breeches tight at the knee, and white or cream stockings and black buckled shoes. The ladies seemed to be wearing beautiful creations in either cream or gold, with long white kid gloves a perfect foil to their partners. When the orchestra struck up and the dancing began, the combination of Oriental splendour and imperial pomp was impressive. From a raised dais, the Viceroy and his distinguished guest, surrounded by the Viceregal party and numerous Indian rulers, sat and watched the gorgeous spectacle; everyone seemed spellbound by the vivid colours, the uniforms and the music.

Though moved by this magnificence, I did not wish to have any part in it. Later when asked to apply for an appointment in Indian States I declined. I could not see myself comfortable and at home in a world of uniforms and red carpets. The informality of the Frontier was much more preferable, where an open-necked khaki shirt and shorts were the usual dress.

The examination in Higher Standard Arabic was due in Calcutta in December, 1920. Time was running short. While in Delhi I arranged to take two months' leave for intensive study in Simla the only place a first class Arabic munshi, and Arab speaker, could be found. With the help of Stanley Webb-Johnson, a great friend and, at the time Assistant Solicitor to the Government of India and a leading personality in Delhi and Simla, a room was secured in the United Services Club. The main season was over. Most departments had moved to the plains for the winter, but a good sprinkling of the more permanent mixed community remained. The air was cold and invigorating at 6,000 ft., the skies dazzlingly blue. What sweet breaths redolent of pine and mountain did I draw into my lungs as my excellent munshi, well versed in the tricks of cramming, grilled me, and my Bedouin speaker fired question after question at me all day long! A difficult part of the exam was the reading of manuscripts, written from right to left in a flowing hand. Getting one's eye accustomed to spotting characters only half-formed was not easy and one had to make (hopefully) an intelligent guess at the distorted shape of a word.

In the evenings I escaped from the concentration of viewing black squiggles dancing on the script and went for long walks. On one occasion I slipped the collar earlier than usual and decided to climb to the top of Jakko, a forest-covered mountain at the end of the Simla ridge and almost 1,000 ft. above it. To reach the foot it was necessary to pass through the main bazaar where the road along the top of the ridge is flanked on either side by flat-roofed native shops, built on stilts, many of them hardly better than shanties. Usually the corrugated iron tops would be crowded with monkeys, making a lot of noise, and now and then dropping to the ground to seize a banana or chupatti, much to the annoyance of the banyas. As monkeys are sacred animals to Hindus, nothing could be done to injure or scare them away. Snapping, fighting, and cavorting, they had it all their own way.

On this particular occasion, surprisingly, the bazaar was completely deserted of langurs (common long-tailed monkeys). As I climbed up through the firs and pines of Jakko not one was to be seen, though normally they were not far from any road or pathway around Simla, and dog owners had to be careful their pets did not stray into the forest, as many had been pounced on and torn to pieces. At the top, the trees ended in a large level open space covered with sand which was nearly filled with thousands of monkeys, sitting in rows on their haunches with their backs towards me, gazing silently towards the far end of the clearing, where, by a hut, stood a Hindu faqir. The holy man appeared to be speaking to them. As soon as he saw me, he beckoned to me to come to him. Walking round the edge to avoid the animals did not satisfy him. With a downward motion of his skinny claw-like hand, he made it clear he wished me to walk straight through the rows. Picking my way carefully to avoid touching the langurs (which were very smelly and tick-ridden) I got about half way, and lost my nerve somewhat as the monkeys showed signs of restiveness. At this the faqir called them sharply to order, waving me on. I eventually reached him and shook hands. The front six tiers were real big fellows with yellow teeth. They did not seem at all friendly. The holy man told me to extend my hand, palm upwards, and dropping some grains of corn from a bag into it, directed me to give them to the largest monkey of all, seated right in front. This huge langur at first looked as if he were going to attack but, prompted firmly by the faqir, bowed his head into my hand and ate the corn. I could feel his two great fangs scraping the inside of my palm. No sooner had he done this than the tension relaxed. We were now friends, and the grains of corn a peace offering. On later reflection, I was amazed at the faqir's control over these beasts, and at the power he possessed to draw them away from the attractions of the bazaar to the top of Jakko for a 'family conference'. And what was the conference all about? It may have been that the faqir's hut was part of a temple to the Hindu God Hanuman,[4] and that the monkeys had assembled

---

[4] A quaint figure in the pantheon of the heroic age is Hanuman, the deified chief of monkeys probably meant to represent the aboriginal tribes of southern India. Volume 13–14, Enc. Brit.

for a religious ceremony. I had little doubt that, for the time I was in his company, I was as much under the faqir's domination as the monkeys were.

Before leaving Simla I indulged in a few days holiday from Arabic, walking out along the Hindustan Tibet road with Stanley Webb-Johnson, and sleeping in dak bungalows, with their inevitable meals of stringy chicken (or goat?) and dried peas. The exercise and the magnificent scenery, coupled with Stanley's company, made this a delight.

Commended by my *munshi* and Arab conversationalist to the mercy of God badly needed for the exam I took the train to Calcutta. This then beautiful city was teeming with life and busy with the industry, trade and commerce, which, largely British owned and inspired, gave it wealth and dignity. The grass-covered Maidan, and the newly constructed Victoria Memorial Hall (memory makes it red sandstone picked out with white), to be opened a year later by the Prince of Wales in the course of his Indian tour, shone in the sun. The Houghly waterfront was a picturesque if rather squalid spot, with its embankment guarding the many sailing ships on the river. Leaving the hotel early in the morning I walked to the examination building. On the steps a telegraph boy stopped me and asked my name. He then handed me a telegram which I tore open and read: "Report as Assistant Commissioner Peshawar as soon as possible."

CHAPTER VI

Assistant Commissioner, Peshawar and Bannu 1921–23

> What lured him to life in the tropic?
> Did he venture for fame or for pelf?
> Did he seek a career philanthropic?
> Or simply to better himself?

So the F and P Department had accepted me after all, before knowing the results of the exam! News did not come until reaching Peshawar that I had passed the Higher Standard Arabic. In the Indian Political Service, I still retained my military rank though 'permanently' seconded to the Civil Administration and received promotion automatically up to the rank of Lieutenant Colonel. Questions of pay and pension were more complicated, but both amounted to more than would have been given in the army.

During the first ten years of service, the Government of India were free to return me to my regiment if they were not satisfied with my work. Conversely, the Indian Army could ask for my return in case of war, or I myself might choose to rejoin.

Sweeping down from the snows of the Hindu Kush, cold clean northern air in winter makes Peshawar one of the most delightful of places, enlivening both mind and body. The sun, after dispelling an early frost, would shine bright and warm from a cloudless sky. To increase the illusion that this was Europe and not India, the sky would be overcast for a day and there might be a light fall of rain or snow. The scanty showers alone could not produce the stately trees pepal, banyan, and shisham bordering the Mall the wide expanses of green grass and flowers which transformed the whole cantonment into a garden and provided cricket ground, race course, golf course and all the amenities of an English provincial centre. Irrigation from the generous waters of the Kabul river supplied all this and much more. A large, richly fertile plain, bounded by a horseshoe of mountains throwing up a line of snow to the north and west, supported fields of wheat, barley, clover, sugar cane and tobacco. Apricots, oranges and other citrus fruits flourished in their seasons, and the peaches were some of the biggest and most mouth-watering I have ever seen, though banned to the services for fear of typhus. Peshawar is situated on the western edge of this plain, separated from the hills by a slope of barren country, across which runs the road to Jamrud and the Khyber Pass. After the deserts of DIK in the South, it seemed a paradise. I was soon to discover that this Garden of Eden is blessed with extremes of climate, so that a bitter winter is balanced by a broiling summer the hottest in India.

Alongside the cantonment lay the walled city, enclosing a largely Central Asian population, densely packed into tall fragile looking houses, high enough to catch a cool breeze in summer over the top of the wall. The City gates bore romantic names, such as Edwardes Gate, Hashtnagari Gate and Lahori Gate, and a visit to the delightfully oriental 'Qissa Khwani Bazaar' or 'street of the story-tellers' never lost its charm.

The Deputy Commissioner in 1921 was Colonel John Keen, a grey haired fatherly figure, who had great experience of Pathans. He invited me to stay in his large comfortable white-washed bungalow, built of mud brick, with deep verandahs and immensely thick walls. It was set in a garden of green lawns and English roses guarded by massive banyan trees, whose branches dropped roots into the ground in a vast barrier. In this house Herbert Edwardes and John Nicholson famous names in the 1850s had lived. During the hot weather Colonel Keen used to give small dinner parties to a few special friends, all men who knew the Frontier well. No women folk were invited. After a tasty pilao of rice, meat and spices, one heard lurid tales of Pathan treachery and brutality and Pathan loyalty. As we sat round the dining-room table sipping our port, the stories would begin. The sole light came from an oil lamp, which, shaded so as to withstand the draught from a slow-moving *punkah*, cast a circle of pale gold, hardly wider than the table. A smartly uniformed barefooted bearer would emerge now and then from the shadows, bend over a glass, fill it from a decanter, and retreat into the darkness as silently as he had come a perfect setting for the kind of real life horror story that makes your blood run cold, the historic associations of the old house adding a dramatic intensity to the scene.

I feel certain one of those present was Mr Short, of the Indian police, holding then a high post in the Frontier Constabulary. Another was a senior member of the Indian Medical Service who supplied much sanguinary detail. Yet another I believe was a Major Campbell of the Kurram Militia who came from the highlands of Scotland. Dark and swarthy in complexion, he had many of the psychic characteristics of his race, and regaled us with a series of ghost stories which would be incredible in broad daylight, but which had a horrifying reality in the dim light of the darkened room.

"I once spent a night at Shabkadr Fort on the Mohmand border," he told us with his rich Highland lilt. "Some years previously the fort had been rushed by tribesmen and the occupants killed. In the room where I slept I was woken at midnight by the blanket rising four or five inches off the bed."

In the year 1930 I myself toured the Charsadda Sub-Division, and arrived late one evening at this same outpost. My bearer got ready for me what I believed to be the same room as that used by Campbell. I remembered his spine-chiller, and wondered, slightly uneasily, if anything unusual would happen. The blanket I made sure was firmly tucked under the mattress. I had a comfortable night and slept soundly, putting down my immunity from ghostly visitations to an interest in psychic research, which led me to join a Christian Society many years later.

As Assistant Commissioner I had to attend meetings of the Municipal Committee of Peshawar City and the District (Rural) Board to learn how their affairs were conducted. In 1921 the political atmosphere was peaceful and relaxed. The intense activity which reached its climax a decade later, when I was once again staying with the Deputy Commissioner, had not yet begun.

On more than one occasion I was called upon to act for short periods as private secretary to Sir John Maffey, then Chief Commissioner for the North West Frontier (later Lord Rugby). I toured the Province with him and developed a profound admiration for this splendid man. Here was one equipped both physically and mentally for a leading part in world affairs. He was not altogether a success on the Frontier as he got embroiled in the Close Border v Forward policy controversy with the Government of India, and was inclined to encourage an 'aristocracy' against the strong democratic instincts and traditions of the Pathan tribes. Disagreement with those in authority led to his early departure from the scene, but his outstanding qualities brought him a distinguished career in other fields.

Talking to an old colleague recently at a Reunion Party of the Indian Political Service (Retired) Association in London, I was shocked to discover that he remembered a story of the days of Sir John Maffey's connection with the Frontier, which still makes me blush with shame.

On a protracted tour, which covered the Tribal Areas as well as the Province, I was responsible for the safety of the cyphers used for secret and confidential communications with the Government of India. Imagine my horror, and the general consternation, when on return to Peshawar all the baggage in the escort lorry accompanying Sir John's car was unloaded *but not the black box containing the cyphers*! The lorry, the escort, the Government House car were all searched to no avail. "Do you realise," said Sir John sternly, "the world-wide consequences of the loss of Foreign Office cyphers?" Rather than pass the baby to a wretched stenographer, I could only hang my head, and take the blame. Fortunately, the next morning the lorries containing the heavy baggage taken on tour arrived in, and the missing box was found.

In 1922 the Prince of Wales visited the Frontier in the course of his Indian tour. I must have been called in from Bannu for special duty in connection with this visit. The Prince objected strongly to some of the precautions taken for his safety for instance on an expedition to the walled city the route was mapped out beforehand and the tallest houses cleared of their inhabitants a situation which prevented the Royal Visitor from having a 'walk-about' and making contact with the people. Sir John Maffey came in for a good deal of criticism, but he was personally responsible for the well-being of the Heir to the British Throne, and the Frontier was not the safest place in which to linger and talk to the populace.

The Deputy Commissioner of Bannu in June 1922 was Colonel Garstin, and I was sent there as his Assistant. As from Colonel Keen in Peshawar, so from Colonel Garstin in Bannu, I received much valuable training in the work of a district officer. I was very fond of them both, and Mrs Garstin was particularly good to me in a motherly sort of way. She made me free of their house, and introduced me to all the folk on the station. In those days an Assistant Commissioner was a very isolated person, with no regiment behind him. I earned Colonel Garstin's displeasure on one occasion.

Soon after my arrival it was decided to raid a trans-border village where a notorious outlaw was known to be lying up. He had recently carried out a number of damaging forays in the vicinity, and it was hoped to surprise and capture him. The raid was planned in the utmost secrecy. It was led by a young police officer named Harold Vickers in charge of a strong force of Frontier Constabulary. Somehow the tribe concerned Bhitannis got wind of it and Vickers and his men were ambushed and had to fight their way back into British India without achieving their object. In the course of the fight Vickers was wounded and seized by the tribesmen. He remained a prisoner across the border for some days. We received information that he was being well treated according to tribal standards: for instance they killed a sheep and skinned it at once, wrapping the warm skin round the young policeman's body so as to cover the wound in his shoulder. They made him sign a request for payment of a large sum as ransom. "Under my signature I wrote the letters UC to signify 'under compulsion'," he told me afterwards. Whether the ransom was paid or not, pressure was brought to bear on the Bhitannis and Vickers was eventually released, only after he had contracted pneumonia. Seriously ill in hospital for some weeks he finally recovered, and although he lost the use of one lung, subsequently had a distinguished career in the Constabulary.

There was a good deal of speculation as to how prior news of the raid had leaked out. I unwisely let slip the remark that I suspected an Indian official whose duty it was to assist the DC in his dealings with the tribe, and who was 'in the know'. The official got to hear what I had said and complained to the DC. Colonel Garstin had me up on the mat and asked me to apologise to the Indian, which I did, because there was no tangible evidence against him.

From my own experience extending over twenty-six years in the civil administration, I can testify that the loyalty of Indian officials to their British superiors sometimes subjected to a great strain was simply magnificent. I cannot remember any other case in which my suspicions were seriously aroused. I do remember an example of the reverse of this, when I was Deputy Commissioner Kohat.

One day a representative of the Criminal Investigation Department came into my office with a personal message from the Governor, Sir Ralph Griffiths, asking me to help investigate a complaint of immoral conduct against my senior Indian Assistant. The accused was a very able man. He had a fine war record and had received a medal for gallantry. "Of course you are free to carry out your enquiry," I told the CID officer, "but I will have no hand in it."

"Unless you help there is no hope of success," he retorted.

"I'm sorry. I can't do it," I said.

There was no court case. On the other hand, the Governor asked for my explanation. "I do not wish to condone any immorality that my Indian Assistant may have committed *in private life*. I said, "His public life is so valuable to the Government and the people he serves (also to me personally), that I cannot bring myself to ruin so fine a career." Sir Ralph accepted my answer.

A severe cholera epidemic broke out in Bannu while I was there. The main weapons at our disposal were a preventive inoculation and saline treatment. Perhaps more effective than either was a rigid diet, excluding all fresh fruit and vegetables, particularly melons and marrows, which was strictly imposed on all military and Europeans living in the cantonment.

But it was useless to expect the civil population to take dieting seriously, and by no means all were prepared to bare their arm to the needle, so the disease took a strong hold among the uncounted numbers in the walled city. As AC I was Vice President of the Municipal Committee and was expected to supervise the burial of multitudes of dead Muslims, the cremation of Hindus, and the burning of all infected clothing.

Early every morning for months I left the cantonment for the city to organise sanitary squads and direct their work, giving what encouragement one could to the scanty medical staff struggling to deal with an epidemic which was beyond their control. I hope never to see such sights again: the terror in the grey faces of everyone, even though not yet afflicted, and despair in the eyes of those who lay helpless in the grip of the disease. There was little one could say or do to comfort, so I concentrated on sanitation, being careful to have a bath and a change of clothes immediately on returning home, but some consternation was caused when it was discovered that I had not been inoculated! All available serum was needed for the city.

At last the epidemic was over. I returned to my main work sitting in a court hearing criminal cases and all sorts of petitions.

A friend named Gastrell in the 9th Hodson's Horse stationed in Bannu was as keen on small game shooting as I, and we both owned motorbikes. A shoot was arranged with a leading Pathan landowner about 30 miles out, who had often invited me to walk over his property with a gun. A court hearing fixed for that date was not expected to end before midday: I had to listen to evidence in a criminal case and record it for committal to the sessions court for trial. The accused were a number of rough-looking tribesmen, who were alleged to have formed a gang and to have committed highway robbery with murder in British India. I found the evidence very unsatisfactory and came to the conclusion that the prosecution witnesses were lying. After the Public Prosecutor had presented his argument, I was still dissatisfied, and exercised my power to dismiss the case and release the accused.

Returning to the bungalow, I collected my gun, got in touch with Gastrell, and we roared off together on our machines. We took the main road southwards towards DIK, leaving the cantonment by the gate in the barbed wire fence, where there was a machine-gun post. The road was safe enough in daytime but dangerous after dark: many travellers had been waylaid and robbed, and some kidnapped by tribal raiders and held to ransom. If the person kidnapped was wealthy, such as a Hindu Baniah, the price would be pitched high say ten or twenty thousand rupees; if payment was not made immediately, the relatives would receive a matchbox containing an ear. If they still delayed, another ear or a nose would follow!

Gastrell and I had excellent sport that day, wading through marshes after snipe. A sumptuous meal followed in the khan's house. What wonderful hosts Pathans can be! We sat talking for a bit after the repast till I suddenly realised it was getting late. "We have to get back to Bannu before sundown, when the cantonment gate is closed," we explained as we hastily thanked our host, and jumped on to our bikes.

Fifteen miles along the road the driving belt of my Triumph suddenly broke. As we could not mend it there was no alternative but to walk, pushing our bikes. The countryside was deserted. All sensible travellers had reached home and safety by now. It was rapidly getting dark. "I know there is a tiny railway station three or four miles ahead," I said. "We might just have time to pick up the last train back." We decided to risk putting on our headlights. There was plenty of time to discuss what to do in case of attack. "As I speak Pushtu," I suggested, "I'll do my best to keep the raiders talking while you move round behind them, and make full speed to Bannu to give the alarm."

It was now pitch dark with no moon, but our lights revealed a straight stretch of road, at the end of which was a culvert and a grove of palms: a notorious spot for highway robbers to lurk. At that very moment a group of men appeared, walking towards us. As they came nearer we could see they were tribesmen. Everyone was armed with a rifle.

"This is it!" I groaned to Gastrell. The ruffianly looking party, dazzled by our beams, advanced, taking up the whole width of the road.

One of them put his hand on my handlebars, bending forward till his face was close to mine. "May you never grow tired. Are you well?" (The usual Pathan salutation) he cried, seizing my hand, and shaking it warmly.

My face must have shown surprise. "You know me, don't you?" he asked. "I'm not quite sure. Who are you?"

"This morning we were all in your court, accused of murder. You gave us justice and let us off."

Starting to laugh and joke, as Pathans love to do, their leader asked: "What are you doing here? This is a dangerous place at night."

I explained what had happened, adding, "We want to put our motor bicycles on the train."

Delighted to do anything they could for us, they escorted us to the station in royal style. Loading our machines in the guard's van, we got back to the cantonment before anyone realised we had broken the rules.

While in Bannu I made contact with the CMS Hospital and heard a lot about the work of the famous missionary, *Dr* Theodore Pennell,[1] who died there in March 1912. I also had the privilege of knowing his great friend and

---

[1]   The story of *Dr* Pennell can be found in *Friend of the Frontier* by Margaret Sinker (The Highway Press).

disciple, Jahan Khan of Karak. I visited Karak, and the church founded by *Dr* Pennell, several times. Because it was in a Muslim area it was not designed to look like a Christian building.

The atmosphere in a Frontier cantonment in 1922 was of course very military. Not only were troops visible on parade, or marching from point to point to man posts on the perimeter, or supply guards in the fort, but from dawn to dusk the air was filled with the sound of bugles blowing reveille: (Charlie, Charlie put on your clothes!), cookhouse (Come to the cookhouse door, boys, come to the cookhouse door!) assembly, retreat, or just bands practising. There was station polo in the afternoons, which I joined when I could get away from court work, or when not on tour. The green grass of the polo ground, kept green by constant canal irrigation, was bordered by low bushy trees, and behind them, rising dark and forbidding like the teeth of a saw, the jagged mountains of Waziristan, constantly changing colour from the pink flush of dawn to a sandy yellow at midday, pink again shading into mauve at sunset, and a cold dark blue at nightfall. At intervals, along the perimeter wire, strong electric arc lights, facing outwards, burned all night to give warning of attack to sentries in machine-gun posts. Infantry patrols moved around inside the wire during the hours of darkness.

Even so, experienced tribal raiders were not deterred by these formidable defences. The military authorities had unwisely allowed a tall sugar cane crop to be grown close to the barbed wire. One night a gang, taking cover in the cane, watched for the approach of a patrol. At the crucial moment, they threw a charpoy over the wire, crossed it, and attacked the defenders, knifing most of them, and, seizing their rifles, decamped across the fence and made off.

Next morning I followed them into the foothills with a force of Frontier Constabulary and a tracker. We found nothing more than the warm ashes of a fire where they had cooked a meal.

CHAPTER VII

Persian and Arabian Gulf
Slaves and Pearls
1922–25

And a bare hill-range in the distance frowning
Dim wrapt in haze like a shrouded ghost,
With its jagged peaks the horizon crowning,
Broods o'er the stark Arabian coast.

I was painfully aware that my education had been neglected and was determined to do something about it. In the spring of 1922 I took my first leave home to England after the war. I went first to Christ Church College, Oxford, and was told that they would accept me for a degree course in Oriental languages, but thought it would be difficult to reach the standard in a reasonable time owing to the necessity for long periods of duty in India. The next visit was to Gray's Inn of Court, London. They advised me that if I worked hard with concessions for war service I should be able to take the Preliminary examination for the Bar that leave, and the Final my next furlough home. This seemed the best plan. I became a Londoner for four or five months, took a course with law crammers, attended lectures at Gray's Inn and 'ate my dinners'. This swallowed up the whole of my six months but I managed to pass the Preliminary. Living as I had for years in the wilds, in an almost exclusively male society, I was shy and uncomfortable talking to the few girls I met. One or two showed some interest, but I had the feeling that they regarded me as an oddity. I was twenty-seven years old, and a thousand miles away from getting married. "Report back to the Frontier." stated a cable arriving towards the end of my leave. I had always assumed that my next posting would be to the Persian Gulf, because the Arabic exam had been taken at the specific request of the Government of India. Already my Arabic was getting overlaid by Pushtoo and a lower standard in Persian which I had managed to achieve at short notice from Bannu.

It seemed a case of now or never. I wanted it to be now, so putting the matter as forcibly as possible in an answering cable to Delhi, I waited. No reply. Wondering at the mighty workings of the GOI's mind, I embarked for Bombay. With the ship only a day's journey from the port, a wireless message was delivered on board. I was posted Under Secretary to the Resident in the Persian Gulf at Bushire.

Looking back forty-five years later, I think that the custom in the F and P Department of giving due consideration to the wishes of their officers in the matter of postings might well be commended to the Church of England, whose clergy are an undisciplined lot and seem to resent the very idea of being posted anywhere by their bishop.

There was a wide range of jobs to be filled in the F and P. Those on the Foreign side along the borders of India and beyond were often remote, sometimes dangerous; those in Indian States on the Political side were more comfortable, and on the whole better paid, because there were more First Class Residencies in States. It must have been a relief to the secretaries to find someone actually requesting to go to a distant outpost.

The mail-boat carried me from Karachi to Bushire in December 1922. Like the North Sea the gulf is shallow, and there are few deep water ports. Bushire is not one of them. The packet had to anchor some miles out to sea, where passengers were transferred to motorised Arab dhows. If the water was rough this often involved a frightening jump from one moving boat to another. Indian women and children, wishing to disembark, were placed in a net, hoisted up by derricks, swung overboard and dropped into the dhow with a lot of shrieking, like so much cattle.

Lying at the north end of a long low desert island, close to the mainland of Iran, Bushire did not look attractive from the sea. As the heaving craft approached the port nothing green could be seen. It was hard to distinguish the island from the distant barren mountains behind. In an old two-storey building there was a town Residency, where the Consul, Vice-Consul and their staff had offices. At the opposite end of the island was a house known as 'Sabzabad' (Green abode) where the Resident lived. This was a large flat-roofed bungalow, built of whitewashed mud-brick, surrounded by a garden with, owing to the lack of fresh water, not much in the way of a lawn. A small bungalow at the end of the garden, similarly constructed, was reserved for the Under Secretary. The flat roofs were in regular use during the hot weather for sleeping out at night. Each had a gallows-like wooden erection from which was slung an electric punkah.

Some of the happiest moments remembered in Bushire were just before falling asleep on a warm night. The punkah moved silently above; fast enough to keep one cool and to drive the mosquitoes away, while all the desert world around, sloping gradually to the distant sea, was bathed in silver moonlight.

Even the far-off call of the muezzin, softened by lack of proximity, was soporific, like bees gathering to a hive.

A lovable and very remarkable man was Colonel A.P. Trevor, Resident at that time. For over twenty years he had been in the Gulf and was nearing retirement. He had two small children from a recent marriage to a young and beautiful wife. A recognised authority on the area, he seemed to be universally respected by Arabs and Persians on both sides of the water. The Government of India consulted him on all Gulf affairs (and many other subjects as well) in strict confidence. One of the wisest men I ever met, his despatches were models of clarity and good sense. Most of his correspondence, secret or confidential was typed by me, much of it telegrams in cipher. I kept all ciphers and coded and decoded all telegrams. I guarded these zealously, unlike an irreverent young friend I knew later in the RAF who, unable to wake his CO one night, stuck a decoded message into his set of false teeth by the bedside. He awoke to find them grinning at him, with the paper clenched between.

Out of sheer necessity, I taught myself to type. I was also keeper of the large Secret and Confidential record room at Sabzabad. Here were to be found copies of correspondence with the Persian Government, despatches of HM's Ambassador in Tehran, and letters to and from Sheikhs on the Arab coast. There were memos about lighting and buoying, about piracy, and the affairs of the Anglo-Persian Oil Company at Mohammerah. The records dated back to the earliest days of the British connection with the Gulf.

Colonel Trevor was a great man but it seems that his predecessor, Sir Percy Z. Cox (always referred to by the Arab Sheikhs as 'the sagacious Cox') and whom I never met, was even greater. Another outstanding figure was Sir Arnold Wilson who had previously been in the Indian Political but who was then general manager of the Anglo Persian Oil Company. On brief visits to us he would receive telegrams, both day and night, requiring decisions on a number of problems, some involving millions of pounds. He made his assessment in every case like lightning, hardly ever requiring time to think it over.

Relations with the Persian Governor of Bushire were very cordial. He often dropped in socially at Sabzabad. During the fasting month of Ramadan a gun was fired by the garrison of the town at sunrise and sunset to mark the beginning and ending of the daily fast, but the Governor did not seem to take much notice of these Islamic rules. He would drink whisky at all times, and even joke about religious observances in general.

The location of a British resident on Persian soil, and the exercise of powers by the Royal Navy to keep the peace, were always a thorn in the flesh of the

Persian Government. A few years after I left, the Residency was moved from Bushire to Bahrain on the Arab side, but in 1923 the whole world was still accustomed to British gunboat diplomacy, and there was even a small detachment of Indian troops still in Bushire a relic of the war, when German agents were active in the Fars Province of Southern Persia.

The Consul and Secretary to Colonel Trevor was Mr H.D.G. Law, whom I succeeded in 1924. There was also a number of British businessmen, bankers and shipping agents. We were all a very happy family. Mrs Trevor was a charming hostess and kept almost open house, particularly when the Navy was in. At one fancy dress dance I wore a smart Cossack uniform bought from an impoverished Russian refugee, while Mrs Trevor was delightfully arrayed in sprigged muslin, a Kate Greenaway bonnet and bronze kid dancing slippers with crossed thongs. The Resident sported a top hat (and very contemporary side-burns) with his cutaway tail jacket and drainpipe trousers.

The cable ship *Lawrence* was used as a touring vessel, and in spite of being a poor sailor, I enjoyed expeditions on her up and down the Gulf. There were visits to Jask, Bunderabbas, Lingah, Qishm, Henjam and Muscat. When we went ashore to call on the Persian governors I bought some Jask rugs, which adorn the floors of my house to this day. They were of primitive style in pleasing shades of red and black, and black with a white square in the centre between the decorated borders.

At Bunderabbas and Lingah curious wind towers dominated the landscape, erected on stilts so that one could recline on a bed or deck chair immediately beneath. The interior of the tower was divided vertically into two parts by a partition diagonally from one corner to the other, so that the strong prevailing wind comes down one section of the structure and up the other, creating a pleasant cooling draught for the persons lying below. If one happened to be reading a newspaper the up-current could easily snatch it away and carry it to the top of the tower.

These buildings were a great boon as, of course, there was no electricity and therefore no fans. The awful heat in summer can best be described by a little Persian story, then popular:

A bad Bunderabbasi died and, on arrival at hell, said to the Devil:

"Ai Hazrat-i-Shaitan, (O Lord Satan) *Kambal bi man bi dahid*, (Please give me a blanket *Ki az sarma me miram."* as I am dying of cold!)

Muscat was fascinating, more like a pirates' cove than the capital of a respectable Arab Sultanate. It was a tragedy that, though so close to the marauding coast of Trucial Oman (graphically described by H. Moyse-Bartlett[1]), we were both tied so much to the office in Bushire there was no time to spend exploring. By 1923, thanks to the Royal Navy, piracy was no longer a live issue.

Many of the little company of Persian servants wept when Colonel Trevor retired. To us it seemed as if the Gulf was losing a father. He was succeeded by Colonel Prideaux, who brought his wife and a private secretary. The colonel was interested in heraldry and genealogical trees and the secretary helped him with this. He and his wife were also experts on European wines and had brought some barrels with them which, when diluted with cold water made a refreshing drink for the hot weather.

I had an invitation to spend ten days on board the ship of the Senior Naval Officer, which was a great experience. It seemed that the Captain's guest was allowed everywhere. Our first meeting had been at the Residency. The SNO was a typical sailor, jolly and sociable, and he was also an artist of no mean prowess. But at sea his character changed. For most of the day he remained in his cabin, silent and aloof. You had the feeling he knew everything. "The Old Man's in a bad temper today," the wardroom officers would remark, with a mixture of awe and affection.

One day we anchored off a desert island and the whole ship's company rowed ashore for a swim. A spit of firm silver sand ran out from one end of the islet, with a sudden drop into deep water. What pleasure to run along the baking beach, almost too hot to let one's feet touch the ground, and dive into the sea! The Naval way of giving a ducking to which I had my first introduction was as follows. With hands on your shoulders from behind the victim is shoved down. Feet are then applied as an added impetus. Fortunately I was warned, and had managed to draw a deep breath before going under.

On other occasions we sailed in the ship's whalers. The captain never accompanied us. One curious thing about the wardroom officers was that the confinement on board seemed to magnify their personalities. One or two never left the gunboat they just could not bring themselves to go ashore rather like the long-term prisoner who dreads leaving jail to face the outside world.

Shortly after this delightful interlude Mr Law was transferred from the Gulf and I took his place. My successor, Capt. W.F.Q. Shuldham, brought his wife with him, a charming couple. The Laws' house became mine and I took over the office in the town Residency as Consul. Here with Indian clerks to assist me, the work was not so hard as at Sabzabad.

---

[1] *The Pirates of Trucial Oman* Macdonald & Co, 1966.

A British merchantman anchored off Bushire one blazing hot day in July and signalled that her wireless operator had died and left a deathbed wish to be buried ashore.

Included in the cable and wireless station (the Superintendent of which was an enormously fat man) was a Christian cemetery; so I arranged for a grave to be dug and fixed a time for the funeral which, as Consul, I had to take myself. The whole ship's company arrived in the evening and stood round the grave, while I read the funeral service rather falteringly for the first time in my life. When the moment came for the coffin to be lowered, the superintendent stepped onto a plank which had been laid alongside the grave to support the crumbling, sandy soil.

His huge weight broke the plank, the side of the grave gave way completely, and the coffin slid out of the mourners' hands and nose-dived into one end of the partially filled excavation. Shocked at this unfortunate occurrence I stopped reading the service, but many of the crew, overcome by the tremendous heat, called on me to continue. I looked at the coffin, one end of which was sticking up grotesquely out of the ground, and refused to go on until the grave was re-dug, and the box, holding the poor seaman's body, properly laid in it. After much grumbling, a few volunteers were persuaded to come forward and dig, while the rest of us waited. Eventually the wretched corpse was well and truly buried according to Christian rites, and the crew returned to their ship.

I had to attend a special training course for junior military politicals at Moradabad in the United Provinces, India in the autumn of '24. Its object was to help us pass departmental exams in Indian law and revenue, also in the general work as a district officer. The local British community made us very welcome, and I lost my heart to a beautiful girl, Gladys Minto, whose family belonged to the permanent English railway staff, truly Anglo-Indian, and who had been born and educated in the land of jasmine and lilies. With her light brown hair and big dark eyes she was tall and slender, and immensely popular with the law fraternity and young ICS officers. She was training to be a nurse, and I could imagine her cool hand alleviating the pain of many a sufferer.

It was not to be that she should alleviate mine. Political friends and their wives soon noticed that I was becoming involved, and pressed me hard to abandon what they said was an unsuitable match. I am ashamed to admit that under this adverse weight of opinion I lost my nerve, as did she, but I was in love for the first time and felt very sad. I think that possibly she did too.

Before the course was over came orders posting me as Political Agent at Bahrain, and the spring of 1925 found me back in the Gulf. A good deal had

يلتمسكم الشيخ حمد بن الشيخ عيسى الخليفه
حاكم البحرين
(اخذ فضوله لكم في غا صيف برليه نيا كظن لندن)

Sheikh Hamad, son of Sheikh Isa, Al Khalifa (with son) Ruler of Bahrain
(photo taken in London at the time of the Wembley Exhibition 1925

PEARL DIVING IN PROGRESS ON BANKS OFF BAHRAIN
Note: haulers, divers, robes, oyster baskets

PEARL DIVERS IN PROGRESS
ON BANKS OFF BAHRAIN
Note: oars, nose clips, goat skins for
fresh water

happened in my absence. Lord Curzon was Foreign Secretary in London. He had been Viceroy of India and knew that part of the world intimately. He was aware that slavery was still widespread, particularly in the pearling industry centred on Bahrain.

Negro slaves were brought across the Arabian Peninsula and made to dive for pearls. The finest natural jewels in the world were obtained from the banks which lay along almost the whole length of the Arab coast, about twenty to thirty miles out to sea. All the rulers, especially the Sheikh of Bahrain, were under treaty relations with the British Government, who undertook to preserve rights of the states to reap the rich harvest as against all foreigners including British subjects. The use of any mechanical apparatus for the purpose of diving or collecting the oysters was forbidden.

Lord Curzon decided it was time to demand in return for these services the introduction of reforms in the industry at Bahrain, to bring about the abolition of slavery. Accordingly, Indian troops landed from Bushire and an ultimatum was delivered to Sheikh Isa Al Khalifa, who rejected this document. He was banished to an outer island of his State, but his son, Sheikh Hamad Ben Isa, agreed, and by the time I arrived negotiations were in progress between the Political Agent (Major C.K. Daly) and the middle-aged Hamad.

It was considered necessary for the whole State to be administered jointly by the Political Agent and the Sheikh at least until the first pearling season under the reforms was over.

Major Daly (later Sir Clive) was due for home leave. This remarkable Arab linguist had endured the fearful climate and primitive living conditions, with his wife and small children, for some time. A bit of a tyrant, he had previously been involved in the Arab revolt of 1920 in Mesopotamia, and had got himself into a tight corner from which he had to be evacuated by air, while an infuriated crowd chanted, "*Rasak ba rameh, Daly!*" (Your head on a spear!).

He was an exceedingly brave man, short and stocky, with a brief stubbly beard. I was required to understudy him, but had the feeling on his departure that quite an awkward fractious baby had been dropped in my lap! Violent opposition to the reforms came from all the rich owners of diving vessels or *zambuks*, who were the slave-owners of Bahrain. They naturally regarded the new laws as an unwarranted intrusion into their private affairs and a damaging interference with the pearling industry that could only lead to disaster. "The slaves, once they are set free will run amok," they gloomily foretold. "Discipline will collapse during the long weeks at sea. They will refuse to dive."

But Sheikh Hamad and I doggedly continued the laborious process of freeing hundreds, one by one, which had been started by Major Daly. We sat together for many hours in a joint court, theoretically with absolute powers of life and death over all Bahrain subjects provided we agreed.

In the event of a difference of opinion a reference would be necessary to the Resident at Bushire on the other side of the Gulf. Extraordinary as it may seem, we never disagreed. We both, however, became immensely weary with the heat and long hours in court. Looking at his watch, and with a twinkle in his eye the court would be adjourned.

This intelligent ruler was full of common sense. He had a high regard for justice that won him the confidence and affection of his subjects. On the bench he looked magnificent: his gold-braided Arab headdress and flowing black robes showing off in style the hooded hawk on his wrist. We became good friends.

Neither of us would take any important decision without consulting the other. How do you free a slave? The procedure was simple. It was easy to get him into court as he had everything to gain. It was not so easy to persuade his master to appear. He usually had to be pressurised. We had at our disposal a small force of armed Arab Levies under a British officer, and I had a personal bodyguard of a platoon of Indian troops. The best safeguard of all was the presence of the Royal Navy 'somewhere in the Gulf', but within call by wireless. By various means a warrant or summons would be served on the master to come to court, and after some delay he would arrive. Then the questions would start, with the owner upon one side and the slave on the other. Was the bondman a diver or hauler? These two worked in pairs, the hauler on deck handling two ropes, one of which had a stone attached to the end, and the other a small basket, above which was a noose. Between operations the diver rested on the surface, supported by the ropes, and perhaps with a foot in the basket. When the time came to dive he fixed his nose clip, the hauler paid out, and he sank, weighted, to the bottom usually about five fathoms. Sometimes the divers operated at depths as great as ninety feet. They were equipped with knives to dislodge the oysters, and to protect themselves from attack by sharks. Should there be a tide running he might be carried well beyond the stern of the ship. Once on the sea floor he released the weighted line, placed his head through the noose above the basket (with a silent prayer to Allah perhaps) and crawled along the sand, sweeping oyster shells into the pannier with his hands as fast as possible. When it was full he released his head thankfully, gave a tug, and was hauled up to light and air. Clearly this man deserved a higher share of the takings. Custom laid down amounts.

For how many seasons had the diver been working for his master?

Generally no dispute. After dealing with many cases we got to know which seasons were good, bad or indifferent, and the diver's portion would be worked out. Had he borrowed money? As there was never any written evidence, an argument would follow, but a compromise would settle it. The final amount owed by the master to the slave (or very rarely vice versa) would be entered in a specially printed account book, and attested by the Sheikh with his signet ring. The last stage of the drama was the production of a 'Manumission Certificate' in parchment with the Union Jack in colours in the centre, containing in Arabic and English the legend:

"To all whom it may concern, (so and so) son of (so and so), once a slave, is now a free man, and no one must be allowed to interfere with his liberty.
(Signed) Political Agent Bahrain."

The smile on the face of the slave, when presented with this passport to freedom will remain in my memory for all time; for with each presentation (and there were hundreds) went a personal pride in the British Empire, which had the power and the will to perform this signal service to mankind.

I imagined Sheikh Hamad reasoning: "These mad Englishmen and their high-minded principles! Do they really think the pearling industry can function without slavery? What free man would spend months of the hot weather jammed into a *zambuk* with eighty or ninety others, dive continuously all day long, and die an early death? The first season under the reforms will be the test." This may be unfair to one whose trust in the British Government, and whose loyalty to his promise to see the amendments through, never wavered for a moment. Many people, however, did express opinions of this kind. It has to be remembered that in those days the State revenues depended entirely on a flourishing pearling industry. They have oil now and are fabulously rich, but then no one dreamed of it.

There were literally mountains of shells in Bahrain enough to pave the streets of London with mother-of- pearl.

Disputes over individual gems arose when a particularly valuable pearl was owned jointly by several persons, one of whom retained possession. "You have sold the precious object without our consent," they would hotly cry, hands on daggers. Or "You have 'doctored' it! We demand compensation if our share has been reduced!"

The doctoring of a pearl is risky and a highly skilled business. It could include cutting, slicing, peeling, filling or polishing. Any of these treatments could enormously enhance the value or destroy it. There was no accurate way of calculating the hazards in advance. Much depended on experience and luck.

I was once shown (out of court) a large silk handkerchief containing hundreds of magnificent round jewels, gleaming with a myriad of soft colours in the sunlight. There is a romance about the oriental pearl, born from the living body of an oyster, and won at the venture of a man's life from the bottom of the sea. Since time immemorial pearls have been esteemed as the most precious of gems. In earliest Hindu literature they were spoken of as having been brought up from the ocean depths by the god Krishna for the purpose of beautifying his daughter on her wedding day. Mythology does not relate the name of the girl. As the god was regarded as the Apollo of the East, owing to numerous adventures with nymphs and shepherdesses, a large number of necklaces could well have been required!

In Europe and America they say "Pearls bring tears", but among Orientals they are worn not only for their shining loveliness but also as a talisman to ward off evil. And the pearl is a child of the East.

I have often been asked, "Did you bring home many pearls from Bahrain?" My answer is "No. Not one." I do possess, though, two greatly treasured mementos of my period of duty there, both gifts from Sheikh Hamad: a photograph of the Ruler and his young son taken in London on his visit to the Wembley Exhibition, and an Arab dagger, the scabbard of which is exquisitely worked in silver and gold filigree. On this visit to England the Sheikh was met by Major Daly and installed, with a small retinue, in a London Hotel. To have all his teeth out, and a set of gold dentures made, was the first requirement. A reputable dental surgeon tackled the job straight away, but Daly had hardly finished a meal at home when the telephone rang.

"Come quickly!" cried the dentist. "Your Ruler is haemorrhaging uncontrollably."

On arrival at the Surgery, Daly found the dentist greatly perturbed. "Why didn't you tell me the Sheikh was a bleeder?" he demanded angrily.

Neither of us had known. Events followed speedily, but by the time a specialist on blood circulation arrived, the crisis was over. The practitioner had staunched the flow and all was well.

To return to the disputes. The plaintiff might claim he owned a half share in a flawless gem which the defendant wanted to sell without his permission. Alternatively, the claim might be that the defendant wanted to cut the pearl without the plaintiff's agreement. This class of case might hang on until, to everyone's relief, and only after considerable pressure had been brought to bear, the precious object was produced in court. It was a tense moment. When the Arab began to fumble in the voluminous folds of his burnous, all eyes were turned on him, until finally, he held in his hand a dirty piece of cloth. After undoing numerous knots the material would be laid open on the table disclosing a glistening pearl. Thereafter a settlement was easy.

Many fortunes were made and lost in these transactions. There were Arabs living in poverty in Bahrain who had once been wealthy. The biggest pearl-fanciers of my time were the Parisian Jews, Rosenthal and Reuben. One or the other would arrive at the beginning of the season and occupy a large house. Crates of furniture, wines and exotic food were unloaded on the quay to make life bearable for them. In their luggage were delicate instruments to weigh and measure. It was not so much quantity they were after but quality. One or two individual shapes were required to match those laboriously collected after many years' search for a necklace. Already nearly complete, I was reminded of the parable of the 'pearl of great price' in the New Testament. One which resembled all the others in size, shape and lustre would be worth far more than its intrinsic value as a single unit. This pearl would put the finishing touch to a work of art. An experienced merchant when he finds such a one does not hesitate. He stretches his resources to the utmost, staking all, not on a gamble, but on a shrewd business deal. This lustrous product of the ocean will buy all the satisfaction of a great enterprise successfully, brilliantly, completed, In Bahrain, every year, it was rumoured that Rosenthal and Reuben spent millions of pounds.

The number of criminal cases was surprisingly small. Compared with the Pathans of the North West Frontier the Arabs were a law-abiding lot.

As the start of the new season drew near the atmosphere became tense. Almost all the slaves had been freed. Would they enter into contracts with their late masters, or would liberation go to their heads, causing them to revolt? The owners confidently predicted the latter, and went about their preparations with scowling black looks, cursing the British for all the evils sure to come. On the other hand, what alternative employment had the divers? Fresh-water springs on the island provided irrigation for a very limited area of cultivable land nothing like enough to produce a living for thousands. Nor was there any hope from the waterless deserts of the mainland. Neither the Sheikh nor I were unduly depressed, though we watched the situation with some anxiety.

The diving season, fixed by long-established custom, was four months and ten days, the time when the water was warmest. It started with the appearance of a star, and ended with the sighting of another star. There was no quarrel about this, nor about the one traditional relaxation. The whole pearling fleet returned in the middle of the season, to allow the divers home for a week to celebrate the Muslim festival of Moharram. The owners warned us this would be the really dangerous period. The men would be worked up by religious fervour and possibly by some liquor as well.

A good start was made, in spite of many forebodings. With the fleet away at sea Bahrain returned to its normal summer routine, with the wet bulb chasing the dry bulb into the hundreds and all human beings, including myself, almost prostrate with exhaustion. A Royal Navy ship put in one day. Some of the officers, including the doctor, came ashore in the evening. We began a game of tennis. "By rights we should be dead," observed the medico soberly when he saw both bulbs on the verandah standing at one hundred degrees. So we gave up and had a drink instead.

In spite of the heat we were far from inactive. In addition to Agency office work, I superintended construction of a new sea wall, and made a golf course with mud 'greens'.

Sometimes the Sheikh invited us to a desert feast in the centre of the island. Circular rush mats were laid on the sand and servants brought huge salvers from the nearby fort containing sheep roasted whole on mountains of rice, complete grilled chickens, and many other delicacies. When the meal was ready guests would squat on their left heel, with right arm and hand (previously ceremoniously washed) extended over the right knee for eating. It was an exquisitely uncomfortable position, jammed in as one was for some time, shoulder to chest with one's neighbours. "You have a very poor appetite," Sheikh Hamad would say playfully at my feeble efforts to engulf the mounds of food. There was always some annoying predecessor to whom he alluded as being a much better trencherman. When the feast finally ended, in the moonlight, out in the open desert, I had to be helped up, as my limbs had become completely paralysed.

As in Bushire nights were spent on the roof, but the small Agency power plant could not rise to an electric fan. For a substitute about half a dozen prisoners from the jail were deputed to pull a punkah in relays throughout the night. Clanking horribly, with chains on their ankles, they would be marched by their guard up the outside staircase onto the level surface, where they sat silently through the long hours till dawn. It was a sign of the times that, although shocked at first, I became used to this service.

In due course the pearling fleet returned for the Moharram celebrations. The zambuks were not dependent on shore supplies for fresh water.

Each diving vessel carried with it one or two goat skins open at the neck. When reserves ran short the Nakhuda, or Captain of the ship, would hoist sail or move through the water with oars until, from the colour of the sea, he could tell he was over a fresh water spring on the bottom. Then a diver with a goatskin leapt overboard, swam, weighted, to the depths and, holding the neck of the receptacle to the mouth of the spring, fillet it with water. He would then be hauled back with, literally, a sweet and drinkable skinful! I have tasted water obtained by these means and thought it slightly brackish, but otherwise good.

Blood flowed over the faces and bodies of fanatics as they cut themselves with swords during the usual ritual processions of Moharram. When the time came for the divers to return to their ships they refused, and there was a general strike. "We told you so! What are you going to do now?" the owners demanded of the Sheikh. This was the dreaded crisis: unless the divers went back quickly the reforms would break down and be acknowledged a failure. The suspected ringleaders were arrested and talked to. They were not open to reason.

One man in particular was organising the strike a bad hat, and Sheikh Hamad recommended him to be punished severely. Corporal punishment was decided on after careful consideration. I was present myself when the instigator was medically examined by the Agency doctor and given six stripes. All the divers knew the punishment had been carried out and that both the Sheikh and I were determined to break the deadlock in the interests of the men themselves, the pearling industry, and of the whole state. We succeeded. Perhaps those concerned realised at last that, unless the new laws could be made to work, there would inevitably be a relapse to slavery. They all returned to their ships and set sail for the banks. The crisis was over.

'Why don't you invite the Ruler and a few leading men to visit the fleet in the Agency steam launch?' suggested my Indian Assistant. This seemed an excellent idea. It might help to smooth over the troubles connected with Moharram. Sheikh Hamad and a number of owners accepted with pleasure. We loaded the launch up with two or three inevitable live sheep, lots of chickens and bushels of rice to feed our guests, and set off for the banks.

Vivid is the memory of that trip. The sea was rough and the mixture of heat and fumes quite overcame me. In the tiny cabin I stayed, trying hard not to think of the sheeps' eyes delicacies, while my noble assistant organised the feast and acted as host. As we neared the oyster beds a forest of bare masts filled the horizon. The vessels anchored close together, to frighten off sharks or other dangerous fish, such as blue jelly-fish or sting rays. There was safety in numbers, both on the surface and on the sea bed. Once among the zambuks our anchor was dropped, and I forced myself to get into a dinghy and be rowed close to some of the largest vessels to watch the diving and take photographs. I daringly went on board one, but the fishy smell of shells which had been opened on deck in search of pearls nearly finished me off. After the Sheikh had made a good inspection of the fleet we returned (thankfully on my part) to port.

Weighing up the pros and cons of that first season under the reforms it began to look like success, but we were wrong. Shortly before the end of the period a deputation of owners came to see me. "It has been a poor year," they cried. "There is a shortage of pearls, but above all, the operation has been upset by your confounded new-fangled laws! The independent Sheikhs up and down the coast have decided to keep their divers out ten days longer than usual. Why shouldn't we do the same?"

If I refused, they added, I would be blackening their faces, because they would be jeered at as slaves of the British.

"I cannot possibly agree to this proposal," I explained to Sheikh. The contract between owners and divers was for the duration of the pearling season no more and no less. The Bahrain fleet must return on the last day. After that the masters could enter into a new contract with their men for another ten days if they wished. After some hesitation, the Ruler agreed that I should give this answer to the deputation.

They laughed derisively. "Did I really think one single slave ... er umph ... freed man would enter into such an undertaking?"

"This is our decision. If you do not accept, you can appeal to the Resident on the other side of the Gulf."

They laughed again. "What is the use of an appeal? All you white faces stick together."

There the matter rested. We waited anxiously for the season to end. On the last day I went out before dawn onto the verandah of the Agency, overlooking the sea. To my intense relief the ocean was literally filled with sail. The vast multitude stretched to the horizon a wonderful sight. The zambuks were making for the shore like hundreds of purposeful white butterflies. The divers spent all morning hauling them high up on the beaches. Not one returned to the oyster beds. The appropriate star had been sighted. The season had ended.

Tired out and sleepy, I sat that night on the balcony after dinner. Some flashes appearing on the skyline I took to be summer lightning. This was the first week in October. No one had ever heard of rain in Bahrain till just before Christmas at the earliest. I had fallen asleep when a loud clap of thunder shook the house and roused me up. A violent gust of wind burst open the French windows leading into the living room, tearing the pictures off the walls and lifting the loose rugs from the floor to the ceiling. A cyclonic storm had hit the island.

The guard was summoned from below and, with the greatest difficulty, fighting the tempest, managed to close the shutters. Meanwhile all the wicker chairs on the verandah were lifted bodily and hurled into the sea. The cyclone raged all night, driving ashore all vessels afloat in the small harbour, including the Agency launch, carrying away many roofs of the houses in the town and uprooting twenty thousand date palms on the mainland.

Next morning dawned calm and clear; but Bahrain was shocked and devastated. An urgent messenger sent to Sheikh Hamaad returned with the answer that he was safe and well. Meanwhile I was asked to meet a deputation of the leaders of the City, including the old crowd of owners, waiting below. Speculating on what they wanted, I descended the stairs. "You have saved the Bahrain fleet and the whole season's catch," they cried, bowing themselves to the ground.

They recounted the dreadful news that all the craft belonging to the sheikhdoms up and down the coast, who had defied the customary diving period, were lost. The divers were drowned, and the ships and the total accumulation of pearls were at the bottom of the sea!

Medical help was needed at once, and the first thing was to get the steam launch seaworthy. Mechanics worked on her for twenty-four hours, but she was seriously damaged. Some time later she returned from the banks with two survivors, one of whom died on the way home. The other was just alive, though half-eaten by fish.

This dramatic conclusion stifled all further dispute on the subject of slavery. It was as if nature had intervened decisively to abolish, in a sensitive corner of the world, a stubborn example of man's inhumanity to man.

The storm was remembered on the whole of the Arab coast for many decades, and the season of 1925 was always referred to as "The Year of the Sinking".[2]

---

[2] Cf. Sir Charles Belgrave's *"Personal Column"*, p.35.

CHAPTER VIII

Arab Oil Back to the Frontier
1925–28

'Doth he curse Oriental romancing,
And wish he had toiled all his day,
At the Bar, or the Bank, or financing,
And got damned in a commonplace way?'

In the meanwhile, Bahrain was preparing to give Sheikh Hamad a warm welcome on his return from England. Staying with me, during this period, was an American named George Gregg Fuller. He was a very pleasant guest, though apt to be critical as many of his countrymen were of British Colonial methods. "My eyes have been opened," he declared afterwards, when he had seen the Ruler's homecoming. The busy port, the streets, the shops and all prominent buildings were gaily decorated; and arches of welcome erected at most focal spots. I donned the white summer 'political' uniform with dazzling topee brass spike, chin strap and ceremonial sword. All Agency and State officials were dressed in their best.

The Sheikh, with great formality, was conducted from the mail steamer to the Agency launch. I received him on the quay. "I was much impressed with Wumbley," he announced, flashing his golden smile. He seemed quite taken aback at the warmth of his reception; large crowds gathered to cheer him unusual in an oriental land and left him in no doubt of the affection and loyalty of his subjects.

It is not strictly correct to say that no one dreamed of oil while I was in Bahrain. The Anglo-Persian Oil Company had sent their geologists some time previously to survey the entire Arab coastline but, beyond this, showed no sign of interest or activity.

At this juncture an Englishman, Major Frank Holmes, appeared and came to my office. He announced that he represented the Eastern and General Syndicate and asked to be allowed to apply to Sheikh Hamad for an exploitation licence for oil.

"Under his treaty with the Home Government the Sheikh can only grant such a licence to a British firm," I pointed out.

"The E. and G.S. is a British firm," he declared.

"Confirmation will have to be supplied by the Colonial Office in London before any negotiations can take place," I replied.

Holmes was annoyed at the inevitable delay. I later discovered that he had first arrived in the Gulf in 1923, and actually approached the Sheikhs of Kuwait and Bahrain direct, without obtaining prior permission of HMG, and succeeded in inducing them to grant, or undertake to grant, to the Eastern and General Syndicate exclusive concessions, for exploitation for oil and other minerals. He had made another visit to Bahrain on 4th June 1924 and improved his position by applying for authorisation from the Colonial Office to bore artesian wells in the town. This was agreed to in January 1925.

With permission from the Sheikh and myself, Holmes selected a stretch of open desert between groups of houses, where water was badly needed, and started to drill. The numerous fresh springs, which are an important feature of the island, together with those that the divers had found at the bottom of the sea, encouraged him to think that he could strike artesian water almost anywhere, and he was right. The drilling had only continued for a matter of hours, when lo and behold, the miracle occurred! Beautiful clear water, sparkling in the sunshine, spouted out of the ground. Major Frank Holmes became an instant hero with the local population and the Ruler.

In the course of many discussions on the subject of oil Sheikh Hamad was quite frank and open. "My treaty obligations will be respected," he told me. But he had taken a liking to the Major (his heart softened, I must add, by expensive presents). "I am convinced he means business and will begin boring as soon as sanction is granted." The Anglo-Persian Oil Company, on the other hand were dragging their feet. The Sheikh had no faith in their capacity for active exploration. Moreover he suspected, possibly with reason, that the British Government owned a controlling share in the Company, and were therefore biased in its favour. Naturally, he was interested in every means of increasing his revenue without delay.

As soon as they heard of Holmes's activities, the APOC at Abadanin the Shatt-al-Arab, were up in arms. They bombarded me with letters full of indignation and alarm: "Holmes is an imposter! The Eastern and General Syndicate is an American and not a British firm the Sheikh must not be allowed to negotiate."

All this gave rise to a lengthy correspondence between the Colonial Office at home and the Resident at Bushire, to whom I wrote expressing my own views. These were generally in support of Sheikh Hamad, but I recalled that the pearling industry, upon which the State then depended for its income, had only just been reformed and would need time to settle down. Any large scale drilling for oil might divert a considerable part of the limited labour force available for pearling into other channels, of employment, and cause a depression in the traditional industry. This, coupled with the possibility that the boring might be unsuccessful, could spell disaster for the State. "I have painted a dark picture,' I concluded.

"Put your dark picture to the Sheikh," came back a telegram in reply.

But Sheikh Hamad was not deterred. He had a hunch that oil would be found. Meanwhile Holmes was getting more and more irritated by the holdup, accusing me of obstruction and threatening to report me to the Colonial Office. "Go ahead," I said cheerfully: but I thought it desirable to press the Resident (Colonel Knox) to visit Bahrain for talks with the Ruler and the Major, which he did. On 7th August 1925 a high level Conference was held, at Whitehall, the outcome of which was that the Sheikh was permitted to grant a concession for the exploitation of oil in Bahrain to the Eastern and General Syndicate. In a matter of months the island was flooded with *American* oil men!

In November 1925 Major and Mrs Daly returned with some of their younger children. I can recall going out to meet the mail steamer; there was a big swell, and as usual I felt pretty green. It was too rough to let down a gangway, so the whole family came over the side one by one on a rope ladder and dropped, or were lifted, into the Agency launch. Looking up from a small boat, on a heaving sea, the mail steamer seemed tremendously high. The Dalys were a tough lot. I was filled with admiration for the entire operation and its lack of fuss.

It was with a mixture of regret and relief at the idea of getting a rest after three busy years that I left the Gulf. My farewell to Sheikh Hamad was perhaps made more formal by the arrival of Daly (the Boss!) His personality dominated such a small State.

The time for home leave had come. Members of the Indian Political Service could rely on six months every four or five years, in addition to a short break every year in India. For those lucky enough to be serving in the North these breaks would probably be spent in Kashmir, one of the world's most attractive playgrounds. The chain of lakes, overshadowed by mountains, and covered in their season by water lily and iris, made a perfect setting for relaxation. The fishing in the hill streams, the Bringhi, the Madmatti, and the Sind, had to be seen to be believed.

Periodical furloughs were essential to lift one out of the highly charged oriental atmosphere and restore a sense of proportion. A bachelor escaped the problems which tormented young families. They were split between the two countries and the need to educate growing children in Europe. Constancy was prayed for on both sides, but marriages seemed to be tougher then. Divorce might mean the end of a career.

When I had been in England about a month, a letter arrived from Daly, written from a hospital in Bombay. "I am still bleeding like a pig from bayonet wounds received when attacked in my office in Bahrain,"[1] he wrote, "but am making good progress, and hope to be out of hospital soon." Daly was one of the most courageous men I have ever met.

The reason for his letter was to give me a message from Sheikh Hamad: would I consider returning to the island at the end of my leave?

After thinking things over carefully, I decided to decline for three reasons: firstly, I suspected that the people of Bahrain thought there was something prophetic about me, because my 'anticipation' of the storm had saved the pearling fleet from destruction. That kind of reputation was impossible to live up to. Secondly, I was now thirty-one and unmarried. I could not be buried for another five years without hope of meeting an English girl who might become my wife. On the other hand, desperation might force me to turn Muslim and take on a harem of four Arab wives! It had been done before. The pull of Islam is very strong, the nearer one gets to Mecca. But there was another, and stronger, pull. I wanted to go back to the Frontier.

On the way home I had hoped to see as much as possible of the Middle East, but I was in a hurry. The journey from Basrah to Baghdad was made by rail. En route the train drew in to a small station. On the platform notice board was written two huge letters: 'UR'. With a shock I realised it must be 'Ur of the Chaldees'. Jumping from my seat, I was half inclined to seize the luggage and get out, but a howling sand-storm was blowing outside and there were many thousands of miles still to travel. Reluctantly I sat down. Ever since I have regretted missing the excavations by that famous archaeologist, Leonard Wooley, revealing relics of the Sumerian civilisation during the period 2500 to 3000 BC. The strange looking burial mounds on Bahrain Island which were dug into by Mr E. Mackay, while I was there, were believed to belong to this

---

[1] Daly had been talking to one of the Indian Officers in the orderly room when a Baluchi Levy man crept to the open window and shot the Indian in the back, the bullet went through him and nicked off a piece of Daly's ear. The other Indian officer ran up and he too was shot. Daly tried, very bravely, to tackle the man, but was stabbed in half a dozen places with a bayonet ... Sir Charles Belgrave's *Personal Column*, p.35.

age; but Mackay tentatively dated them one thousand years later. Many had been entered and rifled, but when they were opened in 1925, the two-tier burial chambers inside the larger mounds contained skeletons and some pottery, but little else of value.[2]

I allowed myself only a couple of days in the Maude Hotel, Baghdad and afterwards regretted that I did not visit the many ancient sites in this valley, such as Ctesiphon. The surviving ruins of the Royal Palace, there, once the capital of New Persia, show the beautiful arch, with its attendant wall and doorway, intact.[3] The huge vault was built over the enormous hall below, without any supporting timbers during the course of its construction. It is 84 ft. across and is the largest masonry vault of its age still standing in Asia. Here the magnificent kings of New Persia held their splendid court, imitated by the weak Roman emperors at Constantinople. Situated almost within sight of Babylon, Ctesiphon was but one in a succession of powerful capitals occupying the river crossing on the great highway between Asia Minor and the East, including Akkad, Babylon, Seleucia and, finally, Baghdad.

A seat in an open Nairn Transport Buick was booked for the transdesert journey to Jerusalem. We started at dawn. Once out of the fertile valley we followed a furrow dug in the firm flint strewn surface of the level plain, possibly to guide land convoys or aeroplanes, or to mark the direction of a new pipeline. There was no road. Travelling sometimes at 70 miles an hour, we reached the oasis of Rutba Wells about nightfall, and after resting the driver and refreshing ourselves with food and drink, we pressed on all through the night with strong headlights. Just before dawn we were slowed down to 2 miles an hour by outcrops of black volcanic rock, sticking up out of the desert like huge teeth, just east of Amman. A civilised road took us down into the Jordan Valley, and we crossed the old Ghoraniyeh (since Allenby) Bridge and up the long pull to Jerusalem. Thirteen years later, in 1938, when I was again in Palestine with Marie we visited the Nairn Transport headquarters in Damascus. When I told them I was one of their first clients we were given VIP treatment and shown over the marvelous modern trans-desert Pullman cars, which now carry passengers in air-conditioned comfort between Jerusalem or Damascus and Baghdad.

---

[2] A description of these mounds and various 'digs' is given in Sir Arnold Wilson's book, *The Persian Gulf*, pp.29–32. See also Mr E. Mackay's report (1925) to the British School of Archaeology in Egypt, and more recently (1970) Geoffrey Bibby's *Looking for Dilmun*, a fascinating account of extensive exploration in Bahrain.

[3] *Ancient Times. A History of the Early World.* Breasted

This was my second visit to Palestine, but the first in peacetime. Not knowing my Bible well enough then, I did not derive the fullest benefit from the dramatic landscape but it left a deep impression upon me. This narrow strip of country with desert on one side and sea on the other was worthy of its undying fame as the land where two of the world's greatest religions, Judaism and Christianity, were born and cradled. Compressed within its narrow bounds is a remarkable variety of scenery. Here a broad fertile plain, there a mountain soaring steeply into the sky: now you are up in the peaks, then more than a thousand feet below sea level. As if nature were still not satisfied, the face of this beautiful country is scarred by a great gash from north to south the steep rocky valley of the Jordan river, flowing ever deeper into the bowels of the earth, until its waters rest in the salt, cavernous blue pit of the Dead Sea. Looking eastwards from the Mount of Olives and climbing the hill behind Nazareth, I felt that this tremendous scenery had lent a hand in the shaping of the Old and New Testament Scriptures; it had fired the imagination of the Hebrew prophets, and drawn the Carpenter's Son at Nazareth away from his father's bench, out into the desert round Jordan. Nature herself had provided the peculiar inspiration needed for the founding of these religions.

My route home meant taking a ship from Alexandria to Brindisi and from there by train to Naples. Here I stayed a few nights with two uncles and my aunt Kathleen: 'the woman with two husbands' as she was known in our family. The trio had retired in Naples and evidently had no regrets at leaving the old country, but basked in the sunshine of these aquamarine shores.

In Rome, and later in Florence, I delighted in the exquisite examples of early and medieval Christian art, but nothing could compare with the grandeur of the 'Mother of Cities'. As I stood uncertainly in the great square of St. Peter's, an American student approached.

"How long is your stay?" he queried.

"Forty-eight hours," I answered.

He offered to conduct me on a lightning tour of the City, which he did in true Occidental style. We rushed from one building or church to another, sometimes running to save time. "You must not look at anything but the cream!" he insisted. The cream was, as I remember, Michelangelo's Pieta in St. Peter's, and a very fine statue of Moses at San Pietro in Vincoli, seated with the tablets of stone, by the same unerring hand. Of course we had to throw our coins in the Trevi Fountain. Neither of us admitted what we had wished for, but I'm sure we were both concerned with the fairer sex.

The winter sports season in Switzerland was at its height. This would blow away the heat and strain of the Gulf, and give the energy needed to tackle the final Bar exam at Gray's Inn. A few hours train journey found me in Villars-sur-Ollon, a lovely mountain resort overlooking the Dent du Midi. Almost immediately I ran into an old friend, Alec Wallace, who had retired early from the ICS and was making his mark as a schoolmaster. He later became Headmaster of Sherborne School, and eventually Dean of Exeter Cathedral. Wallace was on holiday with a gay party of young people, who kindly invited me to join them. What a difference in the skiing then to now: only the snow, the glorious clean air, with its smell of conifers, and the feeling of exhilaration, remain the same.

As to clothes, a sweater, an old pair of riding breeches, stockings, hired boots and skis, sufficed when I stood poised on the top of the nursery slope for the first run down. My new-found friends longed to see an almighty crash and two up-ended skis! They were disappointed. It may be that cavalry training gave a sense of balance that kept me on my feet to the end of the slope, and for many other enjoyable excursions in both Switzerland and Afghanistan.

Once in England, I resumed the old routine of attending lectures and eating dinners at Gray's Inn. The meals were simple: soup, a roast of beef or saddle of mutton, stewed fruit and custard, and a fine Stilton to finish. A jug of beer was passed round from time to time to slake our thirst. Before dinner we robed in gowns, so that the whole affair was conducted with some ceremony. The setting was superb.

The hall, completed about the year 1560, was of handsome Elizabethan design. Here, in previous days, tremendous orgies were held. Students learned to dance, sing, and play instrumental music. Evelyn speaks of the revels at the Middle Temple as an old riotous custom, having relation neither to virtue nor to policy.

The benchers varied in number from twenty in Gray's Inn to seventy and upwards in Lincoln's Inn and Inner Temple. In 1926 there were a number of coloured students who found a smaller Inn more sociable. There was a dais at the end of the hall where the benchers sat at a separate table, while the barristers and students ate in the main body.

Because time was short I went to a crammer in Court lectures, and when sitting for the Final Bar exam with English common law, Statute law, Torts and Equity. The field was so wide one's memory was strained to breaking point. For in the Common Law Paper was (I think):

"Q. Illustrate the Principle in 'Household Fire Insurance Company versus Grant'."

Fortunately I knew the case an important ruling, but still one out of hundreds. Leaving the examination hall, and into the car to visit Oxford friends, I found I could not drive! I was shaking like a leaf. It had been a strain sandwiching the Final between long periods of duty in the East.

In due course my name appeared among the successful candidates, and with my mind distracted by many farewells, I attended the 'Call Night' dinner at Gray's Inn, just 24 hours before leaving for India. Once the Ceremony was over, a rag started. Each one of the new barristers was required to make a speech.

When your turn came, "Get up, get up," they called, "Speech, speech".

But the minute one rose to one's feet, the heckling began.

"What a great honour it is," I started nervously, "to be called in this Ancient and Honourable..."

"We can't hear"..."Open your mouth"..."Sit down"..."Stand up"..."Go on"... etc.

James Almond, afterwards Sir James and Judicial Commissioner of the NWF Province was called at the same time, but I cannot recall that he made a much better showing.

A word about the General Strike that occurred in May 1926 while I was on leave. Though only dimly aware of the real causes, I offered my services to the Government, with car, and was given the job of carrying mail from Whitehall to Cardiff until an advertisement calling for temporary recruits to the Metropolitan Mounted Constabulary caught my eye. I applied as an ex cavalry officer and was at once accepted. There was an admiral in the ranks, and several 'rough riders' from Canada and Australia. Horses were supplied from Smiths' Stables in Cadogan Place, and Mr Smith himself joined us on parade. We executed troop movements up and down Rotten Row and our commander did his best to lick us into shape.

The arms supplied were dummy swords or long truncheons, and as we left for duty a couple of stable boys, with their hands and arms greased up to the elbows, stood at the gates. We drew our 'weapons' through their hands as we trotted out. This left the truncheons so slimy that a striker would not be able to snatch them from us. We convoyed lorries to and from the docks through the streets of London, but got the impression that the authorities were not anxious to let us loose among a crowd of strikers. Fortunately the strike collapsed, without untoward incident, and we were disbanded.

I was appointed District Judge at Abbottabad on my return to India in December, a pleasant job in a good climate. Abbottabad was an attractive hill station, ringed with fir trees, and a considerable European population both civil and military. I settled down in a comfortable bungalow, but in May when the weather had begun to warm up in the plains, a bombshell arrived in the form of a posting to Tank, as Assistant Commissioner. No station on the Frontier is hotter or more remote. I consulted the Deputy Commissioner of Abbottabad, Mr R.R. Maconochie (afterwards Sir Richard, Minister at Kabul), one of the most brilliant men in the Service. He advised me rather curtly to obey orders. It occurred to me that this posting might turn out a blessing in disguise. Although as a barrister I was qualified to be district judge and later sessions judge, my mind was made up not to specialise on the judicial side. To me legal training was a general education. I was interested in executive work which would bring me into touch with the masses of India and all their needs.

Driving down the winding road from Abbottabad to the furnace of the plains there was plenty of time to reflect upon the future. Two hundred odd miles away stood Tank, a small fortified town on the edge of the Derajat, close to the hills and within a mile or two of the border. The AC's bungalow, a grim mud-walled building of immense thickness to keep out the heat, was situated in a tiny cantonment surrounded by barbed wire.

Tank had changed little in the eight years since the interlude with the 27th Light Cavalry in the winter of 1919. During the summer the only other European was the District Officer, Frontier Constabulary, an agreeable man called Scott. Scott commanded a considerable force and was responsible for protection of the district and cantonment against active tribal raiders.

This was my first independent executive charge. The AC of a subdivision and the DC of the district were local representatives of Government in all aspects except the judicial. The separation of the judicial from the executive, save strictly for maintenance of law and order, was an important principle of British administration. There were those who advocated absolute separation, but this seemed impractical in most parts of India, where sudden breaches of the peace could arise from friction between Hindus and Muslims, or from political agitation. It was certainly true of the Frontier, where every district included a stretch of tribal limits, and was open to forays from across the border. So the Deputy Commissioner (and to a lesser extent his Assistant) was District Magistrate and Head of Police, with special powers under the Frontier Crimes Regulation. In spite of this, he could be, and often was the father of his people. They would come to him in any kind of trouble and he would see that their complaints received the attention of the appropriate department. He sat in court to accept written petitions, and in his house to welcome visitors who might wish to make a personal request or discuss local affairs.

My court diary was soon crammed with criminal, civil and revenue cases. A continuous stream of visitors, both from the tribal area and from the settled district, came in daily, and it was here that I first noticed that the incidence of crime in the settled district far exceeded that of the tribal area. Left to themselves the tribe (Bhitannis) had some effective means of dealing with disputes, and of deterring would-be wrongdoers. Many of the cases related to quarrels over the distribution of perennial and floodwater issuing from the hills into the plain in the Tank (or Takki) Zam. This was British territory and disputes would normally be brought into court, with police, pleaders and all the paraphernalia of the regular law.

I took an early opportunity of visiting the distribution point with a surveyor. A permanent system for the division of water was out of the question, as any pukka brick or cement work would be swept away in the first heavy flood. All that was possible was a rough division made by moving stones and earth. It looked a Heath Robinson affair, but it worked. Water is gold in a thirsty land, and an agricultural community usually hangs together.

"Don't you have to keep a perpetual watch?" I asked the surveyor.

"Yes, we pay a Chaukidar to stay day and night in that mud hut, built on high ground for safety. He has a spade and pick to deal with medium sized floods. If the water shows signs of rising to the level of a spate, he runs down to the valley below to cry a warning. It is passed on to Tank by telephone; but usually we rely on prior warning from Jandola, higher up the river."

What about disputes? I queried, my eye following the little mounds of irrigation channels, knowing how quick-tempered Pathans are. "Ah yes, Sahib,' he smiled. "At dead of night men will bring spades and divert the water into their own fields. By daylight the damage can be seen. Even riots can start, as you know, Sahib, when they end up in the courts, standing in front of you in chains!"

During the summer rains, the whole Derajat-Bannu border was subject to serious flooding, produced by the Gomal, the Tank and the Tochi. These three rivers flowed eastwards into the Indus, and cut across the main lines of communication. One day, I was invited to the opening of a fine new masonry bridge over the Takki Zam at Jandola. H.E., the Commander-in-Chief in India, and many important officials, both civil and military, spent the night before the ceremony at the fort. At dawn the bridge had disappeared! Its foundations had been swept away by a huge spate, caused by a thunderstorm in the mountains, which roared down and carried the whole river bed with it. After that disaster, a technique of bridge building described as 'vibro-concrete screw piles', penetrating below the movable bed, proved more successful.

Though on tour whenever possible, most of my time was spent at headquarters hard at work. What a heavy load there was. When the Judicial Commissioner, Sir Hugh Fraser, came to inspect the court, he got out of his car, shook me by the hand and said, "I hear you're overworking. Remember this is the place where P (a previous AC) first went mad!" There were stories that he had been found wandering in the streets of Peshawar, quite alone, and muttering to himself. I was already beginning to think Tank could send anyone mad. The mosquitoes were as big as snipe; they were certainly the largest I ever saw anywhere. Like an orchestra they tuned up in the bathroom, their violin notes echoing from the tin ghusal. Strangely enough, I never got malaria, though exposed to it almost continuously for thirty years.

The Bhittannis, who lived just beyond the boundary, were my special political charge as AC Friendly relations were gradually established, mainly through an old Subahdar-Major of Scouts named Muqam Khan, who had bought land and settled down on the British side. He was a Bhittanni himself and had a good deal of influence in the tribe. Together we persuaded the tribesmen to agree to my doing a tour on horseback throughout their territory. Tents were packed onto camels' backs, and with me went Mr R.H.D. Lowis of the Indian police (later Indian Political Service), with a small escort of Frontier Constabulary. From Jandola into the sun-drenched, soil eroded foothills rode our little cavalcade. There being no roads, rough paths were followed along barren mountain sides or the dry beds of water courses, which in the rainy season turned into angry torrents of brown flood water, pouring through deep gorges to the plains below. A number of armed tribesmen accompanied us, posting sentries round the encampment at night, and reassuring their fellows through whose village limits we passed. Occasionally the route crossed a valley watered by a clear stream channeled into cultivated fields of wheat, barley or maize. These stretches of green, edged by trees, presented a picture of peaceful husbandry, brutally belied by a bare rock face or steep hillside, by a rifle slung over a shoulder and a general atmosphere of vigilance and insecurity.

The journey brought me into close contact for the first time with an indigenous tribal democracy, in its own peculiar setting. The experience was impressive. How did this community, comprising some of the most independent and warlike individuals anywhere in the world, manage to live? They admitted no chiefs or rulers, other than the tribal council of elders, comprising apparently every able-bodied man. They had their blood feuds, and their factions; they were hot tempered; they looked as wild as the mountain wilderness in which they lived. And yet, there was an unmistakable discipline somewhere. Where was it? What did it consist of? I could find no answers to these questions, but they were to haunt me for another fifteen years.

In spite of the forbidding, nature of the country, our progress was uneventful. Contacts were surprisingly friendly except when we arrived near the spot close to the Bannu border where Harold Vickers had been wounded and captured by tribesmen, as described before. Here we encountered the only sign of hostility from the headmen of a village near our route. "What are you doing in our country?" they asked brusquely, refusing to shake my hand.

"We are on a friendly visit at the invitation of the tribe," I replied. We did not hang about.

CHAPTER IX

Frontier Revolt
1929–31

For whether you swelter the live-long day
Toiling under an Indian sun,
Or whether you lie amid English hay
Drinking the summer hours away
What will it matter? when life is done.

When the Shyok glacier slips down a bit further than usual, damming up the waters of the Indus, it creates a huge lake. Sooner or later the ice melts and a great wave cascades down the river gorges into the plain below, carrying destruction in its wake. In the path of this flood lies the eastern edge of the Mardan district, which was my next assignment as Sub-Divisional Officer. A warning of imminent floods made one of my first duties to evacuate to higher ground the villages lying close to the banks. The people were fatalistic.

"There is danger of waters sweeping away your houses and your flocks," I hurriedly told a headman. "You are advised to move for your own safety."

A blank stare would appear on his face and I was usually told: "Allah will provide."

There had been false alarms before. Only a small proportion of the population ever decamped. In this case it also turned out to be unnecessary, so perhaps Allah had provided. However a few years later severe damage was actually done and there was great loss of life.

This was the end of May 1928. Compared with Tank, one was in clover. No longer wearied by interminable stretches of parched desert on plain and hill, my eyes feasted on the green lawns of an ordered cantonment, and on fertile cultivated land, generously irrigated by the Kabul and Swat rivers. The Guides Cavalry were stationed in Mardan, and among the officers was an old friend from Dragon School days Bertie Eales, who was afterwards killed in the Second World War. My youngest sister Joyce joined me from home and moved with me to a new posting as Under Secretary Peshawar in January 1929. Mr C.H. Gidney (later Sir Claude) was an able and experienced Chief, and taught me a good deal for which I was grateful afterwards!

We spent a happy summer at Nathia Gali, the official hill station of the

Frontier Government, 'walking' one of the hound puppies of the Peshawar Vale Hunt, which chewed up all the rugs in the bungalow. In the autumn to Europe by Lloyd Triestino from Bombay to Venice. Thence to England and peace. It was the calm before the storm.

Before leaving India I had been warned that on return from leave I would be appointed Census Superintendent for the Frontier in connection with the All India Census of 1931, an undertaking of immense proportions, yet promising to be a very orderly and sedate operation. No one realised that the whole area West of the Indus was on the eve of one of the most explosive periods in its stormy history. As I had to abandon the Census temporarily to lend a hand in dealing with the crisis of 1930, it will be convenient to summarise some of the main causes here. As a result of the Government of India Act 1919, the whole of India, except the NWFP, was launched into an experiment in democracy. Legislative assemblies were set up in each province and general elections held from which ministries were formed, responsible to the governors, who remained in most cases British.

The Frontier Province was excluded from these reforms on the ground that it was a disturbed area. This proved to be both a psychological and a political blunder, because Pathans are a proud people and consider themselves not only equal, but also superior to the races in other parts of India. When in 1930 the Simon Commission, appointed to review the working of the reforms, again excluded the Frontier Province, the Pathans were understandably furious. In the meanwhile, the All India Congress Committee, a predominantly Hindu body, committed to a policy of complete independence, who had reluctantly agreed to co-operate in the elections, seized upon the Pathan grievances and worked them up into a full-scale revolution. Congress found an ideal agent in Abdul Ghaffar Khan, known afterwards as 'the Frontier Ghandi' a tall man of striking appearance, with black beard and flashing eyes. The fiery speeches of this rabble rouser, to great crowds all along the border, turned many loyal peace loving citizens into red revolutionaries overnight.

Returning in March 1930 to take over the Census I was shocked to find that several old friends in the Mardan Subdivision, regarded as absolutely reliable, were now rabidly anti-British. The agitation spread to the Afridis and other transborder tribes. Before long all British officials found themselves with their backs to the wall.

The centre of the trouble appeared to be in Charsadda, a large and important village, HQ of a subdivision, about twenty miles northeast of Peshawar and ten from Mardan. Here Abdul Ghaffar Khan, whose birthplace Utmanzai lay two or three miles North East of Charsadda, was busy recruiting and training a force of volunteers (Khudai Khidmatgars or 'servants of God') and known to us as 'Red Shirts', being clothed from head to foot in crimson shirts, shorts and stockings. Continuous contact with these colourful characters soon turned my normal dreams into nightmares!

Inevitably the insurrection spread to Peshawar City where serious riots occurred. British armoured cars were sent to quell them and had to open fire with machine guns. The mob, infuriated by this treatment, managed to overturn and set fire to one of them. They also overwhelmed and murdered a British signalman on a motor bicycle. Troops were called out from the Cantonment to assist the civil power, and a regiment of Garwhalis chose this moment to refuse to obey orders. Realising that Congress agitators had penetrated the Indian Army, we began to wonder if we were faced with a second Indian Mutiny. The Garwhalis were disarmed immediately. The other Indian regiments stood firm.

While the position was threatening in Peshawar, Abdul Ghaffar Khan was suddenly arrested by the police on 24th April and held in the sub-jail at Charsadda. This caused a huge crowd to collect, supported by Red Shirts and some trans-border Pathans armed with rifles. The mob surrounded the jail and the bungalow and office of the SD officer, a well-known Pathan named Khan Bahadur Kuli Khan,[1] and threatened to attack him. With only a small force of Frontier Constabulary for protection, K.K. (as he was known to us) managed to telephone for help to Peshawar, before the wires were cut. Whereupon the Chief Commissioner, Sir Norman Bolton, sent for me as the only British officer not on urgent duty, and briefly outlined the situation at Charsadda. My orders were, he said, to proceed at once to Mardan and march with the Guides Cavalry to remove Ghaffar Khan from Charsadda jail and take him to Nowshera. There he would be tried under the Frontier Crimes Regulation, and, if convicted, sentenced to a period of imprisonment somewhere far from the border. "But," said Sir Norman, betraying the strain of the last week, "this must be effected without firing a shot. Any more shooting will bring the tribes down all along the Frontier."

At Mardan all was quiet, and the Guides were ready to march. They lent me a horse, but I took the precaution before we started of getting in touch with one of the leading Yusufzai Khans, a Pathan landowner, whose loyalty could be relied on. He promised to follow us in his car along the road to Charsadda.

Trotting between the Colonel and his second in command at the front of

---

[1] One of the heroes of the Molly Ellis affair. See p.151.

the regiment, I listened to their conversation. "The terms of our assignment are very unsatisfactory," the Major announced indignantly. "When the Army is called out to aid the Civil Power, it is ridiculous to lay down the condition that no shots must be fired. If the need arises for a decision, the only person in a position to judge whether or not to open fire is the officer commanding troops on the spot. Don't you agree?" he asked, turning in his saddle and looking at me. Not wishing to be drawn into this argument on a subject of great controversy ever since the Amritsar incident and the court martial of General Dyer, I simply repeated the instructions given to me by Sir Norman.

We trotted on in a rather grim silence until we reached the outskirts of the village. Here an enormous crowd was surrounding the Government buildings. "I will occupy the high ground over there," said the Colonel, pointing to a low ridge on the left of the road, "and train my machine guns on the mob. What are you going to do?"

"As I want to take the crowd by surprise, I cannot wait for you to get into position," I replied, "I am going to get into the Khan's car and drive straight through to the AC's bungalow."

"Good luck, then," he wished us as we parted.

I leapt into the car, with the wheels still moving, and we went off down the road, driving slower and slower as we penetrated the crowd. Both the Khan, sitting next to me on the back seat, and his driver were armed with pistols. As a matter of principle, I never went armed on the Frontier. We had slowed down almost to a halt when the mob became menacing. "When I saw you being enclosed, and the crowd converging on you from right and left, I nearly opened fire," the CO of the Guides admitted afterwards. If he had, I should not be telling the tale today.

The car had just halted when, pushing their way towards us, came the Red Shirts. When they saw us they took complete command, sending a party ahead to clear a path through the crowd. They climbed all over the vehicle: sitting on the roof, the bonnet and mudguards. They stood on the running boards, holding on through the windows. Some walked on either side, some behind, and so escorted we came quietly and safely to the AC's house.

"*Pah Khair Raghele*" (welcome and very glad to see you) announced a delighted Kuli Khan, and we were thankful to see him safe and well. Disembarking, we held a hurried consultation. There was no time to be lost. The problem was to get our very 'hot' prisoner out and on the road to Mardan without delay. The Frontier Constabulary filled an open truck with armed men, and Abdul Ghaffar Khan was brought from the jail and told to get in. Before he did so, I

FROGS IN THE WELL

spoke to him. I said that I relied on him absolutely to use his influence with the crowd in the interest of us all   to prevent violence and bloodshed. "A single shot would mean great loss of life." I insisted, warning him that the Guides had their machine guns trained.

"Unless you take off my handcuffs," he replied, "I can do nothing, as they will infuriate the crowd."

There was an instant objection from the Police, fearing that he would try to escape. Now I knew Abdul Ghaffar came of a good Pathan family. "Will you give me your word of honour not to run for it?" I asked.

He answered in the affirmative with a smile, and the, handcuffs were grudgingly undone. In order to seal the compact we shook hands. "This is a gentleman's agreement."[2] I said. "Remember, if you try to escape you will be shot!" He smiled again and got into the truck.

He was as good as his word. He stood up, towering above the little forest of rifles, like a Hebrew prophet with his arms in the air. The small cavalcade, led by our car, drove slowly through the vast mob, flanked by Red Shirts, while Ghaffar Khan shouted, "I am being well-treated and will soon be back among you. In the meanwhile there must be no violence, as Mahatma Gandhi has commanded." He had complete control of the people who listened to him in silence.

When we got clear and onto the Mardan road, the Colonel of the Guides galloped up and called out, "Well done". At Nowshera I phoned Sir Norman to say the plan had succeeded, hoping the news would cheer him. But he was on the edge of a breakdown perhaps he foresaw the serious events that were to follow.

Ghaffar Khan was duly convicted and languished in an Indian jail for a twelve-month period, but his followers continued the agitation with increasing vehemence, and once more Charsadda became the centre of a full-scale revolution.

Extraordinary events began to happen all along the Frontier. Red Shirts appeared everywhere, and attempted to take over government of the province. They seized Peshawar city and imprisoned the Police inside their stations.

Immediately he stiffened. "I could never agree to that. It would be against

---

2   Another case of a 'gentleman's agreement' many years later occurred between Pundit Nehru and Raymond Vernede (*Plain Tales from the Raj* edited by Charles Allen) on Allahabad station on a certain midnight. Vernede with a telegram marked 'Release on parole' had to use his discretion how to put this across. Jawarharlal was on his way to Naini Tal where his wife was seriously ill, and like her husband, in prison. "They will release you on parole, providing you give an undertaking," I told him stepping carefully over the white bodies sleeping on the platform.

all my principles to give such an undertaking. I have been in jail for nearly three years."

"Releasing you on parole is an act of chivalry," I pointed out.

"That may have been all right in the Middle Ages, but it doesn't work in India. It doesn't apply any longer. It stinks."

I suddenly had a brainwave. "If you won't give an undertaking to the Government, what about coming to a gentleman's agreement with me?"

He stopped in his tracks ... and a delightful smile came over his face. "Ah, a gentleman's agreement with you? ... I think I could accept that."

The weakness of the government position now became apparent. Faced with a revolt, involving the large majority of Pathans, whose pride and self respect had been injured by the exclusion of their Province from the Reforms of 1919, the few British officials scattered along the border found themselves isolated and alone. The exclusion was intended to strengthen the hands of the administration in a crisis, but in the event it had the opposite effect. The Great Frontiersmen of the past thought that their own direct paternal rule was best suited to Pathans; the most natural form of government for a wild hotheaded race, prone to lawlessness and insurrection. They could not have been more wrong, and many of us, who bore the brunt of the revolt, blamed them for their lack of foresight. The success of the Reforms in the other Provinces exposed the weaknesses of direct rule. There a broad-based administration enabled the British element to retire behind a screen of Legislative Assemblies and elected Indian Ministers. No such refuge was available for the Frontier authorities. The strain on the administration soon produced its first casualty Sir Norman Bolton. He was an able and popular Chief Commissioner. He knew his people; they trusted him, even loved him. It seemed unbelievable to him that he should lose their confidence, and yet that confidence turned into hate before his eyes. The constant stream of visitors to Government House dried up. If he went on tour, he was in danger of being mobbed or insulted. He lost all direct contact with the people, and became a virtual prisoner in his own house. The telephone rang incessantly, with reports of riots in the districts and threatening movements of tribes across the border. He had to preside over one meeting after another of Army commanders and administrative heads to try and deal with emergencies, and bring the general situation under control. This was a heavy strain for one man to bear. The bitterest blow of all the loss of Peshawar City to the Red Shirts and the mutiny of the Gharwalis was the crowning touch. His abrupt departure left us leaderless at the height of the crisis, and undoubtedly increased the tension. We never thought of it in terms of disgrace. He was a casualty, and we were sorry for him. We could only close the ranks, and carry on.

We soon discovered that Delhi took a different view of the situation. The new Chief Commissioner, a big tough-looking man named Sir Stewart Pears, seemed just the kind of man we wanted until he began to say quite openly that the Government of India regarded us members of the Frontier Cadre responsible for Sir Norman's collapse. If we had given him better support, this disgrace, in which we all shared, would never have occurred. This was a bit difficult to swallow! We were faced with a crisis, and there was no time to argue with the 'dreamers of Delhi'.

During this period I was sharing a bungalow in Peshawar Cantonment with my old friend Lionel Jardine,[3] also a member of the Political Service. Mercifully all wives and families were in the hills for the hot weather, so no anxiety was experienced on their behalf. Lionel was an excellent companion when things looked black. He had a great sense of humour and plenty of courage. We both worked in the Secretariat and, aware that the orderlies and many of the clerks were frightened, not knowing what was going to happen next, we made a point of laughing loudly in the corridors on arrival every morning.

I had a golden retriever, Peter by name, of which Lionel was very fond. "Even the ticks are getting uppish," he would joke as we approached the offices. "The Powindah camels (hosts to these bloodsuckers) are camping near the golf course."

"Peter's coat is as infested as a Red Shirt!" I would answer hilariously.

We now began to think in terms of fighting back, and a military operation, in which I took part as a magistrate, was organised to recover Peshawar City from the Red Shirts. This went smoothly thanks largely to the magnificent work of British troops. The sight of those homely white faces filled one with confidence. Tommy Atkins was superb in dealing with the Indian Civil population in difficult times. Holding his rifle with bayonet fixed, he looked rather terrifying, but was always calm and matter of fact, at close quarters with a crowd, and I never saw him lose his temper. Street by street we took possession of the city, removing barricades and reassuring shopkeepers that we had come to stay. There was no serious opposition. The force camped out in the centre for several nights to ensure the insurgents did not return and that the police were once more in control.

After a brief return to my Census duties, I was again diverted by an emergency posting as Assistant Commissioner Charsadda, to deal with the

---

[3] L.W. Jardine, Esq, CIE, ICS.

critical situation in that subdivision. This posting lasted from 15th May to 6th September 1930, the hottest months of the year. It is necessary here to explain my own position in trying to deal with the Census and a revolt at the same time. As Superintendent for the Frontier, I was under the instructions of the Director of the All India Census in Delhi, and my appointment dated from the 1st April 1930. From that date for at least two years, the Chief Commissioner at Peshawar had no claim on my services. Nevertheless, he appealed to me constantly for help in dealing with what might be described as the greatest crisis in the history of the Frontier. The Director warned me constantly of the grave risk I was running in neglecting the essential groundwork needed to ensure the accuracy of the final enumeration, which was fixed for the night of the 26th February 1931, and to provide the vast amount of material required for the Census Report. But he did not put his foot down, he did not press the Foreign Secretary to order the Chief Commissioner to leave me alone to do my job. All he said was whatever I decided to do, the full responsibility would rest on me personally. As Census work forced me to remain on the Frontier in the very centre of the crisis, I was torn between two conflicting loyalties. I decided, rightly or wrongly, that I could not refuse appeals for help from my own Province in its grave predicament. I was young and hoped that I would be able to make up for lost time when I got back to the Census. The excitement and interest of the next four years, however, were dogged by a dark and desperate struggle against strain, overwork and disappointment. I was lucky to emerge alive and sane. It is proverbially dangerous to serve two masters!

I was told on the evening of 14th May that I would be required to take over at Charsadda the next morning. Kuli Khan had been succeeded by a British Political Officer named Kirkbride, whose health broke down almost immediately, leaving this key post vacant. Eager to get my teeth into a challenging situation, I hastily made arrangements for routine Census work to be carried on, and went round to see a friend, a police officer named Lawther, head of the Criminal Investigation Department. Lawther was some years older and a real sleuth he had agents everywhere. There was little he did not know about the personalities and intrigue behind the revolution. He took a philosophical view of all his information.

"Tell you what, we'll go round now and see *Dr* Khan Sahib, even if in he is his pyjamas (it was then 11 p.m.)," he growled when he had heard my news. "We'll get him to talk to us for a few minutes." *Dr* Khan Sahib was Abdul Ghaffar Khan's brother, and I was uncertain what kind of reception we would get.

Called from his bed, and conventionally attired in striped pyjamas, though with a dressing gown on top, he nonetheless gave us a warm welcome. Immediately I fell under the spell of the man who was later to become Chief Minister of the Frontier Province, and with whom I was to have a long and very friendly association. What incredible leaders were those two brothers, standing as they did for Pathan democracy, but driven into a false position by Congress, to whom they had turned in desperation for support.

The Doctor had been educated in England where he studied medicine. When qualified he joined the IMS and was for some years MO to the Guides Regiment. He had married an English wife. During this period the two brothers were deeply involved in Congress intrigue. It was not my business to question their motives. The amended proverb: 'All's fair in love and war and politics', might well have applied to him.

"Mallam has been posted to Charsadda as Assistant Commissioner," Lawther introduced me. "Have you any suggestions or advice for him in his difficult assignment?"

With a beaming smile and eyes sparkling, *Dr* Khan Sahib replied, "There is nothing difficult about Charsadda. All it needs is a little patience. The Red Shirt movement is quite innocent; it is only concerned with Social reform!" Had he his tongue in his cheek? What was impressive was his kindly good humour and a sincerity which somehow shone through the absurdity of his words. "Good night." "Good night." Though disappointed, we had at least established contact with one of our chief 'enemies'.

In Charsadda the following morning, I went at once to the AC's bungalow, where I found several Senior civil and military officials occupying the sitting room, in deep consultation. Finding an empty chair, I sat down and listened with all ears. I gathered that the whole Nowshera Brigade had moved up and was in camp nearby.

"Something must be done immediately to stop the armies of Red Shirts marching round us and hurling insults at my men," announced the Brigadier. "They won't stand it much longer."

"What about the Red Shirt sentries posted round the jail?" was the general complaint of many (some persons recently arrested for seditious speeches had been imprisoned there). "The Red Shirts are behaving as if they represented the civil government."

"My men are bottled up inside their stations and cannot move out to keep order," reported an angry Inspector General of Police.

Everyone agreed that government was paralysed. The military must be called upon to help.

"I am ready to act, but only on the condition that martial law is proclaimed," was the Military Commander's dictum.

Was there a remedy short of martial law as the last resort?

"The position in Peshawar is beginning to deteriorate again," said a doubtful Deputy Commissioner. "Rebels are infiltrating from here, and trans border Afridis are crossing into the District."

No one wanted martial law if it could possibly be avoided. It would mean serious bloodshed. Then someone asked, "Is there not a new AC for Charsadda? He should be given a chance!"

The DC, Mr (afterwards Sir Aubrey) Metcalfe, who had recently received a brickbat in the eye from rioters in Peshawar City, turned to me. "What are you going to do?" he asked.

"If I can be left alone for twenty-four hours, I will produce definite proposals," I replied.

"The situation is rapidly deteriorating but yes, you must have some time to study the position," it was agreed. At this the meeting ended. We all stood up.

"Down, down King George! Up, up Jawarhalal Nehru!" came a chorus of shrill young voices from outside. This was the ultimate indignity. Metcalfe, his face white with rage, seemed about to hurl himself through the window at the chanting children. But an army of Red Shirts was also milling round shouting, *"Inkhilab Zindabad"* (long live revolution).

"Don't worry. I'll deal with the kids," I called out, and somehow persuaded all the VIPs, including the DC, to go their various ways. Their departure removed the temptation to demonstrate and left me alone, except for a Frontier Constabulary Officer on special duty, who shared the bungalow. I looked out through the window and what struck my eye was a hard tennis court close to the house, all marked out and ready for play. "Anyone for tennis?" I asked my companion.

He looked at me as if I was mad. "The Red Shirt sentries are watching us. I want them to think we don't care a damn."

We were evenly matched and had an excellent game. By the end of the second set I had thought up a plan for immediate action, which we discussed across the net. The scheme was simple: to remove the prisoners from the jail in broad daylight, load them into lorries in full view of their supporters, and send them to Peshawar. When they realised the prison was empty, the Red Shirts would not continue their sentry-go, I reasoned. They would go home and good riddance!

My companion agreed; the plan was put into action and succeeded. When the prisoners and their escort were well on the way, I telephoned Metcalfe, warning him that they would be arriving shortly in Peshawar, and asking him to accommodate them there, or send them on to a lock-up in Iridia. He just had to agree.

The rest of the day was spent working on two alternative policies, A and B. Policy A was my favourite: a non-irritant plan which involved the immediate return of the brigade to their barracks in Nowshera while I would mobilise as many loyal elements in the Sub-Division of Charsadda as possible and summon them to a meeting. They would be called upon for active service to Government at this critical time. Failing that, Policy B would come into operation. This policy, a full irritant, involved the return of the Nowshera brigade to Charsadda, this time to assist in the arrest of all suspected of disloyalty, and to occupy or besiege the compact group of villages comprising Charsadda and Prang until all the leading men signed a declaration of submission. I telephoned Lawther in Peshawar asking him to prepare a list of suspects, with a brief note in each case outlining the evidence.

That evening Brigadier Hartley called. "How did you get rid of those confounded Red Shirts?" he demanded, and laughed mightily at the answer. Over a drink, I began to get friendly with the man who was later promoted General, knighted Sir Alan, and in 1942 became Commander in Chief in India. Before he left, I gave him an outline of my plan, and asked for his comments.

"At first sight it seems all right. I'll sleep on it," he announced, after probing me with questions. "I'll ring you in the morning."

"I attach a good deal of importance to Policy A," I told him. "The civil authority should make a last effort to solve the problem on its own."

"It may fail, but it is worth a try," was the encouraging reply.

'Mist and fog' seemed all that emerged from many fruitless visits together to Government House Peshawar. At the first conference my scheme was put forward, supported by Brigadier Hartley, but it hardly received any attention from the Chief Commissioner. "Don't worry," counselled the Brigadier on the return journey. "So long as we agree, we will between us clear up the mess in Charsadda." His confidence was heartening.

Metcalfe gave the go ahead to Policy A and the Brigade returned to Nowshera; the Red Shirts stopped their marching and went home; there was no one left to insult.

But the law courts, usually a buzz of activity inside and out, remained silent and deserted. No crimes were reported to the police. There was no buying of stamps from the post office, no paying of land revenue. The opposition to authority was complete. For several days after my arrival no one came to visit me. Then, by night, came the first man, the Khan of Sherpao, with whom I discussed my plans.

Invitations were sent to everyone, who might still entertain a spark of loyalty, to meet me and discuss the situation. A reasonably well-attended conference was held, but all were ominously unresponsive.

I explained that we wished to reassert the authority of government without the aid of the military, and added that with their co-operation I felt sure we would be successful. The Nowshera brigade, standing by in their barracks, would return to Charsadda if we failed. Finally (and for this I was severely criticised afterwards) I asked them, at a time when many people's loyalty was shaken, to state openly their main complaints against the Power which had served them (I hoped justly) for so many years.

At last the sullenness of the meeting was broken. A few stood up and voiced their grievances. A stenographer was present and the complaints duly recorded. These appeared not to be too weighty. The fact that they were asked at all undoubtedly cleared the air, and enabled the conference to break up with some show of friendliness.

The real causes of the revolt were not of course mentioned, probably because they were too basic, too political they struck at the very roots of British rule.

A report was sent with a copy of the verbatim account to the DC who passed it on to the Chief Commissioner. "A disgraceful communication," exclaimed the latter, after our next discussion. He hauled me over the coals for inviting grievances against the Government at a time like this; only to be interpreted as a sign of weakness. I bowed to the storm and said nothing. It was not the last time I was to incur the anger of the great man.

Work was now put in hand to mobilise all our civil resources and particularly to get the Police moving about more freely. "Are you still there?" asked Metcalfe one day on the 'phone. He informed me that the Afridis from across the border had swept down into the district between Peshawar and Charsadda and cut the telephone wires. Without knowing it, I had been isolated for some days.

"All is well here," I said. "Policy A is at last making some headway."

"The situation is worse in the city and neighbourhood. I suspect all your bad hats have come over here. Policy A is much too slow. Policy B will have to be enforced."

"I'll get in touch with the Brigadier and work out plans."

No sooner had he rung off than I had a call from the Inspector General of Police. "The Chief Commissioner has ordered road blocks to be set up immediately between Charsadda and Peshawar to prohibit all movement. Will you arrange this?"

"There's only a very small force of police at my disposal, and none can be withdrawn from outlying stations. Road blocks would mean a build-up of angry crowds, possibly rioting, and could not be set up without the assistance of the Nowshera brigade, no longer here but due back in about twenty-four hours. I'll arrange it as soon as they arrive."

There was a series of loud cracklings on the line. He seemed annoyed.

The mended wires now seemed red-hot, when next I rang Metcalfe. "Can I come and explain the position to the Chief Commissioner?" I requested.

"You are summoned to Government House on a charge of insubordination," was the strained reply.

"Why have the road blocks not been erected?" shouted Sir Stewart Pears when I entered his study. "Insubordinate officials like you were responsible for Sir Norman Bolton's collapse. I intend to teach you a lesson."

"At this moment the non-irritant policy A is being followed in Charsadda," I explained. Another explosion! "YOUR policies mean nothing to me. I have never approved them."

"But Sir, Metcalfe gave the go ahead, and the Nowshera Brigade has left"

"What? The Brigade left? ..."

There was a prolonged silence. Then, "Go!" he said, and I went. The order for the road blocks was cancelled.

This was the last time I spoke to him. Shortly afterwards he fell from a precipitous mountain path in Nathia Gali, and was killed.

In October 1972 my present wife and I were standing in Nathia Gali by the tiny hilltop bazaar when a small crowd collected. We talked for a few minutes about the days of old. One of the reminiscences was of the death of Sir Stewart Pears, and of his fatal fall down the khud side. It must have been a great shock to all the residents of the little hill station, Indian as well as British.

Apart from the tension, which is apt to fray tempers in times of crisis and the obsession with Sir Norman Bolton's 'disgrace', there was another possible explanation for Sir Stewart Pears' behaviour: the composition of the Indian Political Service. This was 30% ICS and 70% military, the former (nicknamed 'the Heaven Born') enjoying more pay for the same work and equal responsibilities, until this discrepancy was corrected in 1925. The ICS, to which both Sir Norman Bolton and Sir Steuart Pears belonged considered themselves the bosses of India, and I was a mere Captain. It was far more distinguished to be plain 'Mr'.

Early one morning in late June, long before dawn, the Nowshera Brigade crept back into Charsadda, leaving their lorries some way down the road so as not to waken the sleeping villages. Policy B was now in operation, and some thirty arrests were made of leading personalities behind the revolution, while most of them were still a-bed. When the prisoners were mustered, one of them, a Hindu pleader who two years later was elected as a member of the legislative assembly and became a minister, said: "That was a very successful operation." I thought that a generous remark coming from one of the victims!

The Brigade built sandbag posts round the group of villages, comprising Charsadda and Prang, which contained a population of about ten thousand. Their task was made easier since one side of the blockaded area was bordered by the River Abazai, a tributary of the Kabul, which was easily fordable only in one place. A notice was posted up in various parts of the village, and also read out in every street, to the effect that no man, woman, child or any animal would be allowed to leave the blockaded area until the headmen had surrendered to Government authority. Brigadier Hartley then held a meeting of officers. He explained the reason for the Army's return. "The first phase of the operation (the arrest of suspects) has been successful," he said. "Now it is necessary to get the acceptance of the headmen. Have you any comments?" he asked me.

I replied, "As Assistant Commissioner I am responsible for the whole population in these villages women and children as well as men – there are also a large number of animals, mainly buffaloes kept for milking. If the beasts can't get out to graze they'll stop giving milk, and the mothers and babies will suffer."

I visualised that the siege, provided it was effective, would last for forty-eight hours at the most. At this Hartley jumped up, obviously angry. "I'm heartily sick of civil officials calling for military aid, and then putting strings on it," he announced. "Let me make it clear, here and now, the Brigade will maintain the siege for a week or a fortnight or three weeks, just as long as the situation requires it. A definite job has to be done. We mean to do it."

This attack surprised me. I was walking away when he caught hold of my arm. "Sorry to be unpleasant, but my chaps are afraid this visit will be as ineffective as the first. We must really achieve our object." I said I understood.

To my amazement, the siege dragged on for three weeks. Every day I walked through the streets of the villages talking to groups of people, and trying to persuade them to bring pressure to bear on their headmen to terminate it. "We are no strangers to you, we are your friends," I explained. They listened quietly and politely. Office clerks and police warned me against these visits: there were known to be arms hidden in the houses, but I continued as it seemed the only way to overcome the resistance no one in the world can be more stubborn than a Pathan.

Just before the end of the siege, two or three Military Officers came into my bungalow, obviously perturbed. "Who was in charge of the operation, Civil or Military? There is no martial law, so the responsibility must rest with the civil. Is it not so?"

"Sit down and tell me what the trouble is," I said.

I myself was uneasy about the legal basis of the siege. They told me that that very morning, soon after dawn, one of their sentries had shot a villager trying to cross the river and break out of the cordon. "Halt!" called the sentry as the man entered the water. He took no notice. A shot was fired in front but had no effect. The sentry then aimed at the swimmer and killed him.

"Have you recovered the body?"

"Yes. The police have it."

I sent for the Assistant Superintendent of Police. If there was a public enquiry, the legality of the siege would certainly be questioned. The sentry had fired in good faith, of course, carrying out his orders. Feeling distinctly hot under the collar, I greeted the ASP a Muslim. "May I have a report please on the shooting incident this morning? Who was the deceased?"

"The dead man was a Hindu." He gave his name. Was there a smile on his face? Undoubtedly a slight curl of the lips.

"Thank you."

When he had left, I turned to the others. "We are in luck. If the casualty had been a Muslim we might have been in deep water. Since he is a Hindu and possibly a Congress agent, I doubt if we shall hear any more of the case."

The truth was the tide was beginning to turn. The signatures had already been collected of most of the headmen on a declaration of loyalty. The people were tired of revolution and Red Shirt rule. Only a minority was still holding out. The case was dealt with in a routine manner. There was no public enquiry.

The siege ended at last, and the Brigade departed. They had done a good job under very trying circumstances in the height of summer, and their action had brought improved conditions to Peshawar City and its neighbourhood; but the rest of the Charsadda subdivision, a large area stretching to the border and containing forty-odd villages, was still under Red Shirt domination. How to free them? Every hamlet could not be surrounded.

A new Deputy Superintendent of Police appeared on the scene. He bore a name that ought to be written in red letters in the annals of the Frontier Rohullah Khan. A trans-border Orakzai by birth, he was well educated and extremely intelligent. We sat down and planned a tour of the two score villages, in July, the hottest month of the year. Horseback would be the easiest for travel and give us more contact with the people. A small posse of Mounted Constabulary made ready in the comparative cool of the dawn. The only plan was to hold a public meeting in front of every Chowk, or headquarters, to test the temper of the villagers, list their complaints and finally to appeal for their loyalty. The nearest did not present much difficulty. They had seen the main resistance collapse, and were ready to return to the fold.

Our technique was perfected as we moved further out. The headman was approached and asked to convene a meeting. Charpoys were laid in front of the Chowk. Gradually the menfolk assembled and seated themselves on the beds. Others stood behind or sat on the ground. Rohullah and I sat perched on a bed, fronting a sea of faces. I opened the proceedings with a brief explanation of our visit, and of what had been happening in Charsadda. Rohullah Khan, his dark eyes flashing, then let fly with a tremendous pep-talk. A born orator, with a fine voice and figure, he hurled at them his loyalty and affection for the British, his scorn for the Red Shirts and their Hindu masters. This eloquence, coming from a transborder Pathan, was irresistible. Singlehanded (I was a mere onlooker), he won over village by village the whole Subdivision, which had been a hotbed of rebellion. With the aid of a stenographer, I compiled a comprehensive list of complaints, gravely heard, copies of which were despatched to each head of department for such action as was deemed fit. It soon became clear that the masses had been stirred up by agitators outside the province. That it was Rohullah's oratory that turned the scale became evident when, at his final words, all those present rose and escorted us on to the next village. Our tour developed into a kind of triumphal progress.

Before I left Charsadda the All India Congress Party, smarting from their defeat, endeavoured to stage a comeback by sending Red Shirts to picket liquor shops a trick tried successfully elsewhere.

Angrily I ordered the police to move on the picketers, roughly enough to discourage them from coming again. The order was backed by the whole population. Congress leaders in Peshawar then tried to persuade the DC to prosecute the police officer responsible. They had unearthed something unfavourable in his record of which they hoped to make good use. When I said that I would myself give evidence for the defence, the prosecution was dropped.

On 6th September 1930, I was succeeded by Captain Barnes (known to all as Barney) who met a tragic death later on the Baluchistan border.

I was destined to pay a last visit to this delectable spot in the year 1932. By this time the Home Government had seen the light, and agreed that the NWFP be raised to the same status as all other provinces in India: that is a Governor's Province with a legislative assembly and elected Indian ministers.

One morning in Peshawar, as I was struggling with graphs, figures, and charts of population appertaining to the Census, the telephone rang. "This is the Governor," a voice said. It was Sir Ralph Griffiths, first Governor of the Frontier Province. "I have been invited to a garden party at Charsadda this after-noon," he continued, "to be given by ministers and members of the legislative assembly from that area. I have told my hosts that on this first auspicious visit I should like you to accompany me, to which they have readily agreed."

In Sir Ralph's car that afternoon a wave of nervousness hit me as we sped towards the headquarters of my old Subdivision. What about the complaints I had tabulated in 1930? Had anything been done to redress those old grievances? If not, black looks might be forthcoming instead of the cheerful welcome expected by the Governor!

But the warm welcome was there, as heartening as Sir Ralph could wish. They felt themselves really well off now, many old friends assured me. Happy and prosperous looking, perhaps they thought the revolution had been worthwhile after all! It had certainly achieved its object. It had also deepened that mutual respect between British and Pathan, which so often flourished on a temporary confrontation!

And what of the Census? Tired and overstrained by the gruelling summer of 1930 in Charsadda, I had to snatch a few days' holiday in Kashmir, before tackling the enormous backlog of work which had accumulated in my absence. The numbering of every house in every town and every village in the Province, the collection of personal information (in eighteen columns of the General Schedule) regarding the status, extraction, caste, religion and occupation of every human being, the recruitment and training of an army of enumerators, supervisors and superintendents, and the organisation of the final simultaneous enumeration of 2,471,527 persons on the night of 26th February 1931, in their homes, on the railways and the roads, was but a fraction of the planning required. The population of the whole of the tribal area up to the Durand Line had to be estimated (2,242,837 persons) on some reasonably accurate basis. With the approval of my Director I had planned an expedition to remote valleys of the Hindu Kush to record with a dictaphone some of the rare Dardic languages of the tribes inhabiting those high altitudes, and to obtain all possible information about their habits and origin. Alas! Tribal unrest made this impracticable; but some statistics still had to be prepared of the numbers, living conditions, and the large variety of languages spoken by peoples who lived close under the roof of the world. Moreover, the preparatory work needed for the numerous charts, graphs, tables and statistics relating to every conceivable aspect of human life, to be incorporated in the Census Report, was prodigious. The Report eventually consisted of 414 printed foolscap pages, packed with figures and commentary.[4] I cannot speak too highly of the valuable painstaking assistance of my Deputy Superintendent, M. Sultan Mohammad Khan, during this period and throughout the Census from beginning to end.

Battling with fatigue and ill health, I achieved the enumeration successfully, and was beginning to get on top of the Report, when I was again diverted to Dera Ismail Khan as Special Magistrate in an emergency from 17th September to 4th November 1931.

On return to Peshawar, I was kicked by a horse whilst out hunting. The bone in my left leg was broken, just above the ankle. I hobbled to the office, with my leg in plaster, but a discharge from the broken end of the bone entered the bloodstream, causing an embolus in my left lung. Doctor's orders were to lie in bed and keep still. I had no sooner recovered from this setback, than another emergency took me away from Census work in January 1932 to be Additional District Magistrate at Peshawar. Finally, on 8th April, with the Report still unfinished, I was transferred to Kabul, Afghanistan, as Counsellor in the British Legation, at the request of the Minister, Sir Richard Moconachie, with whom I raised the question of the uncompleted report. He assured me that I would have no difficulty in finishing it in addition to my other duties. No one, who has not actually organised a Census, has any idea of the work involved. I was soon to discover that a Counsellor had immense administrative responsibilities: for the upkeep of palatial buildings and grounds, for the salaries and welfare of a large Legation staff (many of them British with a few English wives), for a fleet of cars and lorries, for the accounts covering a vast expenditure, particularly on the heating of houses during the bitterly cold winter, and finally for all official correspondence with the Government of India, the Foreign Office and the Afghan Government. An Under Secretary dealt with passports, British subjects etc. Likewise there was a military attaché, but the overall obligation lay squarely on the shoulders of the Counsellor.

It soon became apparent that I would be unable to complete the Census

---

4   A simultaneous Census covering almost the whole Sub-Continent was the largest and most complex operation ever undertaken by the British Indian Administration and it was repeated every ten years.

Report. I requested that another Officer should be appointed to finish it, and concentrated on tidying up my own work in such a way as to make it easy to give the last touches. Mr A.D.F. Dundas (afterwards Sir Ambrose) got the job. "I was warned in Delhi," he recounted later, "that the Report was in a mess. I did not find it so. It was a tragedy you were unable to complete it."

CHAPTER X
British Legation, Kabul
1932–33

And far from the Suleiman heights came the sound of the
stirring tribes,
Afridi, Hazard, and Ghazi, they clamor for plunder or
bribes;
And Hera is but held by a thread; and the Usbeg has raised
Badu Shan;
And the Chief may sleep sound, in his grave, who would
rule the unruly Afghan.

The mountainous hinterland of Central Asia was in those days a closed book to all Europeans but a privileged few, diplomats, business men, travellers, for whom duty or money provided the key to open the door at the Western end of the Khyber pass. Afghan visas were granted grudgingly, as every foreigner, particularly British and Russian, was suspect. Afghanistan was a great stronghold of Islam, conservative, priest-ridden, backward and resentful of outside influences, particularly Christian, which might introduce unwelcome change. Now I was about to acquire a diplomatic visa that would enable me to travel in and out of the country as often as I wished, at Government expense in a powerful, chauffeur-driven Legation car.

In 1932 few English travellers between Peshawar and Kabul could journey along this famous road, unconscious of its painful associations with British-Afghan history. Just ninety years ago, in the course of the First Afghan War, it had been the scene of one of the worst disasters ever suffered by a British army. In January 1842, when the winter was at its coldest, and snow lay deep on the hills and in the valleys, a force consisting of 4,500 fighting men and 12,000 Indian camp followers, left the cantonment at Kabul. Here they had been besieged for weeks by a hostile enemy. They started to march eastwards towards India in a desperate attempt to reach Jalalabad (a hundred miles distant) where there was a British force under General Sale. Shortly before the retreat began, two English representatives in Kabul had been assassinated: Sir Alexander Burnes, leader of a commercial mission on 2nd November, and on 23rd December 1841, the Envoy himself, Sir William MacNaughten, who was endeavouring to parley with the enemy. The retreat, started in an atmosphere of desperation hostile action, had isolated the cantonment from its supplies and the whole force was already half-starved. The fighting men, having lost faith in their officers, had become demoralised. The camp followers were panic stricken. Worst of all, the men were encumbered by women and children, prominent among whom was Lady Sale, who recorded in a journal,[1] laconically, but with meticulous detail, all the horrors that took place before her eyes.

One sentence of this remarkable diary, describing the first day of the retreat (6th January 1842) runs: "The whole road was covered with men, women and children, lying down in the snow to die."[2] As may be expected, the retirement was marked by many acts of individual heroism, but ended in complete disaster. General Elphinstone, the force commander, and his personal staff, together with most of the English women and children, were taken prisoner; yet the rout continued in utter confusion and in a long drawn out agony for seven days, during which the fleeing army was constantly harassed by a bloodthirsty enemy, who cut off the remaining supplies of food and water, killing and plundering until the road was littered with corpses and the snow stained with blood.

Finally at Gandamak, on a low hill close to the road, twenty-nine miles from Jalalabad, a remnant made a last stand. Here eighteen British officers and fifty men were slaughtered. One commander and eight men were taken prisoner. Next day the sentries at Jalalabad saw a lone horseman approaching the fort. Both man and horse were in the closing stages of exhaustion. The officer was *Dr Brydon*, who believed himself to be the only one from the Kabul army to escape.

On one of my leaves home I saw a print of the picture of this famous scene,

---

[1] *Disasters in Afghanistan 1841–1842*, Florentia Sale.

[2] A note from her book (written in captivity) states:

"There is nothing too brutal or savage for Akbar (Sirdar Mahommed Akbar Khan) to accomplish: he is known to have had a man flayed alive in his presence, commencing at the feet, and continuing upwards until the sufferer was relieved by death." Again on 21st March 1842 she writes a womanly touch: "The *no-roz* or vernal equinox. Mr Melville brought us a bouquet of narcissuses, which we highly prized, for it is long since we have seen even a blade of grass."

Her entry for the 27th, Easter Sunday reads: "I wrote to Sale. Four earthquakes before breakfast, and more at night."

entitled *The Sole Survivor*. It was hanging on the wall of a public house in the New Forest.

As the Legation car carried me up to Kabul in the spring of 1932, I thought of this story, which lives in our military history as a tragic but monitory example of divided counsels and faltering leadership. The road through the Pass was flanked by precipitous hills, many of them crowned by forts manned by the Khyber Rifles. Reaching the top at Landi Kotal, the car dropped down to the Afghan frontier at Torkham. The sudden change from smooth macadam to bumpy torrent bed emphasised the remoteness and inaccessibility of the country in which I was about to make my temporary home, and warned that its people had inherited a legacy of hate.

Much had happened, of course, since January 1842, to redress the balance. In April of that year a punitive force from India under General Pollock thrust its way through the Khyber and relieved the garrison at Jalalabad. It then moved on to Kabul, arriving there in September (a few days before a force from Kandahar under General Nott), having fought and won a battle against the Afghans in the vicinity of the Capital. After releasing the prisoners, the formations returned to India in the following December. This ended the First Afghan War.

The legacy of hate that still remained was intensified forty years later by the aggressive policy of the Viceroy, Lord Lytton, who provoked the Second Afghan War by forcing the Treaty of Gandamak on an unwilling Amir. By this treaty, signed in May 1879, the Amir accepted British control of Afghanistan's foreign policy, and an envoy, Sir Louis Cavagnari, took up residence in Kabul. In July he and all his staff were murdered.[3] Once more a punitive expedition was sent, this time under Lord Roberts. Once more the people rose against the invading force encamped in their midst, and nearly overwhelmed it. But Lord Roberts was made of sterner stuff than Elphinstone. He defeated the

---

[3] Arthur Swinson in his book, *North West Frontier*, p.171, writes of the Amir himself who signaled to General Roberts, via Captain Connolly, PO at Alikhel: "Confusion reached height beyond control: people from city and surrounding country poured into Bala Hissar, began destroying artillery park and magazine. All troops and people attacked Residency. I, Amir, send Daud Shah to help Envoy. He was unhorsed at Residency by stones and spears: is dying; I then sent my own son with Koran, also Mullah, to troops, but no use. Disturbance continued till now, evening; confusion is beyond conception." A second message ran: "Much life lost on both sides; at evening they set fire to Residency…"

opposing army decisively at Kabul, and then, after installing Abdul Rahman as Amir, marched to Kandahar to relieve a hard-pressed British force there.

After withdrawing to India yet again, there was peace for another forty years. The Third Afghan War of 1919 lasted only three months. It began with an attempted invasion of India, and was ended by a pact recognizing Afghanistan's complete independence. From now on that turbulent country entered the circle of free nations on a footing of equality, and her relations with Great Britain, as with all other countries, became regulated by international law and diplomatic practice. This was all to the good, but perhaps it was too much to hope that a mere decade and a half could wipe out the effects of such a bloodstained history.

The British Consul at Jalalabad, an Indian of charming manners, entertained us to coffee, and we continued our journey up the winding road past Gandamak to the Jagdalak pass, through the Tezin valley, and the long climb to the top of the Haft Kotal, 9,000 ft above sea level, where the snow is deep in winter. I thought of the hundreds who had met a frozen death there in 1842.[4] From here the way falls steeply to the Khurd Kabul defile, narrow and menacing an ideal place to lay an ambush for an unsuspecting enemy, and the scene of the massacre of the main part of that first retreating British force. As I entered Kabul for the first time, I recalled that well-known verse from Sir Alfred Lyall's poem, *The Amir's Soliloquy* (1881):

"I look from a fort half-ruined on Kabul spreading below,
On the near hills crowned with cannon, and the far hills piled with snow;
Fair are the vales well watered, and the vines on the upland swell,
You might think you were reigning in Heaven I know I am ruling Hell."

The magnificence of the British Minister's house, built by Lord Curzon, was staggering. It was surrounded by a large and beautiful garden, on the edge of which was a small Georgian-type building reserved for the Counsellor. I prevailed on the Legation surgeon, Captain Teddy Lucas of the IMS, who was also a bachelor, to share it with me and we settled down comfortably.

In order to mitigate bachelor loneliness, I invested in a 16 mm Cine Kodak, with attachments for colour photography, and a projector. I also purchased what I was reliably informed was a connoisseur's gramophone, made by Handmade Gramophones Ltd, London. When the instrument eventually

---

[4] In recent years the road has been re-aligned at a lower level to avoid the Haft Kotal.

HM King Nadir Shah, at the Pillar of Independence
4 August 1933

arrived, the Garage Superintendent, Mr Stranger, exclaimed: "That is the largest crate that has ever been brought up in a Legation lorry from India! Whatever's in it?"

When opened, an enormous exterior horn made largely of papier-mâché and as big as an elephant's trunk, was revealed. The box part, containing the motor, was crated separately and when we put the two together and played a record on the turntable (Scheherezade) the result was marvellous. The players and their instruments, or the singers, seemed actually to be in that room, so far from civilisation. Teddy Lucas, who was exceptionally musical, helped to choose some really good Rimsky-korsakov and other Central Asian discs for the noble gramophone, which was destined to entertain the European residents in Kabul on many occasions. The cine projector, particularly the colour photography which was a novelty in those days, was also very popular.

One of the problems of Legation life shared by a few inmates who saw a good deal of one another, was to keep relationships congenial. Much depended on the head of the Mission and his wife Lieutenant Colonel Fraser-Tytler (afterwards Sir Kerr) who was Charge d'Affaires when first I arrived. He had delightful manners and an endearing way of making everyone feel at home. Inevitably the atmosphere changed when the Minister, Sir Richard Maconachie, returned from leave. Sir Richard was one of the most brilliant men in the Indian Political Service, and he had some of the characteristics that often go with outstanding intellect. We were kept permanently on our toes. His critical eye seemed to penetrate into every corner of the Legation and ruthlessly expose any slackness or inefficiency, which ensured a high standard of work in all departments, but introduced an element of restlessness and discomfort into our restricted lives.

The charm and consideration shown to all by Lady Maconachie mitigated the strain to some extent, and we loved her dearly in consequence.

Life in the narrow confines of the Legation proceeded smoothly as long as nothing untoward happened, and we managed at times to enjoy ourselves. The monotony of work was broken regularly by tennis, hockey, riding and by receptions given by other foreign missions as well as our own. The official dress on these occasions was a morning coat and white topee. The European wives, who were the only ladies present, wore cool and flowery chiffon frocks, floor length, with beribboned hats, smallish in size, but whose brims shaded the eyes.

At the beginning of my appointment we were not on speaking terms with the Russians, but the situation changed suddenly after some months. I can well remember attending their first official reception. We expected our hosts to be as frigid as the wastes of Siberia, but were agreeably surprised when Olga, the wife of the Minister, an ex-ballet dancer and still very pretty, received us most warmly. She paid us the utmost attention and plied us with vodka in tall thin glasses.

The soirees at the Russian Legation soon became the most informal and hilarious of all. On one such occasion some guests from Peshawar happened to be staying with me James Almond, Judicial Commissioner of the Frontier Province, and two or three handsome young officers of the 15/19th Hussars.

With special permission I took my guests to the reception. Olga was transported with joy at the sight of the young officers, and, when she discovered James Almond was an expert pianist, made him sit down and play her piano all the evening, while at times we sang *Under the Spreading Chestnut Tree*, or *Drink to me only with thine Eyes*, with a wealth of meaning.

The climax came when this beautiful dancer lined up all of us Englishmen present, with vodka glasses in our hands, which she proceeded to fill to the brim, one by one. Going down the line, she stood in front of each man until he had drained his cup with no heeltaps. I do not think Sir Richard took part in this frivolity. Olga was always the leading spirit at the Russian evening parties and it was rumoured that her husband, who was rather an austere man, tried vainly to restrain her. It is also true to say that the male members of their Legation appeared surprisingly friendly and seemed to get on with the British better than with anyone else. Perhaps they were enjoying a rare chance of letting their hair down outside the Iron Curtain! The Afghan game was of course to play off the British against the Russians. They were past masters at it. I feel I must quote again from *The Amir's Soliloquy*:

"Shall I stretch my right hand to the Indus,
That England may fill it with gold?
Shall my left beckon aid from the Oxus? the
Russian blows hot and blows cold."

which seems to put the whole situation in a nutshell.

The receptions at other Legations were more formal, but still very friendly the Italians particularly so. One night their Minister gave a fancy dress ball and supplied beautifully made paper costumes for everyone. I can recall a Mad Hatter, with a tall topper, and several monks and friars. We waltzed carefully with ladies prettily decked as Roses or Marguerites, their pink and white petals rustling crisply on the turns. The dance was a great success.

Our own entertainments were well attended and popular but much more devoted to protocol. The palatial buildings, stately rooms and magnificent furniture intended to give the impression of Imperial glory, but too pretentious for a small Central Asian state lent themselves to formality; but the Europeans, and I believe the Afghan Ministers too, loved to come and admire the unwonted luxury of the salons and the perfectly laid out gardens and flower beds, which were always a blaze of colour. Perhaps they came, too, to see the billiard room and huge green baize table under which the inmates of the legation huddled beneath a crossfire of bullets and shells in 1928, while rival factions fought for supremacy during the revolution that accompanied the abdication of King Amanullah. There is something curiously comforting about a billiard table over your head. One was used in the siege of RAF Habbaniya in World War II, when the camp was being gunned by the Iraqis.

In Kabul, however, this safe position eventually had to be evacuated. I can remember seeing the British Minister of those days, Sir Francis Humphries, arrive by air at Peshawar from the beleaguered legation, with the Union Jack tucked under his arm.

Heavy falls of snow and hard frost made the winters extremely cold. At the back of the compound a ridge of high ground rose steeply out of the plain, and was used as a nursery slope for skiing. My Swiss experience gave me a pull at first, but soon practice made us all, including Sir Richard, quite efficient. Skis were piled onto a lorry and we travelled for some distance southwards from the capital, where mountainsides at a high altitude gave some extended runs. The sport in Afghanistan was never easy: windswept snow was constantly encountered. Bitter blasts from the Hindu Kush propelled the soft powder from large areas, leaving a hard crust over which one's skis shot with sudden acceleration, only to be pulled up sharply by a pocket of deep snow, which precipitated the unfortunate sportsman headfirst down the slope.

Some expert Norwegian skiers, staying in the city, came out one day to study the problem. The only way they could devise for coping with the wind-swept patches was to sit down on their skis, just before entering a deep pocket. This made things rather laborious and it was not always possible to judge the right moment to sit down!

The exhilaration of the winter scene stemmed from its extreme remoteness. White mountain capped white mountain in a wilderness far from human habitation. The snow was untrodden; the ranges and valleys unknown to civilisation. Near hills rose two or three thousand feet above a level plain, but away to the north and west, filling the horizon, was the great pearly wall of the Hindu Kush, lifting its peaks eighteen to twenty thousand feet above sea level.

Old Red Fort, Bamian

Remoteness has always held a great fascination for me. Perhaps it was on one of these skiing expeditions that I developed the idea of ending my term of office in the legation by a trek, following the Oxus river to its source through the Afghan province of Badakshan and finding a way through the mountains to Kashgar in Chinese Turkestan. This was roughly the route taken by Lord Curzon some years previously. Circumstances prevented me from pursuing this delightful dream. I had to content myself with a short trek of ten days or so westwards across the Koh-i-Baba range (a branch of the Hindu Kush) into the Bamian valley.

In the spring of 1933 this trek started by road to the source of the Kabul river, and from there, with ponies and mules to carry tents and baggage and an escort of Afghan police, we climbed to the top of the Unai pass. Then crossing the watershed between the Kabul and Helmand rivers, we negotiated the Haji Gak pass, and dropped down into the Bamian Valley.

One of the objectives was to fish for trout in the upper reaches of the Bamian. There was a story in the Legation that one of the staff had done this a few years before. He had made a catch of brown trout (Salmo Oxianus), one of which he had sent in a bottle to the Curator of the Natural History Museum in Bombay, who had refused until then to believe there were any indigenous trout in those northern streams.

Amid magnificent alpine scenery the Bamian river was reached, and camp set up on the right bank. The water was clear, narrow and swift ideal for a fly. The fish could be seen, rising to the surface from time to time, artless and unsophisticated. Selecting, I think a March Brown, I began to cast. In no time six beautiful brown trout, about one pound in weight each, lay on the grassy bank before me all ready to be cooked over an open fire, and how delicious they were!

After two nights in camp the next morning, Mr Stranger, the Legation garage superintendent (who had helped me unpack the gramophone) turned up, having walked some miles from the Bamian road. "I've brought a lorry to take you back," he announced. "But I must see you make a catch first." The fish were only too willing to oblige, and we took home a good supply. I feel glad that Stranger had this quiet interlude in the light of events to come. Lucas, the amiable surgeon, and I, did some short journeys by road together to see places of interest, particularly the sizeable villages of Istalif and Charikar in the Koh-i-Daman plain and up the Ghorband valley across the Shibar pass in the Hindu Kush to Bamian, to admire the great rock cut Bhuddas there. Two of these giant figures, the faces of which have been cut away, stand in niches of the escarpment, overlooking a well-watered plain set with trees, through which passed the old caravan route from China to India. In the 13th Century AD the Buddhas were bombarded with iconoclastic zeal by the Mongol invader Genghis Khan, who at the same time destroyed the ancient Buddhist city of Bamian and the nearby Red Fort of Zohak. One is reminded of Napoleon's bombardment of the Sphinx! From Bamian the car took us to the top of the Ak Robat pass (12,560 feet) overlooking the distant valley of the Oxus.

These journeys did not provide an opportunity for any but the briefest contacts with the local people. It was possible to travel for miles without passing a human habitation. The roads, which were few and far between, mostly followed narrow valleys, flanked by steep and barren hillsides. Unlike the Himalayas, the Hindu Kush was sadly lacking in forest cover, trees and vegetation being confined to the sheltered ravines. The mountains threw up terrifying and dramatic shapes, particularly at the Darra-i-Shikari on the north road to Mazar-i-Sharif, where two vertical walls of rock, rising sheer to a great height, stood just far enough apart to allow the road and Bamian river to pass on their way to the Oxus.

Of the many races that contribute to the population of Afghanistan the Pathans (Duranis) dominated the country, and for many years supplied its rulers. Pathans also occupy the Koh-i-Daman plain to the north of Kabul, and a large part of the country between that city and India to the east and south-east. To the west, round the source of the Kabul river, covering much of the Hazara land and spreading over the Koh-i-Baba range, is a more peaceful people called Tajiks, slightly Mongolian in appearance. Finally the Ghilzais provide an unique feature of northern Afghanistan the two-way seasonal migrations between summer grazing grounds on the slopes of the Hindu Kush and the plains of India in winter. The journey each way is at least 200 miles.

The Gilzais are a Pushtoo speaking people, like Pathans, and in spite of their nomadic life, wield a good deal of influence. They had the courage and audacity not only to cross the International border with their families and camels twice a year, but also, after the main body had settled in the Indus valley for the winter, the menfolk spread out all over the subcontinent, trading camels, ponies and merchandise, and even penetrated as far as Australia several have been known to bring back white Australian wives. Everywhere the countrymen were most friendly and hospitable. I was struck by the intense cultivation in the Koh-i-Daman plain. Here a broad level area, bordered by mountains, is studded with vineyards. Between the vines grew acres of tulips the largest and most beautiful red flowers I have ever seen. In the spring young men would walk along the roads carrying huge bundles of them, long-stalked and blood-red, over their shoulders. Almost every male wore a tulip in his hair or behind his ear. An officer of the 15th Hussars, Dorrien-Smith by name, who chanced to be staying with me in the Legation for the tulip season, was so struck by the sight of these magnificent plants that he arranged to return a little later to dig up some of the bulbs and send them to a large bulb farm run by his father in the Scilly Isles.

Of all the diplomatic occasions in Kabul, the most important and interesting were those provided by the Afghan Government. Ministers would attend the receptions of the various foreign missions, and we got to know them all well by sight. The leading event of the year was Independence Day, August 8, when King Nadir Shah, in full uniform, made a speech from the stone Pillar of Independence. There followed a march past of Afghan troops led by Sardar Shah Mahmud, the king's youngest brother, who doubled up as Commander-in-Chief and Minister of War. The eldest of the King's brothers, Sardar Hashim Khan, was Prime Minister, and a third royal brother Shah Wali, was Afghan Ambassador in Paris. Yet another brother, Sardar Mohammad Aziz, was Afghan Minister in Berlin, and was later in June 1933, assassinated by an Afghan student, as he left his house in Germany. These four remarkable brothers were Durrani Afghans of the Mohammadzai branch, and exceptionally able men. I had the honour of a brief meeting with them all, except the last, and was charmed by their delightful manners. Between them they ruled the country, having wrested power from the usurper Bachha-i-Saqao, after the fall of Amanullah in 1928.

The Diplomatic Corps were present at the Independence celebration in full uniform. What would surprise many Westerners was the fact that if a ceremony continued beyond the time of evening prayer (at sunset), the King, if attending, his ministers and all Muslims would leave for their devotions. Quite publicly, in the open air, they would kneel on a level piece of ground nearby, facing Mecca. Perhaps in five minutes, when prayers were over, they would return invigorated. There were various means at our disposal of keeping in touch with the course of events in this unpredictable country, which was subject to sudden and violent upheavals, but unexpected developments often occurred. The general impression among the Afghans, who were mostly illiterate and deprived of the benefits of a free press and radio news service, was that the King and his Ministers were under the influence of the British Government. This view was encouraged by the unpopular magnificence of the British Legation (hardly less palatial than the King's own residence), and I believe that it was partly at least responsible for a series of events, which shook this small part of the world to its foundations, and which led, incidentally, to my own rather abrupt departure from Afghanistan on leave home.

As the summer of 1933 wore on, I began to realise that my relations with Sir Richard Maconachie were getting strained. He took me up more and more frequently on small details, and his complaints against me personally, although not amounting to anything important, began to cause me anxiety. One expects a certain amount of this sort of thing in a small isolated community, and for a long time I hoped that it would pass. And then something serious happened. I was woken up one night by Stranger, who shouted in my ear: "The Chancery is on fire I am sounding the alarm and getting the fire engine out." Leaping out of bed, I found the Accountant's Office burning freely. Stranger did a magnificent job with the hoses, while I and other wakened members of the Legation did our best to save the files and ledgers, most of which were recovered partly burned and soaked with water. The blaze was quickly brought under control. Subsequent investigation disclosed a defalcation of 20,000 Rupees in the Legation accounts, and the Indian accountant was convicted in the Court at Campellpore in the Punjab near his home and sentenced to seven years rigorous imprisonment, and 25,000 Rs fine. This was a satisfactory conclusion, but it did not improve my relations with the Minister. A month or two before the fire, the Government of India had offered to audit the Legation accounts, and I had pressed for the offer to be accepted, partly to safeguard my own position; a regular audit would make a defalcation almost impossible. But Sir Richard had declined the offer on the ground that we could get on perfectly well without it. No one likes to be proved wrong!

In the autumn of 1933 two more incidents occurred, both far more grave than the fire and its attendant court case.

It was customary at the turn of the year for members of the Legation who were keen on small game shooting to go out before dawn after flighting duck over the Kabul river west of the city. The birds, on their migration from the steppes of Central Asia towards India, would follow the course of the stream, and at first light would suddenly appear out of the darkness above the water, giving the guns exciting sport for an hour or two.

Very early one morning, before dawn, all the officers except the Minister left the Legation in a lorry for one of these shoots. The affair proceeded normally and we got some good bags. The return journey was timed to see us back at our desks at 10 a.m. for the day's work. Half a mile from home, the British Office Superintendent met us. He was extremely agitated and told a shocking story.

It appeared that at 9.00 a.m. that morning an Afghan schoolteacher, carrying a student's satchel inside which was concealed a large eleven-shot Mauser pistol, arrived at the gate of the Legation. He told the attendant, an unarmed Pathan orderly,[5] that he wished to see the Minister in order to obtain a visa for India.

"You cannot see the Great Man without an appointment," replied the orderly. "All other Sahibs are out. They will return, Insha Allah, in an hour's time." At this the teacher's face became dark and desperate. It was afterwards believed that he had drugged himself with opium or charas with the object of murdering a high British official. Drawing the Mauser out of the satchel, he shot dead an Indian translator coming in for the morning's work. The assailant then noticed Stranger, who was fixing an electric pump in a well, which supplied water to the Legation hospital just outside the gate. With Stranger were two Afghan assistants. One tried to run away and was killed in his tracks. The other jumped down the well. There was a parapet a few feet high surrounding the well mouth, and ten feet below ground was a wooden platform with an opening at one side and a ladder leading further down. The assistant fell on the platform, and, with the desperation of fear, leapt up and descended the ladder out of sight of the mad gunman, who now approached Stranger and leveled his pistol at him. After a fatal moment of hesitation, Stranger also jumped down the well but was too late to achieve the ladder. The assassin leaned over the parapet and emptied his pistol into Stranger's body. He died almost instantaneously.

The Pathan orderly then threw himself at the gunman in a kind of rugger tackle and brought him down. In the struggle that followed the powerful Pathan overcame the gunman, disarmed him and handed him over to the Afghan guard outside the gate.

In fairness to the Officer commanding the Guard, it should be mentioned that events moved with such swiftness that he did not realise what was going on and so was unable to intervene. The Pathan orderly afterwards received a medal from the Viceroy for his bravery.

A state of confusion reigned when we returned from our duck shoot. Stranger's body was taken to the hospital, where Teddy Lucas confirmed that he was dead. The widow, who was in the Legation at the time, was suffering from shock. Sir Richard had taken charge of the situation in our absence and contacted the Afghan Government, who acted promptly. The schoolteacher under arrest was tried summarily, convicted and hanged. The remains of the

---

[5]   The Legation was not allowed to employ an armed attendant, but an Afghan guard, armed with rifles, was usually encamped just outside the gate.

poor Indian translator were handed over to his family in Kabul, and it was decided to send Stranger's coffin to Peshawar for burial and that I should accompany it. Mrs Lucas,[6] who wished to go to Peshawar, came with me and went on to Rawalpindi the next day.

When this ugly incident and all that occurred afterwards was finally investigated, I believe that it transpired that the Legation murders were not an isolated case but part of a much wider plot,[7] involving the safety of the ruling family. The conspirators might well have planned an attack in two phases: first against the British Legation upon whom the King was believed to rely for support, and secondly against the King himself.

The Legation murders made us realise how simple it would have been for the assassin to gain access to the Chancery. If he had come during the usual office hours, he would have been introduced as an applicant for a visa to India into the office of the Secretary, Captain McCan. Under the same roof were the offices of the Military Attaché, Major "Tiny" Farwell, and the Counsellor, myself. None of us possessed a firearm, and we would all have been easy targets. The Minister's office was in his house some distance away, and he was comparatively safe. After the shooting we were all supplied with pistols to keep handy in the drawers of our desks.

About this time, I was informed, that I would be relieved of my duties as Counsellor shortly, and could go on home leave. The leave was due, but it would have been normal for me to complete two years in my appointment, and I could not resist the feeling that I was being 'dropped' from the team. It was clear now that the trek through Afghanistan would have to be abandoned.

Then came the second shock. King Nadir Shah was assassinated on the 8th November. Exactly a year previously he had ordered the execution of his greatest enemy, Ghulam Nabi of the Charkhi family, who was leader of the pro-Amanullah party. Though warned of the danger, the King insisted on attending a School Prizegiving in the grounds of his palace on that day. As he was chatting informally with the boys, he was shot by a natural son of Ghulam Nabi, and killed instantly. Fortunately, his two powerful brothers, Sardars Rashim Khan and Shah Mahmud, retained control of the situation and lost no time in proclaiming the late King's son Zahir Shah, a young man in his early twenties,

---

6   In the spring of 1933 a bride arrived from England for Teddy Lucas. They were married in Lahore, and I was best man.

7   The plot involving the notorious Charkhi family and the activities of the pro-Amanullah party is described in Fraser-Tytler's *Afghanistan*, p.239–241.

as the lawful heir to the throne. Huge crowds turned out for the funeral of Nadir Shah and testified that he had been a popular king, and had won the affection of his people. I was also present when the new Ruler, Zahir Shah, faced the whole diplomatic corps for the first time. The ceremony was short and simple, but charged with emotion. I believe that son has been a worthy successor to his father. He has been fortunate to enjoy the loyal support of his powerful uncles.

I left Kabul in December 1933, with many regrets. I had fallen in love with Afghanistan and its fascinating people, and dearly wished to explore it further, particularly in the Northern Province and in the valley of the Oxus, but it was not to be. I planned the journey home via Rhodesia and South Africa, to visit my old friend Cedric Horton of Dragon School days, who was farming in Natal.

Census Operations N.W.F. Province 1931. A large team of excellent Indian Civil Servants working together. A word in praise of the Indian clerk, or Babu – he represented the bricks and mortar of a tall and stately edifice he gave strength and stability to the whole structure of government.

The Development Plan Team working under Leslie as Chief Secretary.

The Kurram Valley and Bannu. A beautiful area, with the mountains beyond.

Assistant Commissioner's House in Tank 1927.

Bhitanni Tribal Territory to the South of Bannu – the temper of the tribesmen in Waziristan was quite different from, and much less friendly than, that of the tribes further north.

Bhitanni Tribal Territory.

Bahrain Burial mounds (probably Sumerian).

Old Portugese Fort.

Sheikh Isa Al Khalifa's Palace in centre of Island.

Deputy Commissioner Kohat 1934–8, Gavagnari gardens – the first home for Marie and Leslie, where all along the front, bordered by a stream, lay well-watered lawns and flower beds, the scene of many outdoor parties.

The Big House. British Legation Kabul 1932. This unpopular magnificence was hardly less palatial than the King's own residence.

Counsellor's House where Leslie lived. British Legation Kabul.

'Doc' Lucas in his car outside Counsellor's House.

King's birthday. 'Doc' Lucas extreme left. King Nadir Shah was assissinated on the 8th November the same year by a natural son of Ghulam Nabi. Exactly a year previously he had ordered the execution of Ghulam Nabi, his greatest enemy.

Legation Sunbeam car with Driver, Bearer and 'Crusoe' on top of Jagdalan Pass.

Old Moghul garden at Nimla, with the snows of Safed Kom behind.

Above The Deputy Counsellor Kabul 1932

Right Mufti Abdul Latif Consul, Jalalabad

Bottom The Khurd-Kabul Defile. Scene of
the Massacre of British Troops 1842

Istalif a few miles North of Kabul.

Above The Rock Buddha of Bamian north west of Kabul.

Middle The Dara-i-Skimari – The Bamian River on its way to the Oxus.

Bottom Just below the Shiba Pass on the way to Damian – Ghorband.

The Akrorat Pass – taken from12,000 ft.

The Ghorband Valley.

Our Afghan Guard "And the Chief may sleep sound, in his grave, who would rule the unruly Afghan." Verses written in India. Sir Alfred Lyall.

The new Family in Eckington Vicarage, Worcestershire in 1955 – the three from India with Sophronia, 'Phro', and Anne.

Return to The North West Frontier in 1972. Phro and Leslie at Dean's Hotel.

Marie and Lady Kaye resting during a ride.

Leslie's faithful khidmatgar, Mohammad Din, one of the two key staff, Marcus and his Nanny (Violet Roach) on and outing in the Peshawar Valley in 1945, Nanny came back to England with in 1947 and lived with the Blenkinsop Family, who already had David, in Sherborne. Nanny had been engaged to an RAF pilot who was killed in action.

Leslie with Lady Wavell on her visit in 1945 to the Lady Cunningham Welfare Centre in Peshawar.

A very relaxed and happy Leslie on holiday In Kashmir, on a Houseboat in the Dal Lake near Srinagar. When seven years old, David boarded at The Garden School Srinagar, and was taken out occasionally by Lady Kaye at the weekend.

Camping in the Swat Valley. Marie centre, with Lady Kaye on the left the mother of MM (Molly) Kaye, who wrote *The Far Pavilions* in 1978.

Marie with Sandy Napier, a close family friend and David's Godfather

Marcus, born in March 1944, with Judith in the garden of Sir James Almond's house in Peshawar. Sir James was the Judicial Commissioner of the North West Frontier Province.

Judith died of Typhoid in April 1945, and Marcus, just a year old, tends her grave.

CHAPTER XI

Deputy Commissioner Kohat
1934–38

My wives I married as was fit,
Some thirteen of the purest blood
And two or three have germs of wit,
And almost all are chaste and good;
But all their womanhood has been
Hen-cooped behind a marble screen.

After a long and arduous journey through Southern Africa, I took ship from Durban to Cape town and went down almost immediately with a high fever, which was diagnosed by the ship's doctor as plague! The rest of the voyage was spent in an isolation cabin in the stern. Nearly thirty doctors queued up to examine this interesting phenomenon when we finally reached our destination. The diagnosis was changed to an obscure glandular fever, and I was subjected to numerous tests ashore. On arrival at a Capetown hotel I collapsed and was admitted to a nursing home, where I was patched up and eventually landed in England more dead than alive.

I went straight to a specialist in Harley Street, reputed to have experience of tropical diseases. He had two assistants. Between them they gave me a thorough 'going-over'. After a final consultation in front of an Xray screen, the conclusion was announced.

"There is nothing organically wrong," the great doctor declared, adding, with a twinkle in his eye, "We prescribe a mixed tonic of liqueur brandy, port wine, a holiday in Aldeburgh, on the East coast, and last, but not least, marriage."

The oracle had spoken and I followed this prescription to the letter. The best tonic of all, however, was Constance Marie Carruthers, whom I met for the first time at our family home in Oxford. She was thirty years old, small, intelligent, gay, and with a sense of humour which I found irresistible. Her naturally wavy auburn hair, which I used to trim later in the Malakand, did not need the attention of hairdressers. She was third of five sisters, four of whom lived in a flat nearby in Banbury Road as their parents were dead. For some time before my return she had been in the habit of dropping in for a chat with my parents. My father, who was legal adviser to the Carruthers family, was charmed with her. I felt wholeheartedly the same.

Marie, who was working as secretary to the Matron of the Radcliffe Infirmary, swept away depression and the ill effects of the African journey. Her gaiety and high spirits changed my whole outlook. We played tennis, picnicked, and drove to many places of interest round Oxford. In the early summer of '34 we went to Bournemouth with a party of friends. We hired horses and rode frequently in the New Forest, galloping over open spaces carpeted with heather, or walking slowly beneath shady pine groves. Marie was fond of horses, and her experience of riding was to stand her in good stead later on. I have memories of bathing in the sea, sunning on the sand, and strolling arm in arm along the whole length of the promenade from Boscombe to Canford Cliffs. My health improved rapidly my hopes revived.

After a dance in our hotel, we sat together in somebody's car, and I proposed to her. She accepted sweetly, but later, as she climbed the broad staircase up to her bedroom, she turned, looking over the balustrade to where I stood in the hall below and said: "There is one reservation. I will marry you, but I will not go to India." The picture is blurred now, but I can still see the small determined figure in the shadows, uttering, over her shoulder, this Parthian shot.

After a restless night I tackled her next morning on the subject of India. "My grandmother was a missionary, and she died there," she answered simply. "I feel that if I go I will die there too." This may have been one of those premonitions familiar to psychic researchers, for ten golden years later, Marie was buried eight thousand feet up in the foothills of the Himalayas.

The marriage took place on 21st July 1934 at St Mary's University Church, Oxford. The Principal of Lincoln College kindly lent his house and garden for the reception, his wife being a relative of the Carruthers.

As we waited for the ship east, a friend lent us her home in Norham Gardens. "There will be a young couple with a baby also staying there." She told us. "As the house is so large, I don't think you'll be disturbed." In due course the pair, whose names were Phil and Eleanor Tollinton, arrived. It transpired that Phil belonged to the ICS and was also a member of the Indian Political Service. Stranger still he had been posted as Assistant Commissioner, Kohat, while I had just received orders as Deputy Commissioner in the same Frontier district. Thus started a great friendship continuing to the present day.

After landing at Bombay in October, we took the *Frontier Mail* to Peshawar and called on the Governor, Sir Ralph, and his wife, Lady Griffiths.

"I have had a number of unfavourable reports about the activities of a lone lady missionary in Kohat by the name of Flora Davidson," the Governor remarked. He did not elucidate much. "Tell her that if she does not behave herself, I will have her deported across the Indus!" Soon after taking charge of the district on 8th October, we met Flora. I had expected to find a formidable female, difficult to handle; but no sooner had she and Marie met than they discovered they both hailed from Scotland and became firm friends. Flora was full of fun and independence. She owned an estate on Deeside and had the means to work free of the established missionary societies. She was a trained midwife and had made a reputation for herself among Pathans, on both sides of the border, as an expert in delivering babies.

This fearless Scotswoman never refused a request to attend a birth however distant or remote the home from which the call came. She did not normally practise in Tribal Territory but had many partisans among transborder tribesmen, whose language she spoke fluently. An Afridi helper named Mirbaz went with her everywhere as an escort. She writes:[1] "One day Mirbaz ... and I were motoring over to try to raise the Banner of the King of kings for the first time in Kohat.

"About two hours before sunset we entered the Pass, which runs for thirteen miles through tribal or Independent Territory. In those days no European was allowed to go a step off Government Road. The Tribesmen could raid and murder as they liked in their own land, but the Road was sacrosanct.

"Gumbat Khan had invited us to go to his house and have a cup of tea. I had not had time to get permission from the PA, and it was most unlikely he would have given it anyhow, so I had to decline. As we came within sight of his house we discovered he was waiting on the road with a retinue of servants, with carpets down, and beds and tables, and a big spread for us."

What they did not know was that hiding among the rocks on the top of the spur three pairs of murderous eyes were watching every movement. Gumbat Khan had several blood feuds on hand. At least five or six different men wanted to do away with him. Now, taking tea with a European on the Road, he would be off guard. Having taken leave, they rose to go, Gumbat Khan himself picking up the tray with all the bright blue Bokhara china. He watched the little party go. Barely had they reached the corner when rifle fire shattered the quiet of the mountains. Mirbaz, looking back, called out, "They've got the Malik!" Gumbat Khan, knowing it was death to remain in the open, flung down the tray, with a crash of breaking crockery, and hobbled to the safety of his door, with his servants crowding after.

He had been hit in the heel. Flora returned to find one youngster with a bad wound in his thigh, groaning and bleeding on the ground.

---

[1] *Wild Frontier*, by Flora Davidson.

"Stop shooting. The Malik has gone," shouted Mirbaz to the swaggering men, picking up bandoliers and blankets.

"Do you like killing people? Are you not afraid?" called the lady missionary.

"Afraid? Why should we? There is no British Government here to catch us."

"Are you not afraid of God?"

"God! God? What is that?" and they went off laughing.

Flora Davidson was a colourful and, indeed, lovable personality. In her late forties or early fifties she was still very active. In spite of our friendship I was well aware that she could be an embarrassment to the Civil authorities. Though unorthodox, her methods were well intentioned. When a Pathan child, a girl, was left on her doorstep half-starved and exhausted from maltreatment, Flora took in the little one and brought her up for some years as her adopted daughter. But when the girl arrived at marriageable age (about fourteen) the father turned up and demanded custody of his child. When Flora refused to hand over the girl there was a row, and almost a riot, in the City. This must have been the case that prompted the Governor to threaten deportation.

I had not been in Kohat many months when another and potentially far more serious incident occurred. Flora was ushered into my office one morning looking very distressed and half-weeping.

"Oh, Major Mallam, what shall I do? I am in such dreadful trouble!"

The story emerged as she sat in a chair, endeavouring to control herself. For some time she had been trying to obtain a suitable wife for the Afridi Mirbaz, whom she regarded as a Christian. At last with the assistance of the Mardan missionaries, a girl was found, and it was arranged for the couple to be married in that town. Immediately after the wedding they came to live in Kohat City, close to Flora's house. On the very first night the girl stuck her head through the clerestory window of her new home, and called loudly for help, saying that she had been forcibly converted to Christianity and married against her will. In the densely populated town the news spread like wildfire and a hostile crowd collected. The doughty Scotswoman had managed to escape – but what was she to do?

Snatching the telephone, I called the Superintendent of Police. He had only just been informed and had sent a strong force to take the couple into protective custody while we sorted things out. Fortunately no breach of the peace had occurred, but there was plenty of emotional feeling and the city was seething with religious indignation. The girl's home was in the Malakand Agency across the border from Mardan. Hastily calling the Political Agent, I gave him her address and asked him to get immediate assurance from her parents that they would have her back. By the evening she was on the train with a strong police guard. I discovered afterwards there was a connection between this unwilling bride and the recent murders of missionaries in Mardan. She was a bad hat. We were well rid of her.

Poor Mirbaz! I never heard whether he managed to find another wife!

These events had a sobering effect on Flora. She never again presented us with a crisis during the whole of my three years' duty in Kohat.

Although forty years have passed, I still feel a strong attraction for that charming District. Even the huge expanses of arid desert and barren hillside are beautiful. The Cantonment was small compared with Peshawar but adequately irrigated from the famous Jangal Khel Springs. There was room for a grass polo ground and nine-hole golf course, and it was possible to grow English flowers, roses, salvias, violets and pansies, in the bungalow gardens.

The Deputy Commissioner's bungalow, Cavagnari House, was the most imposing in the cantonment. It was a domed building in the Italian style, named after Sir Louis Cavagnari, who, with all the members of his mission, was assassinated in Kabul in 1879 in the course of the Second Afghan War. The house was comfortable and spacious, the rooms large and cool in summer, being shaded from the glare of the sun by wide verandahs. All along the front, bordered by a stream, lay well-watered lawns and flower beds, the scene of many outdoor parties given for military, RAF and civil officials and their wives, and for leading local dignitaries, tribesmen and veteran of the Indian Army. Over my mantlepiece now hangs a pleasing watercolour of the house and garden painted by Dorothy Baker, wife of a Brigadier commanding the Kohat Brigade.

No less beautiful than the cantonment were the dramatic shapes of the hills separating the district from the tribal area. The familiar outline of 'The Old Woman's Nose' dominated the plains and the Pass leading northward to Peshawar. From there a range of hills ran westward flanking the Miranzai valley and joining the Samana range beyond Hangu. At the western end of the Samana stood the heights of Dargai, captured by the Gordon Highlanders and Ghurkas, under General Sir William Lockhart, with heavy loss in 1897.

The Kohat Pass and the Samana became famous again in 1923 in connection with the Molly Ellis affair. This strange story[2] began on 14th April when some Afridi tribesmen entered the bungalow occupied by Major Ellis, his wife and their seventeen-year-old daughter. The intruders murdered his wife and abducted Molly while her father was away on duty. In the rescue, organised by Sir John

---

[2] Described in detail in Chapter XIII of Arthur Swinson's *North West Frontier*.

Maffey, the missing girl was eventually located by a party of friendly tribesmen who escorted the brave lady missionary, Mrs Starr, across the mountains to Khanki Bazaar in the heart of Afridi Tirah, where, after lengthy negotiations with Mullah Mahmud Akhunzada, they secured Molly's release and brought her back across the Samana again to Kohat and safety.

The DC's rest house, outside Fort Lockhart, was a cool haven on top of the Samana at 6,000 feet, where I often took Marie. It had a small garden with shady shisham trees surrounded by a stone wall, in direct contrast to the starkness of the fort itself. The wall was patrolled by an armed Frontier Constabulary guard day and night. Occasionally I left her alone with an Indian Assistant for as long as twenty-four hours while dealing with urgent business in the district below, though keeping in touch by telephone.

The Deputy Commissioner's job entailed responsibility not only for the welfare and security of the people living inside the district, but also for the behaviour of the unadministered tribes resident outside British India, immediately across the border. The dual mandate lent an added dimension and a peculiar interest to ordinary district work. The way in which it was discharged contributed decisively to the success or failure of Frontier administration. The location of Political Agents, Scouts and Militias in crucial tribal areas such as Waziristan (where there was also a large military cantonment), Kurram, Khyber and Malakand enabled the Government to bring pressure to bear on the more powerful tribes inhabiting the mountains close to Afghanistan, thus adding indirectly to the protection of the settled districts. The ultimate responsibility, however, for the safety of the British Indian border lay with the DC, who was also District Magistrate and head of the District Police, with special powers, under the Frontier Crimes Regulation, to preserve law and order. He was supported by the Frontier Constabulary and, in the last resort, by the army.

There was an important RAF station in Kohat. One day I was invited to give the Officers a talk[3] about district administration. I tried to give an idea of the varied nature of my work. I mentioned responsibility for the accuracy of the land records, for the records of rights in land and for payment of land revenue, for the maintenance of law and order and general welfare of the people, a duty that took me on tour to every village in the district, and enabled me to know most of the headmen personally. It was an exacting duty. Two aspects proved specially interesting to me: the democratic institutions such as the Municipal Committee and Rural Board, on both of which the DC was

---

[3] In the South Asian Archives of Cambridge University (SAACU).

ex-officio chairman, and the tribes, who were my particular commitment. For the training of the people of India in the difficult art of democracy such institutions seemed to me of paramount importance. Too often tired and harassed officials gave up this very exacting task as hopeless. Soon the elected bodies in many districts were removed and replaced by Executive Officers. I believe the Kohat bodies remained intact almost to the end of British rule. In addition to the scenic beauty of plain and mountain, the Khattak and Bengash tribes, resident within the district, are among the most good looking, well dressed, amenable and attractive of all Pathans, and I am sure that anyone who knows the frontier will bear me out. For several generations they had relinquished their tribal state and had become subject to the laws and practices of British India, while still retaining many of their original characteristics. Above all, they were reasonable and responsive to well intentioned efforts by Government on their behalf. That these particular groups were extensively recruited into the Indian Army was both the cause and effect of their peculiar temperament. The strong 'service' tradition and the presence in their villages of many distinguished pensioned officers and other ranks gave them a steadiness under the constant fire of seditious agitation, which many other districts did not possess. A notable expression of their individuality was the Khattak dance, famous throughout the length and breadth of that wild land. Performed at night, in the flickering light of a bonfire, with the skirl of pipes, the rhythmical beat of drums and a glint of naked swords, the ever-moving circle of young warriors, stamping and twirling in unison, gave an impression of primitive vigour combined with a dignified self-control.

In comparison, the Orakzais, inhabiting the hills beyond the western border, were rough and uncouth, though still fine examples of humanity and moderately well disposed. Their *jirgas* (elders) seldom came down to Kohat; usually I made a journey to Hangu to see them. Relations were friendly and uncomplicated. There were no Government forts or roads in their territory. I longed to drop down the far side of the Samana to pay them a visit in their own homes a project that nearly succeeded when I was asked to help in settling a long-standing dispute between two sections of the tribe over grazing rights in Tirah. Although there was no official jurisdiction in a purely tribal matter of this kind, I spent days in Hangu trying to bring them to a settlement, and eventually succeeded. An agreement was signed by representatives of both parties, and a copy kept in the district record room in case of dispute in future.

Different again were the Adam Kel Afridis, inhabiting the Kohat pass beyond the northern boundary. They were a sophisticated lot, famous for an arms factory on the roadside, where almost exact replicas of the service 303 Lee Enfield rifle were manufactured by skilled men with extraordinarily primitive machinery. Government policy was not to interfere in any way with this somewhat disreputable industry. There were sound reasons for this, perhaps the soundest being that a sudden rush by tribesmen from any part of the Frontier to buy weapons could be easily detected and would give Intelligence in Peshawar prior warning of serious trouble.

Resident in this tribal area (as in some others) were a few distinguished pensioned Indian officers, who had given many year loyal service to the crown. One day, Marie and I were invited to the home of an old Risaldar Major of the Adam Kel, for a cup of tea. His house, simple and rather bare, though strongly built, lay not far from the road. An atmosphere of excitement greeted us on the doorstep. The cause was soon discovered as the old man introduced us to his son, a specially promoted Captain in the Indian Army, who had just returned from London after receiving a medal for gallantry from His Majesty King George V at Buckingham Palace. The pride of the whole family at this signal honour (such medals usually being presented by the Governor or the Viceroy in Delhi) could be felt.

From the Molly Ellis case, as also from the past history of their behaviour before the construction of the road through the pass, I had always thought this tribe was not to be trifled with. Imagine my surprise, therefore, at their attitude when we discussed preparations for celebrating Their Majesties' Silver Jubilee on 6th May 1935.

"Will you agree to set up bonfires on the hilltops overlooking Kohat?" they were asked.

"We are quite ready to do this," replied the jirgas.

Rather daringly we advanced a step further. "Would you like a celebration in the Pass?"

The answer was so favourable that sports and games were arranged close to the road, including a tug-of-war, in which all sections of the tribe were invited to send teams. A rifle- shooting contest was also planned, with white-washed earthenware pots on the hillsides as targets. Written agreements were secured from all sections to suspend blood feuds for the week, including the celebrations. All went perfectly on the day though I cannot pretend to have been free from anxiety when excitement among the spectators reached fever pitch during the tug-of-war particularly as Marie and one or two other English ladies were present, and almost every other tribesman appeared to be armed.

Some of the happiest memories of Kohat are linked with the big agricultural

A Poetry Composed by Hira Lal Mehra, Sub-Inspector of police,
and Presented to Major G. L. Mallam, I. A., Deputy Commissioner,
Kohat, at the Agricultural Show, Kohat, March 1936

Our thanks are due
Major Mallam to you
For restart of the Show
For ages it will go.

This will improve village life
And save the strife
A great seed you have sown
Fruit will be marvellous when grown.

One drives goat – ram others bring
Some send their oxen – other cows and string
The potter is busy with pot and jar
Border and Police with Tug of War.

Village uplift and children's gay
Small girls work and Scouts in play
Fire display and the sweepers run
Camels race is the superlative fun.

Prize will be paid in order they stand
All we admit the show is grand
Credit is due Mrs Mallam to thee
Reward you will get from Al-Migh-ty

This is in a District you did as D. C.
Hale and hearty we wish you to be
In the end Hira Lal sings the song
Major and Mrs Mallam you live long.

AGRICULTURAL SHOW

TRIBAL LAW

Nawab of Peri's Bodyguard

At the ready

Jirga at Gumbat 1935

shows which were held for three years running, reviving an old custom long in abeyance, probably because Deputy Commissioners were changed so frequently, that there was no time for the considerable planning involved.

The first show was somewhat tentative. With experience gained, the second and third were bigger and better. Vast numbers came, many from long distances. The crowds were measured in tens of thousands. They covered an area of old railway embankment overlooking the arena ground like flies. Thousands of animals and birds were brought to the display, including horses, cattle, sheep, camels, hawks and cockerels the various classes being judged by Veterinary Department officers, who ran a temporary hospital in tents for treatment of animal diseases and to give advice on prevention. Every nation-building section of Government was represented and there were large exhibits of local produce and handicrafts. There was wheat, barley, maize and sugar cane to be pinched and exclaimed over, and among the handicrafts were bright lengths of hand-woven cloth, agricultural implements such as ploughs and sickles, harnesses for bullocks, coloured smocks and handsome silver and gold jewelry for the women. Some ladies were in the crowd, clothed from head to foot in the burqa, which could be lifted only in order to examine the goods.

On the last day the Governor and Chief Minister would come over from Peshawar to watch the sports and present prizes. One year, in consultation with the headmasters of various schools, I organised a parade of boys aged between twelve and fifteen for a physical drill display. There were four hundred of them, each wearing a white vest and dark blue shorts so that they all looked alike. With the help of military bands from the cantonment and of school and army PT instructors, the lads were thoroughly rehearsed in simple rhythmic movements. The effect on the final day was most impressive. After the boys had marched off, Sir Abdul Qayum, the Chief Minister (a great man who devoted his life to the advancement of Pathans) came up to me with his eyes full of tears. "I have not seen anything so good before," he said simply.

These were peaceful times as Abdul Ghaffar Khan, that indomitable agitator, was safely shut away in an Indian prison. There were few more able Congress firebrands, and whenever he was free to spread the flame of revolution and to march his Red Shirt army up and down the Frontier, no district official knew any peace of mind!

Overlooking the polo ground was a small but beautiful church. Above the nave hung numerous old colours of the 'Piffer' (Punjab Frontier Force Rifles) Regiments, and the walls were covered with brass memorial tablets to many a British Officer and other rank killed in action, including casualties from the

3rd Afghan War in 1919. A single aisle provided limited accommodation but this consecrated spot held many heart-warming mementos. When the chaplain was away, I often used to take the services. About the spring of 1937 a new electrically-powered organ was installed by the MES. It was dedicated at a special service, when a recital was given by Sir James Almond, who besides being Judicial Commissioner of the Province, was organist at St John's Church in Peshawar Cantonment. A few days later I was woken at 2 a.m. by an RAF officer shouting, "The church is on fire!" Running the short distance along the Mall I could see the blaze. The building was already almost completely gutted. The roof had collapsed, the walls fallen, the colours burned and the brasses just lumps of molten metal. An immediate enquiry was held. The MES were officially exonerated, but no explanation for the cause of the fire was suggested.

This shattering blow much disturbed our local Christian community, as well as many others who knew and loved the little church. Like Kohat, every large cantonment had its own place of worship that meant a lot both to the small groups of Indian Christians and to the Englishman serving his country in a far outpost, to whom it spoke of home. The churches that remain along this remote borderland contain many records of heroism and self-sacrifice.

In the Dera Ismail Khan district, just south of the Bannu border, where the motor road emerges from the Pezu Pass, is an isolated hill, about 4,500 feet high, situated wholly within the district. Towards the end of the nineteenth century, the hill, called Sheikh Budin, was used as a summer refuge for the families of British troops, from the dust and heat of the plains. A zigzag pathway was cut up the side of the hill, so as to allow women and children to be carried on ponies or mules to the top. As the hill is as dry and barren as the plain from which it rises, these animals were also used for transporting in tins all the water required for drinking, cooking and washing from a well at the foot. Until the British came, there was no habitation on the hill; but soon bungalows, even a church, were built high up round the crest, and the hill became populated for the first time in its life. In the year 1927, when I was in the neighbourhood, this little summer station had long been deserted. Fine roads and motorcars made it possible to send families away to the lush, green valleys of Kashmir. One summer in the heat of July, I determined to climb the hill, and spend a night or two in the cool clean air on the top. Setting out before dawn, I reached the crest about lunchtime, and after a breather began to explore the strange, empty hill top world, so full of the ghosts of English mothers and children. Eventually, I found my way to the church a small sturdy stone building, only very slowly crumbling away with the years. All around the church were graves, dozens of them, several infants a few weeks old, and many aged two or three. As I looked down on the sad lonely little stones, each one engraved with an English name, I thought of the tragedy, the awful heartbreak that they represented. I thought of the mothers far away from home in a desolate and unfriendly country and the children sickly and lacking some essential food or treatment. This was only a part of the price that had to be paid for maintaining a great Empire.

When I was a little boy, I had a dream of being a civil official in India, touring my district by river. The dream recurred frequently. The scene was always the same a broad stream overhung on both banks by thick jungle my young idea of one of the rivers of Central India. It could be said that in Kohat this dream came true, with frequent tours by river, though of course the Indus is far from the tropics! These tours were a very special delight to us both. They were mainly confined to the winter months, when the days were warm and sunny, and the nights cold. Travelling usually involved road, river and horseback.

The season would start with a visit to the villages in the dry areas near the Bannu border. A car would take us quickly to the southern end of the district about ninety miles from Kohat. My own pony would be sent on ahead, to await arrival at a *dak* bungalow by the roadside. The same all over the sub-continent, these dak bungalows were built of mud bricks, with very thick walls and deep verandahs, supported by pillars. There was a small resident staff, who, besides cleaning the rooms and serving at table, kept hens. The menu was invariably the same: long-running *murghi* and bullet-hard peas, followed by caramel custard and 'angels on horseback'. It was usually washed down with a *chota peg*. Imagine a hurricane lamp on the table and your wife opposite it seemed a meal fit for a king!

Next morning, a quiet Frontier Constabulary pony would be borrowed for Marie and an early start made, with a small Mounted Police escort, to visit remote villages surrounded by dry, almost desert, country. There were no roads. It was essential to ride.

If we were doing things in style and intended to remain out for a number of days, tents would be sent forward on camelback to a hamlet in a central position from which others could be reached. Accommodation would be ready and kitchen fires burning as soon as we arrived, sometimes late in the evening after a long and tiring round. The khansamah, almost the most important member of the baggage train, would be on his mettle to produce a splendid meal. With the moon coming up clear and frosty it felt incredible to be sitting safe, with an after dinner coffee, in these remote wastes where hardly an English foot had ever trod, and, if they had, were the feet of fighting men.

These tours by a married Deputy Commissioner to the outback were a great occasion for the villagers, many of whom had not seen a white face for years. Poor as they were, they gave us a royal welcome and, with typical Pathan hospitality, one of the larger landowners would lay on a feast of palao rice, sheep, tea, chappattis arid hard-boiled eggs. These eggs, de-shelled, came in a huge bowl, each one covered with black finger marks!

Any Government institution in the locality was a 'must' to be visited, such as a school or hospital, and public meetings were held to which all the villagers were invited, to hear any complaints or suggestions. At a school there would almost always be a guard of honour of boy scouts in uniform lined up on either side of the entrance to greet us, and somewhere on the school building, or on a flag pole in the compound, the Union Jack would be flying. Baden-Powell's great movement for boys certainly stirred the imagination.

A feature of life here was, of course, the shortage of water. Long lines of women, dressed in black, with several water pots balanced on their heads, walked statuesquely to and fro for miles between their homes and water holes dug in the dried-up beds of rivers. In the extended intervals between scanty rainfalls even these sources of moisture began to run out, and there were times when the entire population left their homes to trek to Bannu in search of water and a living. Strangely enough they were a happy people, and the men mostly dressed in clean white clothes.

The knowledge I acquired of the dry areas prompted me, ten years later, to include in the First Five Year Development Plan for the Frontier an agricultural engineering section to be attached to the Provincial Agricultural Department to provide modern mechanical appliances for bringing arid tracts under the plough (locally known as Barani cultivation), and to assist the cultivator in terracing and 'bunding' his fields to prevent wastage of rain water.

The strip of fairly level land between the Indus and the hills, which (including the Hazara district to the east) formed the NWFP, was full of contrasts, none more marked than that between rain-watered and canal irrigated land the former poor, the latter rich. An anomaly occurred here in that folks who scraped a meagre living from poor unirrigated land were often far more cheerful and better dressed than those farming the valuable irrigated parts, every square inch of which was cultivated.

There were economic reasons for this: when canals first came into operation, the value of the land rose enormously, and Hindu moneylenders offered large loans in return for mortgages which the owner could not resist. Exorbitant interest was charged and the wretched owner fell deeper and deeper into debt.

Legislation was introduced to prevent the transfer of property to non-agriculturists (such as the blood-sucking moneylenders), but it did not lift the landowner out of his debt. His status was reduced to that of a tenant of the mortgagee. He continued to till his fields, but could never receive the full value of the produce. The result was that he became badly off, depressed and resentful. Herein lay the cause of a great deal of the Hindu-Muslim friction both in the Frontier Province and in the Punjab.

For most of our touring we made use of the river Indus. Two large boats, rather resembling magnified gondolas with long oars, were hired when we had guests. As the route was always downstream there was no need of a powered unit, and when the craft returned they were dragged back by ropes. Close to the bank the current was not so strong. The crews knew the hazards of the swift-flowing waterway. Starting from Kushalgarh, where there was a road and railway bridge, we drifted smoothly away. The guests would occupy the front boat, taking with them shotguns, fishing rods and picnic baskets, while I sat in the one behind which, with table and chair and room for a clerk, had been turned into an office. With the water lapping gently outside I was left to myself for hours with innumerable files, while Marie and our visitors admired the quiet scenery.

Below Kushalgarh the great river is compressed for many miles within narrow limits, and cuts its way deeply through groups of low, barren foothills. High banks rear up on either side, sometimes precipitous, almost entirely devoid of vegetation. The scene presents a lonely, at times picturesque, desolation. There was very little traffic. We would tie up to the bank for lunch, and the men would have a shoot afterwards pigeons or sand grouse and the ladies some fishing.

Marie once caught a twelve pound *mahseer* (Indian salmon). It was played from the streamside on a spoon bait and gave her quite a tussle. I was head down in the files and did not witness her triumph. Hearing loud noises on the bank I ran to see what was happening. "See what I've caught," she announced, holding it up proudly. "It fought quite hard before he gaffed it" pointing to a happy-looking ghillie. Duly impressed I took a photo of the fish, which turned out to be the biggest catch of the day.

Villages near the right bank (Frontier side) would be warned of the tour and deputations waited at convenient places for interviews and petitions. Towards evening the craft would be moored at a rearranged spot. Climbing up the steep bank, our guests and ourselves would find the miracle of India, a comfortable ready-pitched camp, with an appetising smell of cooking. In addition to the kitchen tent in the rear, there would be several large marquees, outlined by rows of whitewashed bricks or stones, with neatly arranged pathways to each tent; and in attendance, an armed Police guard.

The wide plain, the bare hills and the swelling river, in the late evening and early morning, took on unbelievable shades of pink, mauve and blue. The keen winter air made one rejoice to be alive. To the DC, condemned to long hours of sitting in an office or a court at headquarters, the freedom of camp life in such a setting was a luxury, as well as a duty.

My period of office included a Royal visit. Early in February 1935 the Governor, Sir Ralph Griffiths, rang to say that Princess Alice and the Duke of Athlone would be staying with him in Peshawar, and at the latter end of their stay he would like to bring them to Kohat. "Could you give them lunch on the 21st?" he asked. "We will be delighted to do the best we can for them," I replied, when I had recovered from my astonishment.

Marie practised a curtsy, the Khansamah was commanded to surpass himself and the house and garden were polished up. My faithful bearer, Nasir Khan (who remained in service continuously for thirty years) drilled the house servants, dressed them in clean white clothes and organised everything down to the last detail.

When the day arrived a cavalcade of cars drew up outside. The Royal couple got out and we were presented. It was obvious from the start that things were going to be extremely informal. Princess Alice saw to that. Cavagnari house lived up to its reputation. Silver gleamed and glass sparkled.

Afterwards Marie told me that the Princess had exclaimed, when she was taken into a room to powder her nose: "My dear, you pull the plug here! I have been brought through some of the wildest country I have ever seen, and I expected an outpost of Empire and an earth closet. This is like a palace".

An easier or more charming guest we never entertained. She kept up a flowing and most animated conversation throughout the meal. Everything interested her, especially the Frontier scenery. As the Royal car left the hills below the Pass and entered the irrigated area round Kohat, she had noticed patches of wild dwarf iris appearing in the grass. How fortunate they were in full bloom! "Would you mind digging up some of the bulbs and sending them to us in England?" I was asked. Her request was granted, which led to a correspondence continuing over several months. In 1938, when we were home on leave, we appealed to the Princess as Patron of the National Adoption Society to help us adopt two children. The appeal was not made in vain. Thanks to her, we acquired two beautiful youngsters who attracted much admiration in Peshawar.

After lunch we sat in the garden of Cavagnari House, under a sun umbrella, before the royal guests departed. The visitors' book was graciously signed.

In the spring of 1938 we left Kohat for good, on our first home leave together.

Rather reluctantly we said goodbye to our P. and O. at Port Said and spent a thrilling week in Cairo. On to Jerusalem for Easter: a memorable experience. Marie's company transformed this my third visit to the Holy Land, and it was a delight to discover that she reacted in much the same way as I did to the drama and fascination of that wonderful country. We explored Jerusalem and Bethlehem, dropped down into the Jordan Valley and bathed in the Dead Sea. The insecurity of those days did not deter us from travelling northwards by road through Nablus and Nazareth to Galilee; but we took the precaution to hire a car with an Arab driver. We stayed two nights at a hospice near the Lake run by Father Tapper, a German priest, who was soon afterwards arrested as a spy! He told us that he and his Bedouin assistant had recently made an interesting discovery, when they were digging by the water's edge. Suddenly, their spades revealed a highly coloured mosaic pavement, with a fish on each side. This proved to be the floor of the long lost fourth century Byzantine Church of the Multiplication, last known to have been used for worship in the year 386 AD. Marie and I went to see it, and I felt we were standing at the very spot where Our Lord fed the multitude with seven loaves and a few small fishes.

We continued our journey, skirting Mount Hermon to Damascus and Baalbek; then through the Lebanon to Beirut. Travelling home by sea and land, long before the soil of Europe is reached, one encounters the outposts of western civilisation, such as Alexandria, Port Said, Cairo and Beirut, which are varying mixtures of East and West. These outposts are much the same as those planted by the Caesars to protect the Roman Empire nearly two thousand years ago. Egypt, Palestine, Syria and the Lebanon are dotted with relics of this great Empire in varying stages of decay. The historical sense gained by such a slow mode of travel is lost on those who nowadays go by air.

From Damascus onwards I began to notice a steady deterioration in Marie's health. By the time Athens was reached she seemed to have lost weight considerably; but she struggled on bravely, and at Istanbul we saw the great church of St. Sophia, now a mosque. We rowed on the Golden Horn and entered many fine mosques whose domes and minarets tower above the city and the seaway of the Bosphorus.

Arriving in Budapest by Orient Express, Marie developed a bad cold and had to stay in bed, hovering close to pneumonia. As I had a military rank on my passport, we had to avoid Austria where the Anschluss had just taken place;

instead we travelled north to Prague and were charmed by the ancient city and its freedom-loving people, already chilled by the monstrous shadow of Hitler.

A day's sight-seeing in Nuremburg and the tramp of Hitler Youth; a night in Cologne with a view of the lovely cathedral, then home at last.

It was in a hotel at Canford Cliffs near Parkstone in Dorset, where my parents now lived, that a doctor gently prepared us for the shock that Marie had diabetes.

CHAPTER XII

Marie

Was it there she lived, when the train went sweeping
Under the moon through the landscape hushed?
Somebody called me, I woke from sleeping,
Saw but a hamlet and on we rushed.

As our marriage entered the second half of its short span of ten years, the first of the two monsters which between them were to shatter our happiness, had made its appearance: diabetes. The second was to follow quickly war. From now on, Marie was entirely dependent on daily injections of insulin to keep her alive, and once we had left the shores of England only the postal service, by air or sea, could replenish our stocks of the precious drug, which was unobtainable in India. War soon threatened to isolate us from Europe, and life at times (particularly when our stocks were running low) assumed nightmarish proportions. Strangely enough neither of us was unduly depressed by the constant nearness of danger. It all fitted in with the Frontier setting and with the privations of a world war. A devoted chemist in Oxford never failed us over five critical years, sometimes repeating a consignment on news that a plane or a ship had been destroyed by enemy action. But above all, Marie's spirit rose to the challenge, and our lives became closer and more vivid than ever before. We were assured on medical advice that provided Marie received the amount of insulin that her body required (we had with us the means of testing this periodically) she could lead a completely normal life, and in fact her general health was extremely good. It was not therefore so irresponsible as it sounds that at this particular time we decided to adopt two children and take them out to India with us. Children were what Marie wanted more than anything else; and we persuaded an Irish girl, Florence Thorogood, who was not only a trusted friend and companion, but also an extremely efficient childrens' nurse, to come with us. Looking back now with knowledge of the calamities that lay in store, I think we may have been brave, but not foolhardy. It is strange to recall that India, against which Marie had rebelled so strongly at first, now held no more fears for her; she had become a willing captive.

All this, and her exceptional ability, prompt me to attempt some description of Marie's reaction to the Indian scene, from the moment of her arrival.

What was expected of a Deputy Commissioner's wife in the mid 1930s? In

MARIE

a place like Kohat on the North West Frontier she would be the senior 'civvy' wife. There was of course a large military garrison including Divisional and Brigade Headquarters and an RAF station. Cavagnari House and garden were ideal for entertaining, and Marie was exceptionally good at this, without carrying it to extremes. Her youth and intelligence made her attractive to Senior Officers, and one of our most frequent visitors was the Divisional Commander, Major-General H.L. Haughton an able General and an expert on Greco-Buddhist art, who came to stay with us later in the Malakand.

One of Marie's first problems was 'servants'. My faithful bearer, Nasir Khan, who was the key man of the team, was at first nervous at the prospect of taking on a *memsahib*. I had warned him by letter that I was getting married, and as usual he came to meet us on landing from the ship at Bombay. As I had hoped, in a few days Marie won him over, and with him a really good team of four: all Muslims, except possibly the last: Khansama (cook), Khidmatgar (butler), Mehtar (sweeper). In addition we employed at least one gardener, often assisted by prisoners from the local jail, who seemed to enjoy pottering in the garden, even though it meant dragging handcuffs and ankle chains about with them! Finally, the Government supplied me with a personal orderly, a Pathan, who was as much a friend of the family as a bodyguard and messenger.

In spite of a lively European society, centred on the Club, Marie was attracted immediately towards the local population, consisting mainly of Pathans and a minority of Hindus and Sikhs, most of them living inside a walled 'City' for the sake of protection. She was perfectly natural with them all without a trace of a colour bar; and of course with her experience of the Radcliffe Infirmary at Oxford, she went straight to the local hospital, her first contact being the Women's (Lady Griffith) Zenana Hospital, where a Eurasian lady doctor was struggling against fearful odds. Marie soon discovered with horror that most of the nurses in the wards were convicts – many of them murderesses from the jail. She wrote an indignant letter to the Inspector General of Civil Hospitals in Peshawar, and got these women replaced by more qualified staff, the first, but by no means the last, time swords were crossed with the Department of Public Health.

Very soon a new lady Head Teacher arrived from India to take charge of the Municipal Girls' High School and came to call on Marie. It was then that we first met Sugra Ghulam Khan. We were astonished that so frail looking and gentle a creature could dare to brave the dangers of the Frontier all alone, but soon discovered that she had the heart of a lion. Her family history (which she wrote down many years later) is interesting both for itself, and as an example

167

of the power of Christianity, and the influence of Christian missionaries, in a land teeming with other religions. Born at Ludhiana (Punjab) in 1905, she was of Kashmiri origin, the descendant of a Brahman named Kastari Das, who was the first Governor of Kashmir, during the reign of the great Moghul Emperor Aurangzeb. Later, probably under this mighty ruler's pressure, the family embraced Islam.

Although her father was not interested in any religion, and always treated the question humorously, he was a tolerant man, and sent all his children to Christian Mission schools.

Sugra received a good education, and, being very intelligent, made the best of it. She did, however, come under the influence of the lady missionaries, both Indian and English (in particular Miss Edna Paisley), who became her ideal. When her father died in Burma in 1912, her grandmother took over the family and the business, which did not prosper.

In 1921, at seventeen, Sugra was baptised into the Christian faith by the Revd Abdus Sham in Ambala, where she was doing her teacher training. Conversion in India is a serious step: the convert being completely separated from the family, becoming an outcast, and being disinherited.

Her mother stood by her until her death in 1922, when Sugra was turned out of the parental home, taking with her a little half-sister, aged two-and-a-half years, whom she supported by teaching, being now fully qualified. She worked in Dehra Dun for several years before coming to the Frontier. This is how she describes her departure:

"I was crying my heart out, and my friends around me looked very sad, because I was leaving for the Frontier. The very name frightened them, because it was always associated with murders and kidnapping. I was cursing the day I accepted a post at the Municipal School, Kohat. Only one American friend was consoling me by telling me that there was one good thing that the President[1] of the Municipality was an Englishman. He is sure to look after you. He did, and is still doing it."

The brave girl found an instant friend in Marie, who helped her in the first difficult period, and to this moment I correspond with her regularly. She still resides in Kohat, and has for many years run a private academy of her own, situated in her compound, called 'The Osborne School', teaching the children of Pakistani officers stationed in the cantonment.

---

[1] As Deputy Commissioner, I was ex-officio President of the Municipality.

Marie's main contacts (like those of that doughty midwife Flora Davidson) were naturally among the womenfolk, but she took a keen interest in every aspect of our situation. She shared my views about the quality of British rule, about the need for the rulers to be concerned with other things besides power, especially with all the gifts that Western civilisation had to give India, particularly in the scientific and technical fields. I found in her to my surprise and delight, not only a charming companion but a skilled and enthusiastic ally as well. She saw, so clearly, that in the whole bewildering, heart-rending panorama of Indian suffering, there was no area of greater need than the women and children, especially in a Muslim community where purdah, that dimming veil, was strictly observed.

Straight as a die, she went to the heart of the problem, concentrating her energies on maternity and child welfare and at once came in conflict with higher authority. Midwifery in India was bound up with bewildering custom and superstition, stemming from beliefs and practices of the remote past. It was a hereditary occupation, restricted to a few families, and passed down from mother to daughter. In Kohat, a decrepit, dirty looking old grandmother, with numerous rings on her fingers and bangles on her wrists (regarded as dangerous to childbirth by medical authority) had the largest practice. The net result was very high infant mortality and deformity. The situation cried out for attention and reformatory measures by Government. The subject of maternity and child welfare was not however dealt with by the Public Health Department directly. It was entrusted to the Provincial Red Cross Society, a voluntary organisation administered by a council, the Chairman of which was Lady Griffiths, wife of the Governor.

It was always assumed that the Red Cross Society would be guided by the advice of the PHD, and of the Inspector General in particular, who was a member of the Council. Quite right and proper, but at this time the Department seemed to be committed to a somewhat short-sighted policy.

Marie was elected to the Council and soon began to voice opinions to which official exception was taken. The bone of contention was the training of *dais* (indigenous midwives). The Department insisted that the training should be carried out in a centre in Peshawar to which every municipal committee and district board in the Province must make a contribution. Marie proved conclusively that this policy did not work. Midwives trained at the Centre returned, after qualifying, to their own districts, where it was hoped officially they would attract all the local practice, and force those untrained to apply for tutelage in Peshawar. In effect the reverse happened. The indigenous dais easily held on to the practice which had been in their hands from time immemorial. They skilfully isolated and discredited the trained *dai*, of whom they were jealous, and made it impossible for her to do any work. The time and money spent on her training were wasted.

The Department would not accept the evidence of these facts, nor would they consider a change.

Marie advocated a different plan. Having ascertained the policy in every province of India, she found the consensus was in favour of local Welfare Centres, headed by health visitors qualified to teach indigenous dais the rudiments of modern midwifery and cleanliness. The key to the success of such a Centre must be the determination of the health visitor to make friends with the local untrained midwives, to invite them to make use of the Welfare Centre, and to bring with them the practice which was solely in their hands.

Gradually, dais would be persuaded to take courses, mothers and children would get used to attending the Centre for antenatal and postnatal clinics (run by qualified lady doctors), the victory of modern science over outdated custom and superstition would be complete, and there would be a large drop in infant mortality and permanent injury to the surviving newborn baby.

However, the Inspector General accused Marie, at the Red Cross Meetings in Peshawar, of undermining his authority and of trying to change an established organisation without any experience of Indian conditions. His annoyance increased when he heard that the Kohat Municipal Committee and District Board had decided to discontinue their contributions to the Provincial Centre and to support a local Welfare Centre, which Marie set up in Kohat City in a rented building under a Christian health visitor imported from India.

I think it was true to say that, all over the country, native Christians, both male and female, were the only ones to come forward for training in the nursing and welfare professions, which seems to shed a very important light on a religion dedicated to the service of humanity. There were a considerable number of Christian male nurses on the staff of the Afghan Mission Hospital at Peshawar.

As to Marie's rented Welfare Centre, it was such a success she decided to build a new one with all modern conveniences, a playground for the children and living quarters for a permanent lady health visitor. In this she was backed by the local Branch Committee of the Red Cross, but not by the Department. The attitude of the latter deserves some explanation. The line of thought, put to me personally by the Assistant Director of Public Health, was that as the population was so vast, so depressed and in places so dense, it presented problems far beyond the power of government to solve. The subject of women and children in particular was fraught with difficulty. Hence the limited experiment of training a few dais only in the Provincial school at Peshawar; this did not pretend to be a final solution, but it was at least controllable. Such an attitude could well have been a legacy of the Indian Mutiny that forced the British rulers to reduce to a minimum their involvement in the domestic affairs of the people. None wanted their fingers burnt a second time.

Marie had no such scruples. She could be accused of lacking experience of India, but not of ignorance of human nature. She was convinced that women and children are much the same all the world over, and that the people of Kohat would react favourably to an organisation that set out to meet their essential needs. When the new Centre was eventually built, we watched with pleasure the town youngsters making acquaintance for the very first time with swings, slides, roundabouts, climbing frames and sandpits; they required no introduction they simply moved in and took possession.

Then came the mothers, nervously at first, but taking courage when they saw that the building was surrounded by a high brick wall that would preserve their purdah. Walking into the main reception area, housing the antenatal clinic and labour room, these shrinking violets were welcomed by the lady Health Visitor, who entertained them to tea and showed them round. Last, but by no means least, came the indigenous dais, some of them grandmothers. As the whole midwifery practice was in their charge, they were received as fellow professionals, and were invited to make use of the Centre without any conditions. Slowly they became accustomed to the facilities, and agreed to undergo training, and the Kohat Centre registered nearly one hundred per cent success.

However this happy result was in the future. At present Marie was still at loggerheads with the Public Health Department. After another stormy meeting of the Red Cross Council in Peshawar, Lady Griffith invited her to a cup of coffee in her own private room at Government House. "How are your jolly little dais getting on?" asked the Governor, putting his head round the door.

"This poor girl has had a terrible time at our Meeting. They were all on top of her like a ton of bricks," his wife replied, with a rueful smile.

Griffy (the familiar but affectionate name by which Sir Ralph was known among Frontier officers) beckoned to Marie. "Come into my study," he said. She followed him, and when the door was closed, he opened a safe, and taking out a two thousand rupee note, pressed it into her hand, saying, "You build your new welfare centre and good luck to you!"

With this superb encouragement, it was a remarkably short time before local subscriptions raised the ten thousand rupees needed for the new building, most of the money coming from countless poor folk, who could only afford four or eight annas each. I often think that 'Griffy' realised that if he could capture the support of the womenfolk, the submerged half of the Muslim population, rule on the Frontier would be immensely facilitated.

There was now money to build, but no land to build on. An ideal site was a vacant plot just outside the city wall, belonging to the Jail Department; but the difficulty was that Prisons and Hospitals came under the same Inspector General. Our plans were therefore held *up,* until the tragic news was received that he had been thrown from his horse out hunting in Peshawar and had died from his injuries.

His successor backed Marie from the start, transferred the plot in Kohat from the Jail Department to the Red Cross, and the much talked about building came into being. It is called to this day 'The Mallam Welfare Centre'.

Deputations from all Municipal committees in the Province came to inspect it and ask questions, and in a very short time similar Centres grew up in every town. Marie planned a large Provincial Centre in Peshawar, to include facilities for the training of health visitors, but never lived to see it completed. After her death, I made it my duty, in co-operation with the PHD, to put into effect all her plans for the establishment of Maternity and Child Welfare on a sound and permanent basis.

Apart from public recognition of her services,[2] Marie's breakthrough had other far-reaching consequences. Hitherto the women and children of India had constituted a problem so vast and complicated that the PHD could almost and almost justifiably wash their hands of it, like Pontius Pilate on another occasion. Even after the Kohat Centre had been officially opened by Lady Cunningham, such remarks as, "That clinic of yours, you'll see – as soon as you leave, it will collapse," were endlessly quoted. What people failed to realise was that Marie had achieved not just another nibble at the fringe of the problem, but to all intents and purposes a final solution, something before regarded as impossible.

The Kohat Centre not only survived, it proliferated, gave birth to numerous other progeny wherever the density of population required them. Moreover, the provision of a Provincial Health School for the training of Lady Health Visitors at Peshawar ensured a continuous supply of qualified staff to keep the local Centres working at a high standard of efficiency.

---

[2] After only four years in India, she was awarded the Kaisar-i-Hind silver medal for public service a splendid achievement.

Mallam Welfare Centre, Kohat NWF Province 1937

A local (indigenous) midwife with the largest practice in Kohat, before the Welfare Centre was built

The first health visitor (trained) in Kohat – a Christian. She worked in a hired building (1936)

Front View of Cavagnari House, Kohat 1934

Marie standing by ruin
of Greco Monastery

Old Buddhist Buildings in Swat Valley with
Yusafzai tribal escort, 1940

Above all, Frontier public opinion was now solidly behind the movement, and the Red Cross could rely on private subscriptions to finance most of its projects.

This success in solving one of the country's most intractable problems prompted the question: Why not others? Were we being prevented by defeatism in high places from achieving universal literacy, a Frontier University, new housing, electricity in every home, a final solution of the tribal problem? Such questions as these, inspired by Marie's prowess were my vision of 'Empire with a human face'. They would have sounded fantastic at the time, but some of them were destined to find a place in the First Five Year Development Plan for the Frontier area ten years later.

Before leaving the subject of women and children, some complications presented by the social status of Indian women must be mentioned. On the Frontier all Muslim and many Hindu ladies observed purdah in varying degrees for the sake of protection. In rural areas, tribal women might work in the fields, fetch water or move about the village with a head scarf or covering which could be drawn over the face temporarily; but in the towns all women invariably wore the burqa, which swathed them in a grey sheet from head to foot. Indian women were never visible socially. That alone created a man's world. Marie, like many other English ladies, frequently crashed the barrier by attending purdah parties. I can remember her coming home from one saying: "The wife of Fulana Khan," (a young extra Assistant commissioner) "is stunningly pretty. What a pity you can't see her." How unfair it was, I felt, that Fulana Khan could visit our house without his wife of course and meet Marie and other English ladies, while we men were prohibited from the pleasure of meeting his wife, a rose forever born to blush unseen. The young EAC would probably excuse himself by saying that when they were in Lahore his wife never observed purdah, and often drove the car about town, but on the Frontier that was quite a different matter.

Marie held several purdah parties in Cavagnari House. The windows would be curtained, sheets would be hung in the verandahs and passageways; all the servants would be banished, and I would leave for the office. The guests arrived in heavily draped cars or tongas, each strictly veiled; not a slender hand or dainty ankle would be exposed to the light of day. Once inside the house the whole atmosphere changed. Marie reported that they let their hair down and enjoyed themselves. Among migratory Ghilzai or Powindah tribes purdah is seldom, if ever, practised, probably because they are frequently on the move and women can be adequately protected by their men-folk. A senior Political Officer, who must be nameless, delighted to tell the story of how he once travelled in his car up the Kurram valley towards Parachinar, closely followed by a lorry carrying a strong armed escort of local Militia. At a precipitous point on the road, overlooking the river, the car met a caravan of Ghilzais coming out of the valley towards their grazing grounds in the plain. It was a large *kafila*, consisting of big, shaggy Bactrian camels laden with merchandise, numerous flocks and herds of sheep, goats and ponies, together with whole families of tribesmen. Mothers were seated with babies, live chickens and cooking pots slung on the backs of the camels, while the men mostly travelled on foot with rifles athwart their broad shoulders.

The officer was driving the car himself, with a chauffeur beside him on the front seat. Inevitably the vehicle had to slow down, and eventually to stop, in order to let the caravan go by. The Englishman was in a hurry. He soon got impatient and bored by the long wait. Suddenly, his eye spotted a young Powindah girl walking towards him, her black skirt and baggy trousers billowing gracefully as she moved. She was quite breathtakingly beautiful, with silver ornaments glistening on her forehead, on her nose and at her throat, and wafer-thin silver circlets, like hoops, swinging from her ears. An imp of mischief entered into him; he waited until the maiden came alongside the car, then catching her eye, he leaned back from the driver's seat and opened the rear door just an inch. Instantly he found himself looking down the barrel of a rifle behind which was a pair of fierce black eyes. Gifted with a superb command of Pushtoo he was equal to the situation. "What do you expect me to do in the presence of such dazzling beauty?" he asked, "Sit and twiddle my thumbs? Can I buy the girl? How much do you want for her?"

The incensed tribesman looked at the other, who was relaxed and enjoying the joke, and at the escort, who were becoming restless. "You can't have her," he said. "She is mine she is engaged to me and I am going to marry her."

"You are a lucky man," said the Englishman, sincerely. Then, undisturbed by the incident, the caravan moved on. No Britisher in his senses would risk a blood feud by having any relations at all with Pathan women.

The families of our Pathan orderly, the faithful bearer, Nasir Khan, the *khidmatgar*, the sweeper and not forgetting the malis all lived in our large compound. Their progeny were numerous, and they were all good Muslims. My bearer was extremely religious, and if when summoned, he happened to be saying his prayers, another servant would answer: *"Nasir Khan namaz parta hai,"* and nothing could be done until he had finished. Incidentally the first tee on the golf course so much resembled a green and velvety praying mat, that passing pilgrims would often stop there, kneel down turning obediently towards Mecca, and no one could drive off until their devotions were completed.

"Burra Din Ka Salaam," was the greeting on a typical Christmas Day, regarded as the equivalent of the Id Festival, terminating the Muslim fasting month of Ramadhan. *"Mubarik, Mubarik,"* cried the visitors, adding their congratulations on the happy morning. A personal visit to the DC at Cavagnari House was regarded as obligatory by all officials, from the senior EAC to the most junior clerk stationed at District HQ. When we saw them walking up the long drive of Cavagnari House in a bunch, Marie and I would go into the garden the weather being usually fine, though cold and shake hands with everyone. The occasion was extremely informal, very friendly but not too prolonged. I don't think we ever served refreshments which sounds a bit mean, but, as with so many occurrences in India, we were governed by tradition, which it was dangerous to alter in any way.

After the officials would come local civic dignitaries and *bannias*, the latter invariably carrying rush baskets of fruit or vegetables. One used to hear of such goings on as bottles of whisky concealed among the cabbages, but custom strictly forbade such expensive presents. Last of all, came the house servants carrying a flower, perhaps a carnation, tastefully wrapped with ferns in silver paper. To them we gave, and later our children had much pleasure in distributing, oranges, bananas and apples from the homely panniers that had been donated to us. *"Mubarik! Mubarik! Salaam Sahib! Salaam Memsahib!"* cried the excited youngsters, dancing round us. It was a gay and festive season, and of course, the senior servants received some *baksheesh*.

A last word about Marie's Centre. In 1965, during the war between India and Pakistan, I was watching television in the vicarage armchair at Eckington, when the cameras suddenly switched to Kohat on the North West Frontier, where Indian aeroplanes had been bombing the Pakistan Air Force Station. Up came a picture of a devastated building which I recognised at once. Later news from Kohat confirmed that the Centre had been utterly destroyed, fortunately without loss of life. The Pakistan Government subsequently rebuilt it with money allocated to war damage, and all maternity and child welfare work was placed under the World Health Organisation of the United Nations, and became secure.

In October 1972 with my present wife, I asked a question while visiting the Provincial Health School in Peshawar, which with its high walls looked a little like a prison. "What percentage of the total births in the Province can you claim to have been serviced by a modern trained midwife?"

"Not more than fifty per cent," was the reply of the Lady Principal, *Dr* (Mrs) Hamida.

Of course they had suffered very hard times both during and after Partition.

Medical supplies were desperately short and the increased tribal influence in the Province had militated against the emancipation of women. A more hopeful note was struck when the Principal took us round the lecture rooms filled with young students.

"Will the MAs please hold up their hands?" she asked. Two or three responded eagerly. "And now, if you will be so good, the BAs?" A whole forest of hands appeared, their enthusiasm was very touching; but they were obviously in need of stronger Government support.

On a visit to Kohat a few days later we received an exceptionally warm welcome. The Centre was neat and tidy and the Lady Health Visitor in charge was obviously doing her best; but here again strong official support appeared to be lacking. This support came a year of two afterwards, when all branches of Maternity and Child Welfare were transferred from the Red Cross (later Red Crescent) to the Social Services Department of the Provincial Government. This was followed in the autumn of 1976 by the first 'Women's Week' in Pakistan; and in Kohat many of the activities of the 'week' were held in Marie's Centre.

Writing in December 1976, Sugra describes the marked change for the better: "It was a great joy to see the place looking so well how I wish you could see it." This is most encouraging, but not until the ladies of Kohat are themselves actively associated with the running of the Centre shall I feel happy; nor I think would Marie. If women are to be given their rightful place in society, they must take over responsibility for their own organisations like maternity and Child Welfare, and not leave such matters indefinitely in the hands of men.

Marie died at Nathia Gali (the hill station of the Frontier Government) on 4th June 1944, two months and ten days after the birth of a boy, Marcus.[3] She was only forty years old. I received over seventy telegrams of sympathy, mostly from Indians, and I quote one of them from my successor as Deputy Commissioner, Kohat a distinguished Indian member of the Political Service, Sheikh Mahbub Ali Khan, as a tribute to her memory:

> "Most heartfelt sympathy from us, and sincere prayers for the soul departed. Kohat deeply mourns the death of a true benefactor, who did more for its people, particularly for their womenfolk, than any other person in living memory."

---

[3] In October 1972, Marcus, now a fully qualified architect and town-planner, joined us in Peshawar on his way home from Australia. I was able to show him his mother's grave in the little Christian Cemetery at Kalabagh, 8,000 feet up among the pine trees in the foothills of the Himalayas.

CHAPTER XIII

Political Agent Malakand Part I
1938–41

He is the Reaper, and binds the sheaf,
Shall not the season its order keep?
Can it be changed by man's belief?
Millions of harvests still to reap;
Will God reward, if I die for a creed,
Or will he but pity, and sow more seed?

When medical opinion in Oxford gave Marie only a one per cent chance of having a child of her own, our thoughts turned at once to adoption; and under the auspices of Princess Alice (as mentioned above) we acquired two beautiful children, a boy David, and a girl Judith,[1] and prepared for the return to India. Shortly before leaving, I received a letter from Sir George Cunningham (Governor of the North West Frontier), saying that he intended to appoint me as Political Agent, North Waziristan. At this time Waziristan was in turmoil; the tribes, Wazirs and Mahsuds, were in open revolt and the equivalent of martial law had been proclaimed. The HQ of the PA was at Miramshah, a fortified post inside tribal territory. No wives or children were allowed, Marie would have to live at Bannu (British India) and we would be separated for long periods.

After careful thought, I wrote to ask if we might have a posting where we could be together, in view of Marie's illness and our domestic situation. Sir George was good enough to agree, and I was sent as District Judge to Peshawar.

This appointment lasted only a few months, at the end of which came a temporary posting as Finance Secretary. The, then, Finance Minister was Mr Bhanju Ram Ghandi, a member of the Frontier Congress Ministry which had taken office on 7th September 1937. 'Banjo' was a pleasant, jovial man, easy to get on with. I had occasional dealings with the Chief Minister, Dr Khan Sahib, whom I was soon to regard as an old friend.

Though not well-versed in finance, I was coached for the job by a real expert, Mr E.E.C. (Tom) Price from the Government of India Finance Department who

---

[1] Judith was not available before we left England and came out a week or two later, escorted by a trained nurse returning on duty.

had been loaned to scrutinise and regulate the large Central Government expenditure in tribal areas. Tom and his wife, Frankie, were a charming couple and we be came great friends; his astounding knowledge and ability in coping with complicated problems of finance filled me with admiration. The Prices were about to take long leave in England, and I was required to stand in.

On their return I became Political Agent Dir, Swat and Chitral, Malakand. Here was a charge to warm the heart of any Frontier Political. The Agency consisted of a tangled maze of mountains, rising gradually to well remote and picturesque valleys lived a fascinating variety of peoples under contrasting systems of government, some unknown to civilisation; and away to the north and west on the 'bam-i-dunya', the very roof of the world, was the meeting place of four nations, India (now Pakistan), Afghanistan, China and the USSR. Here the mountain masses of the Hindu Kush and the Himalayas converge, and throw up the great peaks of Nanga Parbat and Rakaposhi, both above 25,000 feet, while away to the west a giant of the Hindu Kush, Tirich Mir, rises to 25,230 feet, and watches over the Chitral Valley, like a great white sentinel in the sky, draped in a rigid cloak of ice and snow.

Looking at this tumult of mountains from somewhere in the south of the Agency, Winston Churchill in his book *Malakand Field Force, 1897* describes what he saw in the following words:

> "By one who stands on some lofty pass or commanding point in Dir, Swat or Bajaur, range after range is seen as the long surges of an Atlantic swell, and in the distance some glittering snow peak suggests a white-crested roller, higher than the rest."

Three swift-flowing streams spring from these northern glaciers, and cut their way southwards in deep parallel gorges towards the Kabul river. Like arteries, they carry the life-blood of the Agency. The western-most stream is known in Chitral State as 'the Chitral', but when it enters Afghanistan, it is renamed the Kunar, before meeting the Kabul at Jalalabad. The centre stream, the Panjkora, flows through the State of Dir, until it joins the Swat below Malakand. The third, and most important, is the Swat, flowing through Swat State, and joining the Kabul in the Peshawar plain. The gorges through which these streams flow, are deep and precipitous in the higher levels, but broaden out lower down to carry a road, and a generous area of terraced fields. This is particularly true of the Swat Valley, which for some distance above Malakand is as much as a mile wide, and supports a considerable population. The lower hills are covered in scrub, but higher up are valuable pine and deodar forests.

The three valleys form the main lines of communication. The road to Chitral starts from Swat, climbs over the watershed to the West, passes up the Panjkora through Dir, and mounts to the top of the Lowarai Pass (10,500 feet), before dropping down into the Chitral Valley. Most of the inhabitants of this mountainous country were the subjects of the three rulers: (in order of precedence) His Highness the Mehtor of Chitral, the Nawab of Dir and the Wali (or Akhund) of Swat. But there were important tribal areas outside the boundaries of these States, in particular the remote and inaccessible tribes of Bajour to the South West, and the Yusufzai, a tribe of pure Pathan origin, occupying the administered area of the lower Swat Valley, which was my main responsibility as Political Agent, and became the object of an important piece of research, described in the next Chapter.

I arrived in the Agency in December 1939, as Europe stood on the brink of the Second World War; and there started for me one of the most satisfying and fruitful periods of my service. The PA's residence and HQ were perched at the head of the Malakand Pass (3,500 feet) and about 300 feet above the motor road which, climbing steeply from the border at the base of the hills, drops down, with a gentle gradient, from the top of the defile into the Swat Valley. At Malakand there was a large fort occupied by the military, but the Political bungalow was situated outside on a steep, craggy hill, overlooking the ravine and ascending ranges of barren mountains beyond. Leaving the car near the entrance to the fort, it was customary to walk to the bungalow. Marie usually rode up the narrow hill path on a pony.

As the tribal situation in the Agency had been quiet for some time, I was allowed to take my wife, the two children and our trusted nanny, Florence Thorogood, and I shall always feel indebted to Sir George Cunningham for this family posting.

Hardly an hour after our arrival, a telegram was received from the Mehtar, saying, "Please come and see me urgently before the snows come down on the Lowarai."

His Highness Mohammad Nasir ul Mulk, Mehtar of Chitral, though senior in order of precedence, was the youngest of the three potentates with whom I had to deal. He had recently succeeded to the Guddi (throne) on the death of his father, who in 1935 had sent him to India to learn district administration. He had been deputed to me as Honorary Assistant Commissioner Kohat for nine months, and was twice a visitor at Cavagnari House. He was a very intelligent scion of the nobility, with a degree at Lahore University and a thorough knowledge of English. We got to know him well and became very fond of him.

Chitral State is a kind of Shangrila, or dream Valley at about 5,000 feet in the extreme north west corner of India and deep in the heart of the mountains. The Lowarai Pass is the only means of approach and was usually closed by snow a week before Christmas. It was already 9th December. There was no time to lose.

Packing some warm clothes, my Indian driver, my bearer Nasir Khan and I crossed the Swat river at Chakdarra and took the long hill road up the Panjkora Valley to Dir. There I called on the Nawab and found him a pleasant, rather reserved, conservative gentleman, who obviously knew how to handle his subjects in a benevolent, traditional style. From the first he expressed fears of encroachment by the Wali of Swat.

After a comfortable night in the Nawab's rest house, we started at first light by pony to climb up to the top of the pass. It was so cold that all the little rivulets on either side of the track were solid ice. A few trees grew on the hillsides, dwindling to rock and scrub as the ascent grew steeper. Dismounting, and walking, which proved much warmer, we followed the steady gradient of the track, and reached the top of the bare and windswept pass by noon.

Here two of the Mehtar's brothers, who had been sheltering in a hut with their attendants, came out to greet us. We shook hands, and, without lingering in the bitter wind, plunged down the far side. The ground fell away steeply and the path zig-zagged towards dark tree tops a thousand feet below.

Short-cutting many of the bends by slithering down the *khud-side*, a rest house at 7,000 feet was reached in time for a late lunch. Then started one of the most hair-raising motor journeys of my life. His Highness owned two or three cars the only vehicles allowed in the State. The chassis had been manhandled over the pass and the bodies built in Chitral. The track (subject of A.E.W. Mason's book *The Broken Road*), had only in the last few years been converted from a mule bridlepath and widened just sufficiently to take a single car. For long stretches it was cut out of a sheer precipice, 400 feet above the foaming torrent of the Chitral river.

The driver was told to hurry *Jaldi, jaldi karo!*, as we had to reach our destination before dark. As we rounded corners, at what seemed breakneck speed, the outer wheels of the vehicle were only inches from the crumbling edge of the precipice, and at times appeared to be momentarily in mid-air. There was no parapet.

The Mehtar's two brothers who sat with me in the back seat, helped to divert my attention from the road by keeping up a light conversation. When we had travelled some distance, the one on my left, the side of the big drop, fell silent. "Do you mind if we stop a few moments?" asked the gentleman on my right.

Only too glad to be released from the terror of the hairpin bends, and perhaps to stretch one's legs, I agreed instantly.

Pointing to where the road, after a slight rise, appeared thin air, but actually took a turn round the sheer face of a cliff, companion said: "That is where, a month ago, my brother went over!"

The driver failed to get the car past the corner. It went straight on, all three of us walked up the road, and looked over the edge. I marvelled to think that anyone could survive such a fall. It transpired that the vehicle had hit a stunted tree, sticking out from the rock face half way down.

"My brother was thrown out and clung to the tree," the narrator went on. "The car and driver fell in the river and no one ever found them. On the opposite bank were some terraced fields being cultivated by our tenants. They heard his calls for help the echoes in the mountains are good – and managed to cross the river, to let down a rope from the road above and to draw him to safety."

"You had a remarkable escape," I congratulated the sufferer. "You're very brave to come this way again."

We continued our journey in high spirits, both men telling one story after another about the history of the road. One tale was about a very portly General, commanding the Peshawar District, whom I knew well. He was paying his first visit to Chitral. The brothers sat him in the back seat of an open tourer, as I was sitting now. When the dangerous bends were reached, the General became so excited, that he seized and shook the two sides of the car with his hands, shouting, "This is sheer madness!"

I visited Chitral twice a year from the Malakand and the route became less and less terrifying each time. As my subsequent trips were in the summer, there was no need to hurry.

His Highness received me as an old friend, and made me very comfortable in his guesthouse, where the standards were simple and homely. He was obviously anxious to establish contact with me before I succumbed to the blandishments of the Wali who provided a first-class hotel for his guests. Chitral had a chequered history of dynastic strife and murder, fanned into war by Pathan interference from outside the State in 1895. No ruler could afford to ignore the possibility of another invasion by an ambitious enemy.

I can remember stepping out early on the following morning into a world of snow and ice; very invigorating. Bare hillsides rose to great heights on either side of the narrow valley, and overlooking it to the northwest, was the white, majestic bulk of Tirich Mir, so close it seemed to lean towards me out of a clear blue sky.

A visit was paid to the Assistant PA and to the Officers' Mess of the Chitral

Scouts. I dined in mess that evening and was waited on by some of the famous Everest Sherpas, men of magnificent physique, temporarily located there for mountaineering purposes. Everyone of the British officers present was a climber in his own right. They had already carried out an expedition on skis at 9,000 feet, and were planning a much longer one when the snow came down.

There was a challenge in those mountains. It could be felt in the air. Men stationed there had either to accept it and start climbing, or ask to be transferred. It was not possible to stay quiescent in such a place without being overtaken by a deep depression perhaps induced by the claustrophobic effect of a narrow valley enclosed by mighty peaks, and subject to earthquakes.

Not anxious to be isolated for the whole winter, I hurried back over the Lowarai. During my summer visits to that dream valley and its peaceful, happy people, I was privileged to join in their national game of polo or *chaughanbazi*, as the Persians called it. As level ground was restricted, the game was often played in village streets, the ponies had to be small and handy and the rules were different from the modern game. The finest ponies of all, the Badakshani breed, were like miniature racehorses. The Chitralis were experts; they had eyes like hawks and seldom missed a shot. Their Captain would start by galloping full split up the ground, with the reins in his left hand and the ball and his stick in the right. About half way up the field he flings the ball high in the air with a fearsome yell and smites it before it touches the ground. The rest of the team charge madly behind.

Miangul Gul-Shahzada Abdul Wadud, Wali (or Akhund) of Swat, was the most junior, but by far the most powerful and energetic of the three rulers in the Agency. In the year 1926, by his religious influence, astuteness and resource, this remarkable man created Swat State out of a turbulent assortment of tribes, inhabiting the mountainous regions between the Swat and Indus rivers, and ruled them with a rod of iron. So far as the British administration was concerned, he was the 'blue-eyed boy' of the Frontier. Almost by a miracle he had appeared as a stabilising element in an area of lawlessness and hostility, which had provoked large scale military operations under Major General Sir Binden Blood in 1897. Although autocratic, the Wali was a progressive ruler. He built forts and made roads. Hospitals and schools were erected and the considerable economic resources of the State, such as timber and agricultural products, were developed. The sporting instincts of the average Englishman were well catered for, and his duck shoot was the finest in Northern India. The *chikor* (or grouse) shooting was unrivalled. The best shots in the country jockeyed for invitations, similar in prestige to a day on the Scottish moors.

Buddhist Stupa in Swat Valley, 1940

HIS HIGHNESS MOHAMMED NASIR-UL-MULK, MEHTAR OF CHITRAL
On the roof of his palace – Tirich Mir in the background
1939

One of the Wali of Swat's Forts in the Swat Valley, 1940

"What a waste to send Mallam to Malakand," was a remark heard in sporting circles, when my posting became known. I did not altogether care for large shoots involving the slaughter of vast numbers of birds often over one thousand in one day. Sir George Cunningham was an excellent shot, and seldom brought home a bag of less than three hundred I always gave up after shooting twenty-seven this was my outside limit my satiation point. By kind permission of the Wali, I was allowed, as PA, to invite a fixed number of guns beside my own. It was not surprising that the Wali's popularity in British circles became so great that many experienced Politicals envisaged him becoming King of a much larger State, and ruling the unruly Pathan along the whole length of the Frontier, thus solving all its knotty problems. The psychology of the Pathan, however, strongly resisted such dictatorial ambitions. The Wali's success was partly due to the fact that most of his subjects came from a more amenable race, whose origin and affinities belonged to Central Asia.

The Political Agent was not required to concern himself with the internal affairs of Swat State, nor with those of Dir or Chitral, unless the rulers were to ask for advice or assistance. But the Wali was not above thoughts of expansion perhaps *liebensraum* was in the air and when he began to cast envious eyes on the Garvi tract, a mountainous area round the sources of the Swat river, containing valuable virgin *deodar* forests just beyond the limits of his State, I felt bound to intervene, particularly as the independence of this tract was officially guaranteed by the Government of India.

The Garvi tribes, often referred to under the names of their two main villages, Kalam and Utrot, were of great anthropological interest. Their language was never specifically classified by the expert Sir George Grierson, but was linked by him with Kashmiri and Kohistani under the general term Dardic.

As Census Superintendent in 1930, I had been required to go to the Swat Valley to visit these distant tribes, taking a dictaphone to record their speech. Frontier disturbances, unfortunately, prevented my doing so. Equally, with their language, the tribes themselves were a mystery to anthropologists, mainly because of their remoteness. One theory held them to be an indigenous race of possibly Greek origin, who took refuge from successive invaders of India by retreating higher and higher up their valley until eventually the top was reached.

Reliable information warned me that the Wali was using agents to sow dissension among the Garvis, paying and arming his own fifth column and generally softening them up for invasion and annexation.

I reported my fears to the Governor, noting that the Wali seemed to be using the same techniques as Hitler in Europe. "Why don't you go and tell him so?" was the reply.

Accordingly, I went to Saidu, the capital, and asked for an interview. The Wali received me, as always, most politely. We sat down to talk. Putting my information before him, I pointed out that the Garvi tribes were covered by a treaty, and on the same principles for which we were fighting a World War, I was bound to protect them.

Silence; and then, "What I am doing to these tribes I was encouraged to do by your predecessor." he answered.

"I must ask you to withdraw rifles from these tribes and allow their leaders safe conduct through Swat State to visit me in the Malakand," I persisted.

"Of course I will do as you wish," said the Ruler, standing up and closing the interview.

The Wali was as good as his word. The Garvi elders flocked down through Swat State, and hundreds were entertained by us for a few days at Malakand. They were a happy crowd. Some of their spokesmen could talk Pushtu or Hindustani and it was easy to make friends with them. The question that was asked quite openly was would they be protected from invasion? I reminded them of their treaties and reaffirmed my intention to protect them so long as I remained there.

I must record that throughout these proceedings, and in all my dealings with him, the Wali behaved with absolute propriety and politeness; but regrettably, after this incident, his personal relations with me became formal, rather than friendly.

When we had been installed at Malakand for a few weeks, one day we heard footsteps on the verandah outside the house, accompanied by the sighs and gasps of someone exhausted by a climb. Being a bit nervous about the effect of the steep pull on anyone with a weak heart, we rushed for the whisky bottle. "Come in," we both called, welcomingly. The young couple who entered were complete strangers. It transpired that they were Swedes, who casually mentioned they had just been up to 20,000 feet on Tirich Mir!

We had many other visitors, lured by the mountains, the most famous of whom was Sir Aurel Stein, in his day the greatest living explorer and expert on Central Asia. He was a fascinating guest, and, in spite of advanced years, most entertaining. A Hungarian Jew by birth and a naturalized British subject, he was a little man, hardly reaching my shoulder, but a most prodigious writer. "If all my books were placed flat on the ground, one on top of the other, they'd be taller than I!" he used to say, his face crinkled up with good humour.

Heights drew him like a magnet, but there was always a purpose, mainly archaeological, in his travels. In my library today is an autographed copy of one of his main works, *On Alexander's Track to the Indus*, and a number of pamphlets on particular journeys, illustrated with beautiful photographs.

After his second visit in October 1941, he set out at the age of seventy-nine on a hazardous tour of Indus Kohistan, involving the crossing of passes nearly 15,000 feet high on the watershed between the Swat and Indus valleys. He describes this journey:

"The Bisao pass ... was likely soon to be closed by snow. It was crossed just in time, but proved trying. After a long march had brought us to the highest of the huts to which the Duber people, like all the others of the Kohistan, repair in the summer for grazing, it took us a day and a half of exacting climbing before the height of the pass was gained. The ascent on the first day lay over a succession of old glacier beds and moraines. The recession of glacier ice, apparently not very distant in geological time, had left here huge masses of rock debris in utter confusion, very trying to the feet, especially to mine, which had lost many toes from frostbite thirty-four years before on the high Kun-Lun range. It was long after darkness had set in that the narrow rocky ridge was gained, where room could be found for a night's halt."

His object was to trace the route followed by pilgrims from China to the Buddhist sanctuaries of Swat, where a remarkable civilisation, flourished from 100 BC 100 AD and flowered in the magnificent, world-famous Greco-Buddhist sculptures recovered from the ruins of monasteries scattered along the hillsides above and below Malakand. In these sculptures Greek culture, introduced by

Alexander the Great and by the subsequent Greco-Bactrian Empire, meets and fuses with Oriental culture from India. Long after this ancient civilisation had passed its zenith the Swat valley continued to be the goal of pilgrims from China and India. In the annals left by the Chinese pilgrims, and particularly by one Fuchsine in the year 400 AD, the route followed by them along the gorges of the Indus is described as 'The route of hanging chains', ie tree trunks suspended by chains over the precipice. The sides of the mountains reaching down to the river were "like a stone wall ten thousand feet in height". Sir Aurel reports that when the "recent" track was constructed "men had often to be suspended from pegs while they were at work boring holes to blast the rock or to fix in fissures the tree branches which were to support galleries".

In spite of many adventures, this brave archaeologist and historian returned triumphantly to Swat with his mission accomplished and an increased admiration for the powers of observation of the old Chinese travellers. "These fair border valleys," he wrote, "dotted with sacred Buddhist sites, thus acquired special sanctity for monastic communities so far away as the Yellow Sea, and attracted the visits of those pious Chinese pilgrims whose records now serve to guide us among the ruined sanctuaries of Swat, their Dyane, the Garden".

When he stayed with us in Peshawar for the last time in 1943 he was much frailer and once, when he went to sleep in a chair, we feared he might never wake.

Just before his death he was allowed by the Afghan Government to visit Kabul. For years he had longed to look at some of the archaeological sites there, but had been refused permission. He died in the capital on 26th October 1943, at the age of eighty-one and perhaps to make amends for their persistent repudiation the Afghan Government honoured him in his death by allowing his body to be buried near Barbur's tomb in the Christian part of the cemetery at Kabul.

Another name to be conjured with in connection with Greco-Buddhist sculptures was that of Major-General H.L. Haughton, CB, CBE, CIE. When he was commanding the military District at Kohat he had been a frequent visitor at Cavagnari House, and he stayed with us on three separate occasions in the Malakand. Tall and good-looking, with grey hair and a dignified manner, he had an old-world charm which made one feel that if he had not been a successful general, he would have made an even more accomplished diplomat. He used to say, "I regard the Malakand, and particularly the Swat valley, as my spiritual home." He was very well informed on the subject of the Greco-Buddhist civilisation.

A total of 144 guests signed our visitors' book during 1940–1941 at

Malakand, most of whom were British officials and their wives. It was no lavish entertainment but a simple wartime board and lodging which gave tired officials a rest and change in comparatively peaceful surroundings. I was either engaged in day to day office work or out on tour. Being literally 'in the wilds' a radio set was relied on for war news.

Three of our guests were of political importance, the first two being Dr and Mrs Khan Sahib (an English lady), from Utmanzai village in the Peshawar District, in January 1940. All Congress Ministries throughout India had resigned in protest against the committal of India to participation in the war without, in their view, prior consultation with the elected representatives of the people. Dr Khan Sahib, himself, had given up office early in December, and Sir George was administering the province under powers given by Section 93 of the Government of India Act 1935.

So the Doctor was a man of leisure for a while, and being a great exponent of chess, we played several games together. He almost always beat me, but I like to think I gave him a run for his money! The 'resting' Chief Minister of the FP (to be returned to office again in 1946) was, of course, a brother of 'the Frontier Ghandi', Abdul Ghaffar Khan, and as a leading member of the Congress Party was deeply involved in anti-British agitation. He had still managed to preserve intact many of his old friendships with English officials, however, although his aim was the complete independence of India.

The third important guest was Mr M.A.H. Jahanzeb, eldest son and heir of the Wali of Swat, who honoured us with two visits in 1940. Jahanzeb was a smart, athletic young man of faultless manners, and very Anglophile in his outlook. His father had already handed over to him part of the administration of the State, and he took his responsibilities seriously. He used to drop in to see us sometimes on his way to or from the Peshawar plain, but these informal visits unfortunately ceased after my 'brush' with his father over the Garvi tribes.

The Swat river was well stocked by nature with mahseer as well as other kinds of fish. In order to prevent disputes, the river below the Swat state border was parceled out for fishing between the Political Agent, the Army and the Levies. This had been done many years before, the Political Agent being allotted a stretch in the lower reaches, in the vicinity of Malakand. Included in this stretch was a pool called 'Rocky Point', reputed to be bottomless and to contain the biggest fish in the river. My largest catch was a twenty-six pound mahseer, but one of my successors caught one weighing eighty pounds!

One January, Major Robinson, head of the Frontier Intelligence Bureau and known to everyone as 'Robbie', with his wife and small son were staying with us for a few days. He was a keen fisherman and suggested we should try our luck at the pool. It was the off-season for mahseer and I was not particularly keen. We settled down to an afternoon's spinning, not expecting to catch much. The sky was overcast. It was very cold. We fished from a little shelving beach below a steep cliff overlooking the pool, on top of which stood an armed sentry belonging to the tribal levies. The pool looked dark and sinister, sheltered from the main stream by a little promontory of low rocks jutting out from the cliff. On the far bank the hills covered with thin scrub rose steeply, shutting out much of the meagre daylight. I had a short, very strong spinning rod and was using a wire trace, weight, and spoon, with a triple hook strong enough to hold almost anything. After many fruitless attempts I decided to test where the pool was really bottomless. Casting as far as I could, I let the weight carry the spoon deeper and deeper, paying out more line, and pulling at it now and again to see if it had reached the bed. Almost all the line had been paid out when the hook suddenly engaged, and I started to pull. Using all my strength, I was thinking of abandoning the tackle, when the object I had hooked began to rise. It was a heavy, inanimate object straining rod and line almost to breaking point. When at last it reached the surface the black clothes and body of a dead woman appeared, which, horrified, I drew towards the bank. Robbie was so revolted by the sight of the partly decomposed body that he was sick. I was too busy signalling to the sentry for assistance to feel squeamish. In due course we got the village *jirga* on to the case. The woman was identified and her husband prosecuted and found guilty of murdering her by tying a stone to her leg and pushing her into the pool. He paid the customary trial fine, and must have cursed me for spoiling his thousand to one chance of getting away with it!

CHAPTER XIV

Malakand Part II
The Yusufzae

It's not that I care for the money, or expect a dog to be clean,
If I were lord of the ryots, they'd starve ere I grew lean;
But I'd sooner be robbed by a tall man who showed me a yard of steel,
Than be fleeced by a sneaking Baboo, with a belted knave at his heel.

Most Frontier Politicals would not regard the Malakand Agency as a particularly difficult or dangerous assignment. And they would be right although it is never safe to rely too much on the patience or restraint of the Pathan. The Yusufzai of the lower Swat Valley what is known as the Swat Ranizai and the remote assortment of tribes in Bajour had been quiet for some time.

The Yusufzai, who speak a purer form of Pushtoo (or Pakhtoo) than their kinsmen in the south, enjoy a reputation as some of the most intelligent and advanced of all Pathans. Many of them were settled in the Mardan district, and had become amenable to the laws of British India. Outstanding among these were a few individuals who had acquired wealth and became *zamindars* or landowners in a big way, thus breaking with the tradition of their own people, which placed severe restrictions on individual holdings. These landed gentry called themselves Khans and Nawabs, and formed a local' aristocracy of their own. They were highly cultured and charming to meet. As Political Agent, I was concerned solely with that section of the community, which lived outside British India, still in their tribal state. In December 1939, there was peace; a luxury on the Frontier throughout the Agency. But that does not mean to say that these tribesmen did not know how to fight.

Consider this description of them by Winston Churchill, written only forty-three years previously:

"The inhabitants of these wild but wealthy valleys are of many tribes, but of similar character and condition. The abundant crops, which a warm sun and copious rains raise from a fertile soil, support a numerous population a state of warlike leisure. Except at the times of sowing and of harvest, a continuous state of feud and strife prevails throughout the land. Tribe wars with tribe. The people of one valley fight with those of the next. To the quarrels of communities are added the combats of individuals. Khan assails khan, each supported by his retainers. Every tribesmen has a blood feud with his neighbour. Every man's hand is against the other and all against the stranger ... Every influence, every motive, that provokes the spirit of murder among men impels these mountaineers to deeds of treachery and violence.[1]

Thus spoke Sir Winston, who, one has to remember, was at that time a war correspondent. The above is a portrayal of the enemy in wartime, written to impress home readers to set the stage for a romance of blood and bravery on the side of the British and only turbulence and fanaticism on the side of the Pathan!

For the time being all was quiet. So quiet that Marie and our nurse and the two children were able to tour with me several times in the Swat valley, camping out at night and using ponies to take us to distant villages and to the ruins of Buddhist monasteries dotted along the hillsides.

To camp at night with women and children in a tribal area was unprecedented. I was firmly against the idea, until my Indian Assistant came up with the suggestion that we should borrow a couple of tribal flags, as a guarantee of our safety, in addition to a guard of tribal levies. The flags, triangular in shape and brightly coloured, had been used in the fighting forty years previously, and, readily offered, were planted alongside the Union Jack at the entrance to our camp. This gave us a feeling of security. It was also a token that, here at least, between British and Pathan there was now peace. We received a remarkably warm welcome wherever we went.

As the Bajouris needed little attention, I could concentrate my energies on the administered area of the lower Swat, and it was here, among the Yusufzai, that I found an ideal opportunity for a careful study of the indigenous judicial system, that mysterious inner working of the tribe, that for many years I had wanted to investigate. It did not take long to discover that in the day to day handling of civil and criminal cases, no trace could be found of the original system. The cases were dealt with under the provisions of the Frontier Crimes Regulation, just as if the parties were resident in British India, the final order in every case being passed by the Political Agent, Sir Olaf Caroe, linking Kurram with the Malakand, reflects the official view of this situation: "a loose form of administration, much on the Sandeman model, which has continued to the satisfaction of all parties to this day".[2]

The 'Sandeman system'[3] was applicable to Baluchistan tribes, accepting

---

[1] Malakand *Field Force 1897*, p.4.

[2] Caroe, *The Pathans*, pp.380, 386.

[3] *Ibid.*, p.376.

the authority of feudal chiefs. It has never 'worked' with democratic Pathan tribes, certainly not in Waziristan. So far as I know it has never been introduced either in the Kurram or in the Malakand, where I could find no trace of it. Let the Political Agent Kurram speak for himself: in 1927 he wrote a note commenting on the administration of justice in the valley: "When we took over the Valley in 1894, we did so at the invitation of the Turis and agreed to administer their country as far as possible in accordance with their *Riwaj*, that is their standard of right and wrong. Now the difficulty is that the Valley Riwaj has never even been properly classified or recorded. There are a few rough notes left by Mr Waterfield but they do not help much. My experience is that the Turis themselves do not know what their Riwaj is. If one cross-examines the people, the answer … is generally more in the nature of a personal expression of opinion than any representation of custom and usage … The circumstances above explained results in similar crimes being in some cases ignored or punished with a nominal sentence or in others punished with transportation for life. It has always seemed to me curious why the people of the Valley have not objected to what must strike them as the waywardness of justice." On 12th May 1944, the then Political Agent forwarded a copy of this note to the Frontier Governor with the remark that "its contents are generally true today".

The situation I inherited from my predecessors in the Malakand was almost identical with that in the Kurram. The Sandeman system has been described as one of 'indirect rule',[4] but if the indigenous rule itself is unknown, indirect rule is impossible, and Sandeman flies out of the window! We are left with a 'loose administration', amounting to sheer improvisation and all its attendant evils; a waywardness of justice, corruption and bribery extending from subordinate officials to individual tribesmen; a political Agent, with a minimum of legal training passing thumping sentences of rigorous imprisonment with hard labour, sometimes even transportation for life,[5] without hearing any evidence and solely

---

[4] Caroe, p.376.

[5] The following figures are significant:

1 Sentences of rigorous imprisonment aggregating more than 100 years were passed by Sir George Cunningham in the course of two days in court as Assistant Commissioner Hangu, in 1920 (p.40, Norval Mitchell's *Sir George Cunningham*).

2 I personally imposed sentences aggregating 110 years' rigorous imprisonment in the course of one month as Assistant Commissioner, Tank, in 1927. These huge sentences were only made possible by the exclusion of regular court procedure by the provisions of the FCR.

on the recommendation of four or five elders 'chosen by his Indian assistant'. All this on a sensitive frontier! To describe such proceedings as 'satisfactory to all parties' was to mask by smooth official language a disgracefully low standard of administration.

My legal training rebelled against a continuation of this state of affairs, and I was determined to change it. This decision linked up well with a desire to investigate the inner working of the tribe, and I got down to business. I had to tread carefully. There were obviously some vested interests in the present system. I represented the Government to the tribe, and could not step out of my shoes and pretend to carry out an impartial, scientific enquiry. Again, I ran the risk of my motives being misunderstood by the local Mullahs and Qazis (Muslim judges). There were rumours that a previous PA had made an attempt to codify the riwaj and had to abandon it, because of powerful opposition from these religious dignitaries. I proceeded warily therefore, confining the investigation within the framework of my ordinary judicial powers under the Frontier Crimes Regulation. It was soon clear (as in the Kurram) that verbal enquiries would be useless, so I concentrated my attention on the tribal record room. Here were files of many hundreds of cases going back fifty years at least, all slowly rotting away. On the principle that the older files, decided before the recent corruption set in, would be more likely to reveal the correct tribal usage, I made a careful selection of a few outstanding cases under the main heads of crime, noting that each case contained an unanimous finding by a strong Council of Elders, giving a clear indication of the riwaj applicable.

I then waited for a similar new case to come before me for orders. It was not long in arriving. I called the members of the jirga to discuss their finding, which gave no indication of any tribal riwaj, but simply stated that the accused was guilty or not and gave answers to the issues framed by the Indian Assistant. "Is your finding in accordance with tribal riwaj?" I asked.

"Oh yes, Sahib," answered some. The others remained silent.

I took up the old file, crumbling away with age, and read out the names of the elders who had signed the finding, with their fathers' names.

"Do you know these men?"

Silence. Then one man said: "Is that A—, son of B—, of P— village?"

"It is."

"Oh! He was my grandfather. He died two years ago."

The jirga then identified another and another of the old signatories, until ten or twelve were properly traced as well known (dead or alive), to the jirga before me. As all the elders were illiterate, they had signed by affixing their thumb impressions, against each of which the *muharrir* (clerk) wrote the name, the father's name and sometimes the village, for purposes of identification.

"Were these all good men and true? Could they be relied on to state the tribal riwaj honestly?"

In chorus, unanimously, "Yes," came the answer.

I then asked the muharrir to read out the facts of the old case, and the finding of the council.

"Is this finding in accordance with riwaj?"

"Yes," replied some of the elders, but others were beginning to look uncomfortable.

"The two cases before us are very similar," I pointed out. "As the offences committed are of the same nature in both, should not the riwaj applicable also have been the same? Why have you made a different finding in this new case?"

There was an astonished silence, the elders realising that they had been caught out. I hastened to spare them embarrassment by returning the file of the new case, to them for reconsideration. Within an hour I got it back with a revised finding, identical with the old one. I had both cases recorded in a new register of tribal case law, much on the lines of the Common Law of England, to which reference could be made in a few minutes. This process was continued for all the main categories of crime and civil dispute until the true tribal riwaj for civil and criminal cases was revealed and put into practice, simultaneously.

The result was startling. The spirit of the tribe revived, with a renewed confidence in their own peculiar law and procedure, which now became the rule for deciding almost every case. A few were still referred, at the request of the parties, to arbitration, and some went direct to the *qazis* for trial by shariat. All the local Islamic dignitaries assured me of their satisfaction at the results achieved. My impression was that the tribal law closely resembled *shariat*, with important differences, particularly in regard to punishments, such as cutting off a man's hand for theft, which was rejected. These results, with a good deal of administrative detail, were incorporated in a note entitled *Tribal Reconstruction* which I forwarded officially to the Governor, suggesting that a single representative council of elders for the whole of the administered area should be formed, to deal mainly with local matters, such as education, hospitals, and agriculture, much on the same lines as a district or rural board in British India. This proposal was pigeonholed, but a minor one, which accompanied it the construction of a *jirgahall* (or committee room) where Council Meetings could be held in more dignified surroundings than sitting on the ground under a tree must have been sanctioned. I possess a photograph of Marie laying the foundation stone of the new hall, the site of which was a level piece of ground close to the road at the top of the Malakand Pass.

One aspect of my research calls for special mention. In considering the whole subject of tribal self-government, one question above all others demanded a satisfactory answer: "How did the tribe decide a question of fact, such as the guilt or innocence of an accused person?" I can confidently say that in official circles no one knew the true answer. It was well known that disputes, both civil and criminal, would normally be referred to the tribal jirga consisting of anything up to fifty or more persons. How did such a large body of men, often faction ridden, come to a unanimous (or even a majority) decision? "They just fought it out," some officials would say, and others: "It was simply a matter of which party in the case could bully or out-bribe the other, and so win a majority of votes." The general impression was that in a lawless society, power, brute force, or bribery always won the day.

The truth revealed by my inquiry was very different. A fixed procedure was prescribed for each class of case, and it was *impersonal*, dispensing altogether with judge and jury. The function of the jirga was to lay down the procedure and to make sure that it was followed correctly. There was seldom any dispute about this, as the procedure was simple and well known to everybody. It would usually involve the taking of an oath. For instance, in a murder case, the complainant (son or nearest relative of the deceased) would be required to produce two witnesses from the village limits, within which the murder occurred, to take oath on the Holy Koran before a mullah in the mosque, in the presence of the accused and anyone else involved, that the accused committed the murder. If the oaths were taken, the accused was guilty, and the jirga would then prescribe the punishment, say a fine or banishment from the tribe. It is important to note that the sanctity of the oath as a solemn religious act, was relied on absolutely. In a tribal community, where everyone knew everyone else's business it was impossible for anyone to make a habit of giving false evidence (so common in British India) with the result that if the tribe was left to itself, without interference or pressure from outside, it could maintain a high moral standard of behaviour. It was this that enabled these Pathan democracies to survive for centuries in a dangerous environment.

I would not claim to have made an exhaustive study of the Yusufzai judicial system, or that my discoveries were anything more than a rough guide to the procedure in other Pathan tribes. I was too heavily occupied with routine work. What was needed was a scientific study of each tribe separately although all had a great deal in common, particularly their peculiar democratic structure, and their religion.

The suggestion in my 'note' to build up again the government of the tribes by the tribes for the tribes, and to reinstate the ancient system of law, adapted to modern conditions, was put unofficially to a number of experienced politicals on the Frontier, and their replies covered the whole range of views from wholehearted agreement to thorough-going dissent. There were more perhaps who wanted to let the tribe die, because it was worthless, than those who were prepared positively to build it up. There were some who thought it would have to go anyhow, because it was out of date. The few opportunities I had for discussing the matter with Sir George Cunningham were unproductive. The lack of a clear lead from higher authority, and the absence of any consensus of opinion about the future of the tribes, augered ill for a British solution of the problem, and for lasting peace.

Nevertheless, there was one reply that more than compensated for any disappointment from the others. The Deputy Commissioner Mardan, an experienced Frontier Political, informed the Chief Secretary (copy to me) that he was in agreement with the policy I advocated, and enclosed a copy of a report by a prominent Congressite of the district, Ghulam Mohd Khan, ex-President, Provincial Congress Committee (and therefore a declared 'enemy' of the British), whom he had asked (unknown to me) to visit the Malakand and make enquiries. This is the report:

"According to your intention I went to Malakand, though the time was little; yet I found out the following facts in brief: Political Agent Malakand has found out a new, and in reality the old, system of Pukhtoon, in connection with the jirga system. He himself does not nominate any jirga member, but he gives order to those who are living in that village, where the occurrence has taken place, to come and decide the matter according to oaths laid down by the Riwaj. Every person of such village can become a jirga member, who possesses some immovable property those who have got no such property could not sit in the jirga. When these persons of that village come, the file of the offence is handed over to them, and thus they decide the matter unanimously, and the Political Agent approves the same decision without any objection, and if the members of that village fail to give their findings finally, then the same file is put to another jirga, which contains the Masheran (important people) of the whole ilaqa (area) and thus they decide the matter once for all. Alas that such a jirga system of the ilaqahas come to an end in the districts, which is still alive in the tribal territories and agencies. Such kind of jirgas is the sign of the

improvement of the Pukhtoon and also the welfare of the country …
In reality it is very useful system in putting a stop to offences."

This report confirmed that my research had at least established contact with the true original Pathan law and judicial procedure. A reliable foundation had been discovered on which to build a more modern structure, closer to the pattern in British India.

More than this. There was now proof that the Pathan tribes were far from being lawless. In the heart of these primitive communities lay a core of justice and morality, capable of controlling every individual, however headstrong, and of raising the standard of tribal life to a high level. Unfortunately, since the internal structure had become corrupted almost beyond recognition by external pressures, few Politicals would believe that it existed. Accompanying the official report on the result of my research was a recommendation that a Bureau of Tribal Information should be set up to assemble, test, preserve and complete the knowledge already gained from various sources about the tribes, and to use it in the training of Political Officers. These Officers rendered magnificent service, sometimes under dangerous conditions, but they spent a great deal of their time away from the Frontier, in Indian States, in the Delhi Secretariat, in the Persian Gulf or Baluchistan. Unless supplied with precise information about the tribes, he was dealing with, and supported by higher authority with a firm intelligible policy, understood and accepted by the tribesmen, the Political Agent was thrown back on his own resources. Too often, like Bruce,[6] and his long line of successors in Waziristan, he would pursue the ends of government through the medium of individual tribesmen, judged to possess influence over their fellows, thus splitting the tribe into 'friendlies' and 'hostiles', and causing consternation and dismay to Mullahs and Faqirs, trying to hold the tribe together. As Political Agents were changed frequently, the friends of one could easily become the enemies of his successor. In spite of this, Caroe rejected my suggestion for a Bureau of Tribal Information: "Such a Bureau is quite unnecessary," he wrote, "because our officers on the Frontier already know collectively all there is to be known about Pathan tribal organisation." Even supposing such a claim to be true, no sum total of their knowledge could possibly be arrived at, nor could it be compared with the whole range of history, composition, folklore, mythology, religion, law, custom and usage, without the help of a scientific and official body of this

---

[6] Caroe, p.398.

kind. There were other factors too that Caroe failed to take into account, such as the possibility of error on the part of a busy Political Agent, and increasing corruption within the tribe. In order to do justice to Pathans, the indispensable information needed was the true unspoilt order and pattern of tribal life, as they existed prior to contact with the British.[7]

A word is necessary here about what may be called 'frontier psychology', as revealed in the correspondence relating to my research in particular comments emanating from Waziristan. Here, more than anywhere else, the unrelieved atmosphere of confrontation caused by the continuous military presence for the 'last twenty-five years', affected the mentality of the British and the tribesmen alike. Replying to my 'note', on Tribal Reconstruction, the Resident (a Senior Officer in a key position) wrote: "My opinion is that the transborder tribesmen are for the most part, savages, whose main desire is not to be governed by anybody ... my own conviction is that we can only successfully control the tribes by breaking down their tribal spirit, as has been done with the tribes in Scotland ... The best form of government, so far as the tribes are concerned, is paternal rule." He could not have said (or thought) anything more certain to arouse the anger and hostility of a transborder Pathan, obsessed by a passionate love of freedom. Here again, as in the case of the Kurram and Malakand, is this strange reliance on the efficacy of paternal rule, which, whether you call it that, or 'a loose administration', belongs to the lowest grade in the administrative scale the rule of expediency. Regretfully, it has to be admitted that sentiments of this kind occupied an important place in Frontier psychology, even as late as the 1940s.

Caroe, describing the manner in which the jirga, as the instrument of the tribe, arrives at decisions, provides a good example. He purports to be describing a jirga acting as a Court of Law; but in fact he is describing one discussing the day-to-day affairs of the tribe. "The unwritten law," he says,[8] "is that the jirga takes decisions, which in the end overbear opposition, and are accepted as unanimous. Minority opinions will be given, but unless the argument or personality is strong enough to sway the jirga, they are borne down by rude eloquence, by the personality of the most persuasive or forceful, and in the last resort by force or threat of force." This description is slightly contemptuous, but it could pass (apart from the last sentence) as a fair

---

[7] Caroe's book, *The Pathans*, which is mainly historical and too late to be of any use to the British administration, is of course an important step in this direction.

[8] The Pathans, p.411.

description of the proceedings of our House of Commons! Anyone unfamiliar with the working of a democracy might be scandalised at the behaviour of our Members of Parliament, and the verdict might well be 'anarchy and chaos'. And if the observer happened to notice a powerful Trade Union holding the country to ransom, a group of teenage vandals smashing up public seats and telephone kiosks, ripping up flower beds in public parks, dismembering toilets, mugging old people let alone terrorism in Northern Ireland, he might be excused for calling us all a lot of savages! We would of course hasten to protest that appearances can be deceptive. "Do not jump to conclusions," we would say, "look below the surface: study our democratic system in depth: look, for instance, at our religion and our law." That is exactly what a Pathan Mullah would say, and he would add: "You British have no respect for our way of life. You have threatened us with your superior armaments for nearly a hundred years; many times you have been on the point of destroying us physically; your representatives have undermined the moral fabric of our people in order to enforce your will upon us. How do you expect us to behave in the face of such provocation?" Caroe expresses the conviction[9] that had the Mahsuds exchanged their democracy for a single leader, "they might have laid the foundations of a state as stable as the Swat of Miangul." The 'stability' of Swat State (with British backing) lasted for hardly more than a single generation, while the tribal democracies stretch into the remote past, and are still very much alive today.

And what of the Pathan contribution to Frontier psychology? I do not want to suggest that he is a saint any more than the Viking, the Scottish Highlander, or the Welsh border raider. Arthur Swinson has described him[10] as "possibly the most ferocious, independent and warlike race ever known". Against this rather dramatic description must be set the strong personal attraction that undoubtedly existed between Britisher and Pathan. What they had in common was a respect for the individual as an equal, a sense of humour, and an instinct for fair play. The Pathan loved a fight, provided it was conducted on roughly equal terms. He strongly objected to the use of aeroplanes, as giving the British an unfair advantage. Many British Politicals put a high value on these personal friendships, though few realised the danger of conducting official business on a personal level, when the tribal customary procedure was deliberately impersonal.

Pathans were extremely proud of their own social system, and customary law, and were prepared to defend them to the last man. In consequence, the

---

[9] *The Pathans*, p.405.
[10] *North West Frontier*, p.18.

Frontier Crimes Regulation, as applied to British India and to administered tribal areas, like the Malakand, the Tochi and the Kurram, was deeply resented, because it introduced a foreign element, the British jury system, into their indigenous legal procedure.

The need for special legislation to provide for the trial of tribesmen accused of murder in British India in furtherance of a blood feud or some other offence such as the kidnapping of a girl, involving tribal custom, was generally recognised. Tribal custom was also involved in certain classes of Civil dispute. The regular procedure for the trial of these cases was long, complicated and expensive. Police investigations were forced to stop short at the administrative border, while the roots of many disputes, both civil and criminal, lay in areas beyond the ordinary jurisdiction of the Courts. The tribesmen themselves were unfamiliar with British Indian law and court procedure, including the rights of the parties to be represented by pleaders. The intention of the Regulation was to cut out these complications, to save the tribesmen the expense of litigation, and to provide for the withdrawal of such cases from the Courts for trial by a 'Council of Elders', in accordance with Pathan custom. All very reasonable, but the unforgiveable sin was to make no determined effort to ascertain the true customary procedure, and to substitute for it a witch's brew of arbitrary rule, official expediency, and the British jury system. The presiding magistrate selected from a list of local notables, a Council of Elders consisting of four or five persons, and after hearing objections if any from the parties, required them to give findings on the guilt or innocence of the accused in a criminal case, or on the points at issue in a civil dispute. The Council were permitted to make independent enquiries out of court and to visit the spot, if they wished. Their verdict was accepted, as if it were that of a British jury. I can imagine English lawyers wincing at the thought of a jury being allowed to leave the precincts of the Court, to listen to all kinds of inadmissible evidence, and to be exposed for long periods to opportunities for bribery. If the Regulation was unpopular in the districts, it was far more so in the protected tribal areas, where it clashed with the true customary law, and became an offence to Mullahs, Faqirs and Qazis responsible for upholding shariat and the moral standards of Islam. Caroe admits[11] that "it was a failure as it fell between two stools". It could well have been a potent cause of Frontier unrest. There is no doubt about what the tribesmen thought of it. In the preface to "MIZH", Howell[12] puts the Mahsud argument like this, quoting the words of a leading Malik:

---

[11] *The Pathans*, p.354.

[12] Sir Evelyn Howell, KCIE, CSI.

"a civilisation has no other end than to produce a fine type of man. By this standard our own social order must surely be allowed immeasurably to surpass that of British India, with its law courts and assemblies. Therefore, let us keep our independence, and have none of your law ... let us stick to our own customs, and be men, like our fathers before us."

Howell sympathised with this point of view; and there seems no moral reason why the true Pathan customary law (carefully ascertained) should not have been incorporated in the Frontier Crimes Regulation. On the other hand, it is disturbing to contemplate the injustice inflicted, and the extent to which the tribes were corrupted, by a vicious Regulation. For my part, I decided that, within my jurisdiction as Political Agent, Malakand, I would ignore the Regulation altogether, and follow the true customary procedure, as revealed in my research, for the settlement of all civil and criminal cases. This decision was supported wholeheartedly by all the local Mullahs and Qazis, and has now remained in force for over thirty years. When I visited Malakand again in October 1972, I was informed that it was still working satisfactorily.

One final conclusion must be mentioned: the influence of religion in tribal life. This influence was supreme without it the tribe could not live. In a community where no individual could be trusted with absolute power, the sanctity of the oath, administered as a religious act, was universally relied on. This meant that considerable power, both spiritual and political, was often centred in the Mullah, or other religious dignitary, such as a Faqir. If this had been fully understood, many wars, many lives and much money might have been saved. Throughout the whole period of British rule, the 'holy man' of the tribe was invariably regarded (and was in fact) the arch-enemy. As the Mullah and the tribe were inseparable, it is not unreasonable to visualise the possibility of these two and the British seeing eye-to-eye, discovering an identity of interest and working amicably together. It has to be remembered that this desirable result was achieved effortlessly in the case of the Wali (an autocratic ruler) and Swat State. It should not have been impossible for one democracy to understand another.

My chances of getting this message across to higher authority were remote. Even in peacetime, all that the outside world required of the Frontier Governor was to keep the tribes 'quiet' and there was a war on.

CHAPTER XV

Chief Secretary
1941–44

Hath he come now in season to know thee,
Hath he seen, what a stranger forgets,
All the graveyards of exiles below thee,
O Land of Regrets?

All the clerks lined up in a row, when I went to my office in the Malakand, to say goodbye. Before I shook hands with them, the head clerk made a little speech. They were very pleased, he said, that I had been promoted to Chief Secretary, and they wished me luck. He ended with these words, which have always stuck in my memory: "Sir, you are leaving us on appointment to a high office, but we are remaining here like frogs in a well. Please do not forget us."

The words seemed to emphasise the chasm that lay between us. While I belonged to the tiny circle of Englishmen who could move from one highly paid post to another, they were lost in the vast anonymity of five hundred million Indians to whom life offered hardly more chance of individual achievement than a frog had of leaping out of a well. Of course one had known clerks, particularly stenographers, who had risen to posts of great responsibility in Government office, and the Army provided means of promotion from sepoy to high commissioned rank, but these were few and far between. For all but one or two exceptionally fortunate men, the head clerk's words were true. I was determined to do what I could to improve their lot.

One of the most obvious ways open to me as Chief Secretary was a revision of scales of pay, not only for clerks, but for all provincial services. This was an immense task, but before giving up my duties had complete proposals to put before the Provincial Government. One advantage was that when the Five Years Development Plan for the Frontier Area came to be prepared, I was able to incorporate my revised scales of pay into all the schemes, thereby enabling them to get off to a good start, properly financed, and without delay.

It is commonplace in England today to see low-paid employees striking for more pay, but in the Indian services, twenty-five or more years ago, such a thing was unheard of. The war has caused a considerable increase in the cost of living, and the loyalty of lower-paid government servants was constantly threatened by subversive political agitation. It was essential to make them aware that their interests were being considered.

This opportunity must not pass without a word in praise of the Indian clerk, or Babu. He was often a humble, rather depressed-looking individual, struggling to maintain a large family on a meagre salary but to the power he served he was worth his weight in gold. In thirty odd years, first in the army and then in the Political service, I was 'boss' to literally hundreds of Indian clerks and I cannot remember one who was either blatantly disloyal or stubbornly disobedient.

What would the British Empire in India have done without its Babus? When I think of the long hours of hard, uncomplaining work these men put in, often in stuffy, ill-ventilated offices, in the cold of winter and in the scorching heat of summer, I know that I was privileged to witness a devotion to duty unsurpassed anywhere in the world.

Perhaps a Babu on the Frontier might be less sophisticated than his counterpart in, say, Bengal; but scattered in his thousands in Government offices all over a vast sub-continent, he represented the bricks and mortar of a tall and stately edifice he gave strength and stability to the whole structure of government, and his patient observance of office rules and procedure supported many a jaded British official through long hours of tedious work in an insufferable climate.

As the result of my new appointment, Marie and I and the children could look forward to an interesting spell in Peshawar, the social and political centre of Frontier life. Only the width of the Mall separated us from the gates of Government House, and our contacts with Sir George and Lady Cunningham were frequent and friendly. To us, 'Robin' Cunningham was pure gold. One of my most vivid memories of her is at one of Sir George's Investitures, when it was my duty to read out, before a large and distinguished audience, the names of those about to receive honours, and the citations in the case of bravery awards. I must have looked a bit nervous, because she fussed over me, plying me with glasses of sherry, and telling funny stories to lighten the tension.

Robin was very fond of Marie, and both became deeply involved in Red Cross work. As the war was at its height, there was plenty to do for the wounded, for those on active service and for their dependants. Robin soon became equally interested in the main peacetime activity: Maternity and Child Welfare. When the large new Provincial Welfare Centre at Peshawar (with the School for Training of Lady Health Visitors attached, which Marie planned) was finally completed, it was named 'The Lady Cunningham Provincial Welfare Centre'.

Sir George and Lady Cunningham had no children of their own, but after

Marie's death, Robin mothered our little adopted daughter, Judith, who was then about five years old, and a beautiful child.

I was one of Cunningham's many admirers. He had a coolness of temperament that could take the heat out of any crisis, and an air of authority equal to any challenge. He seemed to excel in everything he turned his mind or his hand to, and he had a slow irresistible smile that could disarm his worst enemy.

As Chief Secretary, I dealt with him direct on all matters connected with the transborder tribes.

Ever since the creation of the North West Frontier Province in 1901 it had been considered essential for strategic and administrative reasons for the Viceroy and Central Government to retain direct control over all official relations with the tribes inhabiting the areas beyond the administrative border. This control was exercised through the Chief Commissioner as Agent to the Governor General and through the officers of the Indian Political Service subordinate to him in the agencies and tribal areas; but when, in 1932, the Frontier Province was raised to the status of a Governor's province, like those in the rest of India, it was ruled by elected Indian ministers. The distinction between local administrative control in the Province and central control in adjoining tribal areas now became artificial and cumbersome, and it was embarrassing to the Provincial ministers to be barred from all dealings with their own tribes across the border. Right up to the end of British rule, the Central Government persistently ignored this problem, and refused to abandon direct British control in tribal areas or to associate the Provincial ministers in any way with the administration of their tribes.

Cunningham (like Caroe, then Foreign Secretary in Delhi), was a staunch defender of the status quo. On 12th September 1945, he had a talk with *Dr Khan Sahib*, then Chief Minister, who pressed that the tribes should come under the Provincial Government, adding, "The great cause of all: our trouble is the hard and fast administrative border, and we should aim at linking each tribe with its adjacent district."[1] This was plain speaking. It had no effect on Cunningham.

During my period of office as Chief Secretary these were not 'live' issues. While the war was on, big administrative changes were out of the question. However, in the course of a close association with ministers, one could not help sensing their views on matters which, although outside the strict scope of their responsibilities, yet concerned them and their Province very intimately.

---

[1] *Sir George Cunningham* by Norval Mitchel, p.113.

Since 1932 there had been periods during which the party in power (usually the Congress), refused to take office as part of an all-India protest against some aspect of British rule or policy. The Governor was then obliged to administer the Province, under Section 93 of the Government of India Act, 1935.

Such was the situation on 4th November 1941 when I took over charge. It continued until 25th May 1943, when a Muslim League Ministry was formed under Mohammed Aurungzeb Khan.

This Ministry remained in office until 12th March 1945, when it was succeeded by a Congress Ministry under *Dr* Khan Sahib. Thus during only the latter half of my term of office was a ministry functioning. During this period, on Provincial affairs I worked under the instruction of the Chief Minister, and had occasional dealings with all Ministers. And yet, this was not the sum total of my experience of 'diarchy' (that is joint British-Indian rule under the Government of India Act of 1919). As Finance Secretary in 1938–39 I had taken orders from Mr Bhanju Ram Gandhi (Finance Minister); and later as Planning and Development Commissioner I was closely associated with all Ministers, who in the last two years of British rule belonged to the Congress Party.

There was at one time a good deal of doubt among Europeans, both in India and England, as to the capacity of Indians (and particularly Pathans) to rule themselves. That doubt was dispelled on the Frontier, and I believe throughout India, as soon as the democratically elected Ministers took over their duties many of them straight from long periods of political detention in jail. From my own experience I can testify that, in spite of such an inauspicious beginning, the experiment of diarchy was immensely successful. Not only were relations between the Ministers and their British Governor and Secretaries uniformly good, but the Ministers themselves proved responsible and business-like in the execution of their duties. My own conclusion is that during this period the Frontier Province experienced the most efficient form of administration it ever knew under British rule or possibly under any rule.

Good government is of course something more than the mere capacity to rule, and the very success of diarchy made it inevitable that it could never be more than a stepping-stone to full independence.

In the meanwhile, the Province was enjoying the benefits of a happy relationship between the officials and the Ministers they served. Curiously enough this was particularly true when a Congress ministry was in office, in spite of the fact that throughout the war, and almost to the end of British rule, the All-India Congress Party maintained a virulent and anti-British attitude. This friendliness was very much to the credit of all concerned, especially the

Governor and Chief Minister. In his biography, Norval Mitchel emphasises the extraordinarily warm personal relationship existing between Cunningham and Khan Sahib, which helped substantially to maintain peace on the Frontier during the vital war years.

Why did not these 'turbulent, lawless' tribesmen seize such a god given opportunity of embarrassing their British overlords, caught in the toils of a life and death struggle? Experts in guerilla warfare, they could have practised their art in a hundred ways against road and rail communications, against forts and cantonments on both sides of the border, against defenceless civilians in British India; and they could ferociously have engaged thousands of Allied men fighting men desperately needed in other theatres of war.

Instead, the North-West Frontier, notorious in peace time for a chronic state of insecurity, became for the duration one of the most trouble-free areas in all India.

For instance, in 1942, not only were British and Indian troops heavily engaged with the Japanese on the Burma border, but six provinces in India were torn by armed insurrection, and for three weeks traffic on the railway line between Delhi and Calcutta was at a standstill. "My main impression is that the North-West Frontier is about the only pleasant part of India nowadays," recorded Cunningham in his diary. Why? I suggest: first, no leading Islamic nation was deeply involved against us. "Do you anticipate trouble in the event of war?" Cunningham asked Khan Sahib on 28th April 1939.

"Not from the tribes, because Turkey, Persia and Afghanistan would stick together." was the reply. From my experiments in the Malakand I knew that the whole tribal system was steeped in Islamic culture. If their religion had been in danger, Pathans, who regard themselves as the champions of Islam, would not have remained passive.

Secondly, it was well known that the British were so involved in other theatres that they could not contemplate any further extension of control, at any rate for the time being. On the other hand if the tribes caused trouble, they might draw upon themselves some of the deadly armaments being used elsewhere.

Lastly, the war intensified the lurking fear of Russia. Pathans had a keen international sense. Although illiterate, they could not be regarded as 'ignorant savages'.

Most of my time was spent in office, dealing with hundreds of files on provincial and tribal matters. Almost every evening boxes of them had to be taken home and worked on before going to bed. One great advantage was that every year the bulk of the Secretariat moved to Nathia Gali, the summer headquarters, located in the Hazara district east of the Indus, 8,000 feet up in the foothills of the Himalayas. Here, scattered along the tops of pine-clad ridges, chalets and bungalows, including a delightful Government House, had been constructed to accommodate high officials and their families for the summer months. The cool, clean air, the magnificent views of Nanga Parbat (unhappily often veiled in cloud) and other snow-capped giants, the remoteness and yet the comfort, the friendliness of a small, isolated European community, the limited duration of the season, all added up to a rare dimension of living that few who experienced it will ever forget. Those were happy days for Marie and me and our little family.

That happiness was soon to be shattered by three personal tragedies. Our nurse, Florence Thorogood, besides being an excellent nanny and loyal friend, was a good-looking young girl. In the spring of 1942 she became engaged to a smart young Sergeant Major in the 25th Dragoons, stationed at Peshawar, named George Devenport. As the marriage seemed obviously suitable, we did all we could to encourage it. A date in January 1943 was fixed for the wedding in Peshawar. Florrie arranged for her wedding dress to be made.

Being of Irish extraction, she was a devout Roman Catholic and often, particularly in the Malakand, we had a priest to stay with us and give her Mass. On Christmas Eve 1942 she went to Midnight Mass in Peshawar, and some days later fell sick. We nursed her for six days in our house before her illness was diagnosed as smallpox. She was removed immediately to an isolation hospital. We never saw her again. She had contracted the very worst type of smallpox, called 'the Tiger'. After being desperately ill for several days she survived the crisis, but her heart gave way suddenly and she died. I had the unpleasant duty of breaking the news to George Devenport.

In September 1943, just after our return from Nathia Gali, Marie discovered that she was pregnant. This disturbing news was confirmed by *Dr* Henderson of the Afghan Mission Hospital, with whom we were friendly. We knew that in view of her diabetic condition, the birth would be dangerous. For the whole period of her pregnancy, however, she remained well and cheerful, and kept to a regular round of engagements, not forgetting, of course, the Red Cross and Maternity and Child Welfare. The doctors were optimistic, but as we were aware, India was not geared medically in those days to deal with diabetes.

On 25th March 1944, Marie's baby, a boy, was born by Caesarian section in the Lady Reading Hospital, Peshawar. One of the Indian doctors who attended the birth told me afterwards he had never seen such extreme precautions taken at any operation. The staff of the Lady Reading were assisted by some from the Afghan Mission Hospital.

There is no doubt that everything possible was done to save both mother and child, but Marie never recovered from a severe haemorrhage within a few hours of the birth. We moved her to the cool air of Nathia Gali in April, but she got steadily weaker and died on 4th June. Her coffin, draped with a Red Cross flag, was carried by a sturdy band of Gurkhas along the narrow mountain path from the motor road to the tiny cemetery at Kalabagh among pine trees.

So ended ten years of great happiness. Marie lifted me up, when I was down, and gave me all that a husband could wish for. Her death was a great shock to her many Indian, as well as English, friends. The Indian Red Cross Society placed a memorial in the form of a brass plate in St John's Church, Peshawar Cantonment, with the following inscription:

'IN LOVING MEMORY
OF CONSTANCE MARIE MALLAM
KAISAR-I-HIND MEDAL (SILVER)
WIFE OF LT. COLONEL G.L. MALLAM CIE. IPS.
WHO DIED ON 4TH JUNE 1944 AT NATHIA GALI

* * *

This tablet is erected by the Chairman and Members of
North West Frontier Provincial Branch of the Red Cross Society
To commemorate her devoted work in the interests of the
women and children of the Province.

* * *

I was now left with three small children in India in wartime, and it was very difficult to find a suitable nurse or governess to look after them. As Chief Secretary I was tied to the office for long hours during the day and had little time to give them, although having lost their mother, and nurse as well, their need was great. As may be expected, friends rallied round in a wonderful way and somehow we got by.

After Marie's death, Judith, our little girl, spent most of her time in Government House and out shopping or paying visits with Lady Cunningham. The third tragedy occurred when she fell ill on 4th April 1945, and was admitted to the Lady Reading Hospital, four days later, with typhoid fever. The fever raged for twenty-one days.

I had ceased to be Chief Secretary in the autumn of 1944 and was now Planning and Development Commissioner for the Frontier area. Every evening, as soon as I could leave the office (and, whenever possible, earlier), I went to see Judy in hospital. As the fever made her delirious, she received me always with the same refrain, "Why are you so late, Daddy?" Her voice is as clear as ever to me now, so many years after, with its sad and piteous appeal.

On 24th April, *Dr* Maidie Shearburn, the well-known lady missionary doctor from Tank, on the Waziristan border, was visiting Peshawar. I begged her to see Judy, who had been completely unconscious for more than twenty-four hours. Just before midnight we stood in the corridor outside the ward, discussing her condition, when a nurse brought word to say that both her temperature and pulse were down. *Dr* Shearburn seemed to think that this meant the crisis was over, and insisted on my going to bed. Early next morning the hospital phoned to say that Judy was dying. By the time I reached the hospital she was dead. She was only six and a half years old. It seemed that all Peshawar attended her funeral the Governor and his wife, the Indian Ministers, most of the British residents and a large number of Indians. Judy was so young and such an attractive little girl. She had already made her mark as a gifted dancer in some theatricals in Peshawar. At this time David, now seven, was at a boarding school at Srinagar in Kashmir. Marcus, just a year old, knew nothing of these events.

To return to my period of office as Chief Secretary, I made a short tour of Waziristan in the spring of 1943, which was a relief from office work and very educative. Boarding a small open Auster, with an Indian pilot, at Peshawar aerodrome, I was strapped into the seat, to which a parachute was attached (I had not the foggiest idea how it worked!).

The pilot flew to Miranshah and then, dropping to a hundred feet, steered the plane westwards up the narrow Tochi valley towards the Durand line and Afghanistan. Manoeuvering in limited airspace among high mountains required a good deal of skill, but the intrepid aviator was obviously enjoying himself following the turns and twists of the winding valley and skipping over intervening ridges. The acrobatic display was exhilarating, but I wondered whether the tribesmen in the fortified villages below thought we were 'buzzing' them if so, we might expect a bullet any minute!

Landing safely at Miranshah, I stayed the night with the Political Agent, North Waziristan. The following day Remake was reached by road. This military cantonment in the heart of tribal territory used to be called the largest monastery in the world, housing as it did, thousands of troops both British and Indian in a sexual desert. No women were allowed. The strange Imperial outpost had one advantage; it was located high enough in the mountains to ensure cool air and freedom from mosquitoes in the summer, but there seemed to me a menacing atmosphere about it a feeling intensified the next day when Charles Duke (later knighted), the PA South Waziristan, took me on the road to Wana.

We travelled in an armoured lorry into which were crammed a small armed escort of Scouts and five Mahsud tribal elders in the back, while we sat in front with the driver. The tribesmen were not travelling for pleasure. A more sullen, unwilling lot it would be difficult to imagine. Dressed in dirty clothes, they had not a smile between them. They were hostages for our safety and they knew it. The mountain road was lonely and sinister. There could have been an ambush round any corner. The tour did not leave a happy impression, but it gave me a tremendous admiration for the courage of Englishmen like Charles Duke, whose duty it was to handle hostile tribesmen under those conditions. I was of course no stranger to Waziristan. I had taken part in the Third Afghan War, in 1919, with the 27th Light Cavalry; a closer acquaintance had been made as Assistant Commissioner, Tank, in 1927, when I travelled over most of the newly-made roads. Finally, for almost two years, I had dealt with all correspondence and reports from this area as Chief Secretary. My tour convinced me that the temper of the tribesmen in Waziristan was quite different from, and much less friendly than, that of the tribes further north. I could not resist the conclusion that all the money and effort concentrated on this region were producing unpromising results.

CHAPTER XVI

The Frontier Development Plan
1944–47

He was touched with the tales of our glory
He was stirred by the clash and the jar
of nations who kill con amore
The fury of races at war;
'Mid the crumbling of royalties rotting
Each cursed by a knave or a fool,
Where kings and fanatics are plotting
He dreamt of a power and a rule.

My three years as Chief Secretary came to an end in the autumn of 1944. I was getting senior in the service and the number of higher posts on the Frontier was extremely limited. Just after Marie's death, Cunningham had pressed me to consider leaving the Frontier and applying for a post in Indian States. His view was that, apart from other considerations, it might do me good to get away from it all. This suggestion was I am sure, made out of kindness, but my mind ran in exactly the opposite direction. Now that I had lost Marie, I felt more than ever that I belonged to the Frontier where her interests lay.

I was intrigued with the subject of post-war development, which, during the summer of 1944, had begun to loom large in the correspondence addressed by the Government of India to the Provincial Secretariat. The war was drawing to a victorious conclusion and it had become vitally necessary to think and plan ahead. Post-war plans fell into two main categories: first, plans for the political future of India, involving a transition to Dominion status, if not full independence; and secondly, the economic development of the whole sub-continent. There was nothing I could do about the first, but the second offered real and exciting possibilities. The Government of India had already begun to press every province including the Frontier to prepare post-war development plans in consultation with the economic departments of the Central Government. Why should not the Frontier have such a plan, to cover both the tribal areas and the Province, and to link the two in a natural whole? I went to the Governor and asked him to appoint me as Planning and Development Commissioner for the Frontier area, including of course the tribal areas. Cunningham looked at me blankly. A guess at the working of his mind would go something like this: "Development on the Frontier? The very idea is absurd even slightly effeminate. The Frontier is a place where MEN live and fight and kill, and they will go on like that for ever." What he said was, "What is there to develop in these rocky hills and stony valleys?"

He did not expect an answer, but I gave him one. "I will give you a list," I said. The list I sent him eventually formed the basis of the first Five-Year Development Plan, costing seven million pounds. It ran as follows:

> Apart from minerals, the extent of which is as yet unknown, there are four commodities for which the Frontier provides climatic and other conditions unsurpassed in any other part of India:
>
> 1   Fruit
> 2   Drugs (medicinal herbs)
> 3   Sheep
> 4   Poultry.

Years later, revisiting my old parish in Kidderminster, a rather bleak industrial town in the Midlands, and the centre of an important carpet weaving industry, I was to hear the manager of one of the leading factories remark casually, "The finest carpet wool in the world comes from Peshawar in West Pakistan." Cunningham would have been surprised to hear this!

I was not dependent entirely on him for the furtherance of my plans for development. The Muslim League Ministry was in office. I talked to the Chief Minister and others on the theme, "All other provinces in India are preparing post-war development plans; should not the Frontier Province do the same?" And, "Is not the productive potential of the Pathan just as good as, if not better than, that of any other people in India?'

As was to be expected, I obtained an immediate response; and was appointed in due course Planning and Development Commissioner for the Province and tribal areas.

At the outset an extremely circumscribed official attitude[1] towards development had to be overcome. All that was expected of me officially, was one or two immediately productive, irrigation or other schemes of an agricultural nature serving a limited number of people, and costing not more than a *lakh*[2] or two of rupees each.

---

[1]   For some explanation, see Appendix I.
[2]   1 lakh = 100,000 rupees.

I collected a small but intelligent team of Indian assistants, led by one of the best brains in the Secretariat, Sheikh Abdul Hamid, who had for some years been Secretary of the section known as Development Departments, covering a limited field of education, agriculture and industry. Development with a capital D was such a new subject to India that we had to start by defining what we meant by it. We soon came to the conclusion that we could not be bound by any arbitrarily imposed restrictions on our thinking and planning, whether financial or other, and rejected absolutely the productivity restriction. There was so little basis on which to build the progress of the people that the early stages of Development would have to consist in laying those essential foundations, which could not by their very nature be immediately productive. Again, it soon became clear that if our plans were not to be stifled at birth, we would have to create a 'development climate' both among the public and in official circles. Most educated Pathans, particularly the Ministers, were immediately receptive to these ideas; the uneducated masses would present a problem later at the implementation stage, but in the meantime their ears were open to any news of our aims and activities. Perhaps following the lead of the Governor, the British officials, with a few notable exceptions, were either hostile or indifferent. Their fear was that if development was introduced and allowed to take the centre of the stage, individuals would have to give way to scientific planning and teamwork, and a clear-cut policy would take the place of expediency. On the other hand some British officials, to whom development was a subject so new and strange that they never gave it any serious thought, regarded it as nothing more than a gimmick. Finally, some of the most brilliant Political Officers with honours degrees at Oxford or Cambridge were opposed in principle to planned, development initiated by Government. They had been educated on the Conservative theory of laissez-faire and to them a government development plan was socialistic and anathema.

To meet this situation, shock tactics were decided on. We prepared first of all a long-term plan including a number of final objectives which could conceivably be attained during the next twenty-five years. Among them were:

Universal literacy.

A Frontier University (The Edwardes College and the Islamia College at Peshawar and the Vedic Bharatri College at Dera Ismail Khan were already in existence to form the nucleus of a full university independent of Lahore).

Teacher training colleges at various centres.

A medical college with training hospital of five hundred beds.

A health school for the training of lady health visitors.

Research stations for fruit and fruit technology.

Research stations for medicinal herbs, sheep and poultry breeding.

A large expansion of the existing research station for agriculture.

An agricultural engineering section.

A research station for forestry and school for the training of forest officers.

A greatly extended hydro-electric scheme.

Extension of existing roads and railways.

Housing and town-planning schemes.

We defined these objectives in some detail and gave a rough estimate of the cost entailed and a description of the methods advocated for attainment. It was made clear that our object was to raise the tribes eventually to the same standard of living as their non-tribal brothers resident in the Province. The Frontier Printing Press prepared proofs of the Plan and we suggested that it should be published for information to encourage wide discussion and comment. Having completed this work, I left for England on leave in order to take David home for schooling, in May 1945, just after VE-Day, leaving Marcus and a nurse in charge of friends.

I must now go back a few months to the spring of 1944 to describe the steps I took to prepare the ground for development in tribal areas. On 25th February 1944 (while I was still Chief Secretary), I sent the following note to the Governor, but have no record of his remarks on it:

"As we are about to start work on a programme of post-war development in Tribal Areas, this is perhaps a suitable moment to consider the conditions it is necessary to create in these areas in order to obtain maximum results. It is a truism to say that no economic or cultural progress is possible in an atmosphere of anarchy and disturbance. In those tribal areas therefore, which are not peaceful, to try to implement the programme would be a waste of money. There are of course other tribal areas where conditions are not constantly disturbed and where we may expect some return for our money; but wherever you look along the border, nowhere is it possible to say that political conditions are conducive to economic development. It is hardly surprising that the Frontier tribes are politically backward. They have for years been in a state of suspense, their political future has always been uncertain, and their old traditional tribal system of government has been slowly crumbling. There is at present nothing to take its place. I feel that we must fill this vacuum before we start spending money on post-war development, or at least do both simultaneously.

There would be few who would deny that if it were possible to organise the domestic affairs of the tribes in such a way as to produce a fair degree of just and effective tribal government, this would satisfy the Government of India, the outside world and the tribes themselves and lead the way to a peaceful and constructive future. Opinions differ mostly as to whether this is possible or not, but why should it not be attempted? The alternatives are barren enough: British Indian administration up to the Durand Line, preceded by a bloody and expensive conquest and maintained by a huge, recurring and unproductive expenditure; long years of sullen ill-will which the British would not have time to live down; or a retreat to the line of the Indus, leaving a turbulent area to become still more turbulent, and condemning the peace-loving to years of submission to anarchy and bloodshed. To continue as we are, even if it were possible, would not satisfy a post-war world, which will demand a set purpose, clearly defined objectives and a carefully worked out programme.

As a first and indispensible step I recommend the institution of a bureau of tribal information to study the indigenous system of tribal government and to prepare a manual on which to base the training of political and subordinate officers who would be called upon to handle the scheme."

Having failed to get any answer out of Cunningham, I sent the note privately to Sir Olaf Caroe, then Foreign Secretary at Delhi, and responsible for Frontier policy. In his reply he agreed, in principle, that we should work for a system of tribal government in tribal areas but refused the means of achieving this. He was (as already mentioned) dead against a bureau of tribal information.[3]

On the 1st November 1944, as soon as I was appointed Commissioner for Post-War Planning, I addressed an official letter[4] to the Chief Secretary at

---

[3] See p.200
[4] SMCU.

Peshawar, much on the lines of my note of the 25th February, stressing the point that plans for the development of tribal territory would inevitably be met by questions, if not suspicion, as to the ultimate intentions of Government in regard to the future of the tribes. I thought it extremely unwise therefore to attempt any appreciable economic development of their territory without simultaneously taking steps to settle and secure their political future in a manner that they would understand and appreciate. With this letter I enclosed a note[5] on 'the case for tribal self-government', giving my proposals in some detail for the establishment of organised tribal government as the ultimate political objective in these areas.

I received no answer in writing to this letter. I was however instructed verbally by the Governor to get on with the planning of economic development and to leave the political future of the tribes alone. As my assignment was the planning of economic development only, I had no alternative but to accept this decision, but I did so with a heavy heart. Time was running out fast and my chances of influencing tribal policy before the British account closed were rapidly diminishing. I felt that I was up against a mental paralysis, largely induced by the war, a built-in resistance to change, and perhaps above all the obsession with Waziristan and a military solution of the Frontier problem.

Nevertheless, as I prepared to leave for home in May 1945, I was not quite as depressed as I ought, logically, to have been. I believed that I had one trump card left in my hand: if I could get the Government of India to approve a plan for the economic development of the tribal areas to the same standard as for the Province I would then be able to ask "How do you propose to implement this plan? Are you going to use force, like a Stalin steamroller, or will you consider the use of more civilised methods?" Fortunately for my peace of mind whilst on leave, I did not know that the mice would be at the cheese while I was away.

'Victory summer' gave me an impression of wartime England that I reproduced at the request of All India Radio in a broadcast[6] from the Peshawar studio on my return. I visited relations and friends and got David settled into a new home with his uncle and aunt, Mr and Mrs Blenkinsop at Sherborne. As they had no children of their own, they kindly agreed to look after him. Alison was Marie's sister, and 'Blenky' was a master at Sherborne School (he also was a nephew of General 'Pug' Ismay who worked as a key member of Churchill's team in WWII). With his help, backed by the Headmaster, Canon

---

[5] *Ibid.*

[6] SMCU.

Alec Wallace, an old friend of mine, David was accepted as a boarder at the Preparatory School. I embarked on a troopship at Southampton in September 1945, for the voyage back to India.

One look at the faces of my little band of planners on my return from home leave was enough. They said that all was lost. A high-ranking Secretary from the Government of India Finance Department (a Hindu) had visited Peshawar while I was away and held a ministerial meeting, the outcome of which was a decision that our long-term plan was completely unrealistic. It was not to be published in case it raised hopes that Government would never be able to fulfil; but worse still, I was instructed to prepare another plan at a cost not exceeding three *crores*[7] of rupees. We all agreed that this would not be worth the time and trouble involved. What were we to do? Resign? I went along to see Mr A.P. Low, then Finance Secretary. He was very critical of our long-term plan and completely in agreement with the decision imposing a limit of three crores. "Now," he said, "you will have to cut your coat according to your cloth." He added that he believed in the principle of laissez-faire and was against the planning of economic development by Government. The only thing I could think of saying at that moment was that my *mali* had just left a heavy roller on my lawn for a couple of days. When the roller was moved it left a patch of dead grass behind it. A laissez-faire Government which refused to plan development was like that roller, and the poverty-stricken people of India like the dead grass beneath it.

I went to *Dr* Khan Sahib (Chief Minister of the Frontier Congress Government in power at the time), and talked things over with him. I expressed deep dissatisfaction at the decision arrived at in my absence and suggested that I should now prepare the First Five Year Development Plan, containing a selection of schemes from the long-term plan, to meet all the essential needs of the Province and Tribal Areas capable of execution during this period. The cost of each scheme would be carefully estimated and when the total expenditure was known we would go again to the Government of India and try to persuade them to finance their share. *Dr* Khan Sahib agreed, our hopes revived and we got down to serious work. The second plan was drafted in consultation with the Provincial heads of departments and also with the corresponding technical departments of the Government of India, to whom each scheme was sent for approval. This was a laborious business as it involved for each one the four stages of formulation, estimation, Provincial and Central

---

[7] 1 crore = 10 lakhs = 1 million.

approval. Among these plans were many for strengthening of the existing departments of the Provincial Government, to enable them to take on large extra responsibilities, and several of a preliminary nature were added for execution during the pre-plan year.

At last our ideas and activities were getting known and public interest in the subject of Development increased. I was asked to broadcast a talk from the Peshawar studios of the All India Radio, and to give the Convocation Address[8] at the Islamia College, Peshawar, on 23rd February 1946, a sure sign that we were now being taken seriously by responsible opinion in the Province.

In the Address, which was published in full by the Frontier Mail on 10th March, I mentioned the attempt to limit expenditure on development to a ridiculously low figure, and the advice 'to cut my coat according to my cloth'. "No good tailor," I said, "would try to do such a foolish thing. As in tailoring, so in development, the main consideration is not the amount of cloth or money available. It is the shape and size of the body to be clothed, the needs of the people, and the resources (human and other) to be developed."

For all our efforts, it was the autumn of 1946 before the Plan was ready for publication. In the meantime Sir George Cunningham had retired on 2nd March 1946, and had been succeeded by Sir Olaf Caroe.

In September, as soon as the Plan was ready and the cost fully estimated, a meeting of all ministers was held in Peshawar under the chairmanship of the Chief Minister, *Dr* Khan Sahib. The Governor was not present. I was asked to attend, also Low, Finance Secretary. I have vivid memories of this meeting at which I presented the Plan in its final form and requested permission for printing and publication. The Plan contained one hundred and thirty-one individual schemes separately formulated, costed and classified under the headings, Agriculture, Animal Husbandry, Co-operative, Medical, Public Health, Industries and Marketing, Forests, Education, Public Works and Drinking-Water Supply. Of these, twenty-eight were exclusively for tribal areas and fifty-five for the Province and tribal areas jointly. The whole Plan was estimated to cost nearly ten crores of rupees (about seven million pounds). Nothing had been seen like it before on the Frontier. There was an atmosphere of suppressed excitement and enthusiasm at the meeting. No discussion of the schemes was necessary as each minister had already seen and approved those relating to the departments for which he was responsible. Permission to print and to publish was readily given. It was essentially a plan for Pathans. It linked

---

[8] SAACU

the tribal areas and the Province as a single economic unit; and, by setting a common educational standard for both, it forged strong cultural links between the tribes of the mountains and those of the plain, thus partly obliterating the administrative border that had run along the foot of the hills for almost a century. By providing two new degree colleges, one at Abbottabad and one at Peshawar (for women), a new medical college and five-hundred bed Provincial hospital at Peshawar, the Plan brought the Frontier within a step of academic independence. It might be called[9] a 'Plan for Pushtunistan' though that name had not yet been coined.

The discussion turned to the all-important question of finance. Low pointed out, quite correctly, that the Plan flew in the face of the decision reached a year ago that development should be limited to three crores (I intervened here to remark that the trouble with that decision was that it was made in my absence) and that therefore the second Plan was as unrealistic as, the first. Low was quite sure that the Central Government would never finance the vast expenditure proposed. I replied that it was common knowledge, at any rate in official circles, that the Government of India was about to receive from the United Kingdom huge sums in the form of Post-War Credits and that most of this money had already been earmarked for development in all the Provinces of India. The Frontier Province was the smallest and poorest, but it was strategically placed on an important international frontier. The departments of the Province were the only agency available to the Central Government for carrying the benefits of development into the tribal areas; but they had for years been under-financed and were so weak that unless considerably strengthened, they could not possibly carry out the duties assigned to them in the plan. Now was the psychological moment to press our essential needs on the Central Government; the opportunity might never occur again. This just about carried the day. It was decided that as soon as the plan was printed it should be despatched to the Central Government asking them to finance a development grant of five crores to the Provincial Government and direct expenditure of four crores in tribal areas. It was further decided that, after a reasonable interval to allow the Central Government to study the plan, a deputation consisting of the Chief Minister, one other Minister, myself and Low, should fly to Delhi and present our claim in person. Before the meeting closed, one other subject was briefly discussed: the problem of implementation. Owing to the proximity of Peshawar to the Russian border, all the Ministers were

---

[9]   For further information see the Plan itself SAACU and India Office library

fully aware of the economic 'miracle' being performed by Stalin in that country, in spite of the war. *Dr* Khan Sahib stated that "India is a democratic country; in the execution of our plan we cannot possibly make use of the totalitarian methods adopted by Stalin for forcing development upon his people."

The plan, consisting of four hundred and sixty-three printed foolscap pages, was forwarded to the Government of India in November. A month later, *Dr* Khan Sahib, the Minister of Finance, Low and I boarded a small passenger plane at Peshawar for Delhi.

We were delayed at Lahore for a couple of hours while repairs were carried out to the plane, and eventually made a night landing at Delhi. I shall never forget the breathtaking beauty of the view to right and to left as we sped along over the level plains of India, slowly disappearing into the darkness. Westward, above the rim of the far horizon, was the fading glow of a magnificent tropical sunset, while eastward the snows of the distant Himalayas turned pink and then silver in the brilliant moonlight.

In the vast building which housed the Imperial Secretariat we were ushered into the presence of the Secretary dealing with our case in the Central Finance Department once again, a Hindu. *Dr* Khan Sahib asked me to state our arguments. The face on the other side of the desk showed not a glimmer of interest; we were not even asked to sit down. When I finished, he said that, so far as he was concerned, we would not get an *anna* more than the three crores promised a year ago! It was useless to plead any further; we came away feeling somewhat humiliated. When we got outside the Secretariat, Low said, "I told you so."

We sat down on some seats in the sunshine and all I could say was, "I am not beaten yet." In the silence that followed I turned over in my mind the thought that had been lurking there for some time, that so long as we dealt with Hindu Secretaries we should get nowhere. The idea of Pakistan, involving the partition of India, was rapidly becoming a live issue, and I doubted whether any Hindu would allow Central Government money to be spent in an area that might soon form part of Pakistan if he could possibly prevent it. The subject was a delicate one to discuss with *Dr* Khan Sahib, who, with his brother Abdul Ghaffar Khan, was a member of the All India Congress and therefore committed to Hindu-Muslim unity and of course a united India.

In desperation, I turned to him and said, "Is there no leading Muslim that you know in Delhi, preferably on the Viceroy's Executive Council?"

After a moment's thought, Khan Sahib, eyes sparkling, replied, "I know the very man, Sir Akbar Hydari on the Council and he is also concerned with development."

We found a telephone and Khan Sahib rang up the great man and begged an interview urgently, as we had to return to Peshawar that afternoon. Within half an hour we arrived at a palatial residence in Kingsway and were shown into an elegant drawing room. As we stood waiting, the door opened and a fine looking, rather elderly man came in. He shook hands with *Dr* Khan Sahib, whom he knew, and the rest of us were introduced.

"Well, gentlemen, what can I do for you?" he asked, "I have only a few minutes to spare before a Council meeting, but I understand your business is urgent."

I felt confidence in him at once. Again I was asked to do the talking.

"We want money," I said; "for a Frontier Development Plan."

"How much?"

"The Government of India have already offered us three crores but we want six crores more," I replied.

"That's nine crores and a lot of money isn't it? Why do you want as much as that?"

"The Government of India is already spending as much and more on the Army and the Air Force on the Frontier, and that expenditure is largely unproductive. Our plan is constructive and it is the best hope there is for a permanent and peaceful solution of the Frontier problem."

"Has the plan been approved by the technical departments of the Central Government?"

"Yes."

"I will have a look at it," he said, "but now you must go as I have to be off to my meeting."

As he saw us out he assured us that he had always been interested in Pathans and in the Frontier problem and that he would do all he could for us. He was as good as his word. The schemes for the pre-plan year 1946–47 had previously been approved and were already in operation. By February 1947, the whole Five Year Plan(1947–52) received the sanction of the Government of India, and I recorded these words on the fly-leaf of one of my copies on 9th February:

"This plan has now received the approval of the Government of India
it owes its form and existence to team work on the part of many people,
but to me it gives practical shape to the dreams of many years on the
North-West Frontier."

CHAPTER XVII

The End of British Rule
1947

Let the wide waste sea for a space divide me,
Till the close-coiled circles of time unfold,
Till the stars rise westward to greet and guide me,
When the exile ends, and the years are told.

The sanction no sooner reached Peshawar, than I was informed officially that the post of Development Commissioner was abolished, and that I was appointed Revenue and Divisional Commissioner, a Senior post with heavy routine duties, covering the whole Province. This meant that I would be unable to play any part in the execution of the Plan.

Money, and the power of money, had now reached the Provincial Administration, and I suspected that *Dr* Khan Sahib and his ministers were determined to keep this power in their own hands, which they were perfectly entitled to do.

I soon discovered how wrong I was. One of the ministers came to me in a state of despair, and said, "Do you not think that the best man to implement the Plan is the man who devised it?"

I replied, "Yes. I am at your service whenever you need me." It was now clear that the Ministry had not been consulted before the post of Development Commissioner was abolished. This decision must have been a blow to *Dr* Khan Sahib, who was relying on the Plan to help him meet the rising challenge of the Muslim League and the pro-Pakistan movement.

The political situation in the Frontier Province during the last few years of British rule was anomalous. In the elections of January, 1946, the Muslim League, who stood for the partition of India and the creation of Pakistan, were defeated by *Dr* Khan Sahib and the Congress party, who stood for a united India and for Hindu-Muslim unity. To those who knew little of local conditions this looked like a rejection of the whole idea of Pakistan by a predominantly Muslim province, and may well have given Pandit Nehru and the All-India Congress the impression that, so long as *Dr* Khan Sahib remained in power, the creation of Pakistan was a practical impossibility. But appearances can be deceptive and Pakistan was not, in fact, clearly and specifically a main issue in the elections of 1946. At that time the departure of the British was not considered imminent. The final 'Quit India' announcement by Prime Minister Clement Attlee was not made until a year later on the 20th February, 1947. It may be historically of some interest to enquire what were the main issues in the elections of January, 1946, which returned *Dr* Khan Sahib and his anti-Pakistan Congress Party to power with a comfortable majority only twenty months before the actual creation of Pakistan and the end of British rule.

Arthur Swinson in his book, *North West Frontier* (page 335) suggests, "For the last twenty years this great party (the Congress) had seemed the only organisation which could rid them (the Muslims of the Frontier Province) of the British." It is true that the Congress party in the Province was anti-British, but far less so than in other parts of India. During the whole of the war it had refrained from attempting any violent anti-British agitation, while the rest of India was in a turmoil. Moreover, by January 1946, it was clear to all that the British were already searching for an opportunity to bow themselves out. I am convinced, therefore, that the main issue in the elections of January 1946, was neither the expulsion of the British nor the creation of Pakistan (though both of these all-India issues lurked in the shadows), but something else. As in other countries, elections would often be decided on local issues, of more immediate concern to the voters than remote ones, however important they might be.

The local issue that had carried the Congress party to power in all previous elections was the common people versus the landed gentry (the *khans*). The Congress represented the former and the Muslim League the latter. This explains the poor showing of the Muslim League in almost all elections and their meagre representation in the Legislature. The Muslim League ministry only came to office in May 1943, with the tacit consent of the Congress, who had a majority in the Assembly but refused to take office themselves; and the Muslim League ministry was ousted in March 1945, by a simple vote of no confidence without an election.

Thus, the Provincial elections of January 1946, served to mislead all but the closest observers of Frontier politics and Pandit Nehru was not one of these. Against the strongest official advice, he flew from Delhi to Peshawar in October of that year and stubbornly carried through a disastrous tour of the Frontier. His appearance as Foreign Minister brought the Pakistan issue abruptly for the first time to the doorway of every home on both sides of the border. The easily foreseeable result shocked Nehru, but brought the Frontier Pathans into the all-India picture in their true colours. No political issue, not even a class war, could withstand the power of religion in the tribal mind. Pandit Nehru's tour was the danger signal for Islam. If Pathans had to have a ruler, he must be a Muslim. From that moment the common people of the Frontier began rapidly to switch their allegiance from the Congress to the Muslim League, preferring for the time being the company of the hated khans to the worst of all evils Hindu domination.

While Khan Sahib and Nehru for a long time refused to face realities, the dwindling power of the former and rising communal tension forced the Viceroy, Lord Mountbatten, to visit Peshawar in April 1947, to find out for himself. He was greeted by a great crowd of Muslims, estimated at 100,000, demonstrating in support of the Muslim League demand for a referendum on the subject of Pakistan. Mountbatten saw and was convinced. Against the wishes of Nehru and Khan Sahib, he agreed to the referendum that took place on 20th July, and produced an overwhelming decision in favour of Pakistan.

This referendum was at the centre of a political storm, which forced the Governor, Sir Olaf Caroe, out of office, caused the downfall of the Congress ministry, made the partition of India inevitable, and hastened the departure of the British.

From the dull security of my routine duties, I watched these events. As a senior official, I was allowed three minutes on a sofa in Government House, Peshawar, on different occasions with each of three leading personalities involved in the transfer of power Lord Wavell, Pandit Nehru and Lord Mountbatten. The three-minute conversation in each case was a pure formality, but enough to give me a lightning impression of three contrasting characters. Wavell was the only one to give me a glimpse into his mind. Nehru's name was mentioned, possibly in connection with his visit to the Frontier, and I noticed a flush rising from Wavell's neck and spreading over his face. Relations between Wavell and Nehru were, I believe, badly strained at this time and I felt sorry for the Viceroy. I was sorry, too, when my three minutes came to an end.

Nehru left me with one impression only intellectual arrogance. I was Development Commissioner at the time and one would have thought that as Foreign Minister he would have been interested in someone who was trying to plan the future of the Province and the tribes. But no he treated me as if I were a *Naib Tehsildar* (junior district official). This may have been due to his anger with Frontier Politicals generally, whom he held responsible for the failure of his tour.

Lord Mountbatten gave me the impression of a man who lived and worked under such terrific pressure that he could not stop and notice the present always he had to be just one half step ahead of time.

In the early part of 1947 the officers of the Indian Political Service were accused of trying to influence the Frontier Muslims, most of whom had voted for the Congress only a year previously, to transfer their allegiance to the Muslim League and declare themselves in favour of Pakistan. It is true that a number of my colleagues sympathised with the khans who supported the League, believing them (the khans) to be the most stable element in the country, and because they were generally pro-British. About this time, a number of British Socialist MPs landed in India and sent a circular to all of us politicals on the Frontier, warning us that we were backing the wrong horse. The Congress party in India, they said, possessed the power. We should therefore back the Congress and not the Muslim League, and make it easier for Britain to hand over power without delay to the Congress leaders as representing the whole of India. What right had these MPs who knew nothing of India, to teach us our job? From long experience of the Frontier we knew that once the cry 'Islam in danger' had been raised, few Muslims would be able to resist the call of Pakistan. But what interested me was the mentality behind the circular, which centred on the principle of majority rule, equated with democracy by many people in England. I suspected that this view had been transported from England into India, through schools and universities founded on the English pattern. Millions of Hindus, including Nehru himself, had been taught from their youth up that, because they were the majority community in India, they had the moral right to rule the whole country non-Hindu minorities and all and that any Muslims who dared to oppose them would be acting immorally, undemocratically. Almost every day during the last year of British rule, I listened to the stream of words issuing from Gandhi's prayer meetings over the radio. Not one shred of hope did they offer to Muslims eager for some alleviation of total Hindu domination. Each day it seemed to me that one more nail had been driven into the coffin of United India. Gandhi was a saint, but more than that he was a politician, and more than that he was a Hindu. Neither he nor Nehru could hide the arrogance of the caste Hindu, which precluded any possible understanding with Muslims on the future of India.

To what extent are we British responsible for this attitude that led to partition? Is it not time that we developed a view of democracy capable of world-wide application and not limited to the tiny, until recently, homogeneous, community of this small group of islands we call the United Kingdom? In the interests of peace and justice I suggest that the principle of majority rule should be modified by the precept that where there is in any large community a sizeable ethnic or religious minority, the onus rests on the majority community to satisfy all the reasonable demands of the minority, and that the minority have a clear right to secede if their demands are not satisfied. If the Hindus of India had been educated long before the transfer of power to realise this, they might have saved the Muslims of the Frontier Province from changing their minds at the last moment and opening the door to Pakistan. In any case, the Hindu majority community and not the Muslim minority should be held responsible for the partition of India. Even now acceptance of these principles would be the best hope of peace between the separated components of the sub-continent.

The same principle could well be applied as between Nigeria and Biafra, Ireland and Ulster, Greeks and Turks in Cyprus and other similar problems.

Forming a sinister background to the momentous events of this year, and often intruding into the foreground, was rising communal tension. The Frontier Province, where the population was over ninety per cent Muslim, the Hindus and Sikhs constituting only a small, though significant minority, was more fortunate than the Punjab, where the various communities were more evenly dispersed; but there was a large colony of Hindus and Sikhs in Dera Ismail Khan to the South of the Province and here communal rioting broke out in April, 1947, which was only suppressed after great damage had been done to life and property. The disorder spread to Tank, forty miles from Dera Ismail Khan, and attracted the unwelcome attention of thousands of Mahsud tribesmen from across the border. They surrounded the city, breached the walls in several places and started to loot and burn. The attack, prompted by revenge for severe casualties inflicted on Muslims in the Punjab, was directed primarily against Sikhs and Hindus, who had for years monopolised the banking and commercial interest in that area. Once the tribesmen's blood was up, there was no knowing where they would stop.

There were a number of English ladies in Tank, including three remarkable lady missionaries Dr Shearburn, an eminent surgeon, Miss Studd and Miss Hadow, both trained nursing sisters. About twelve years previously these courageous ladies had set up a hospital, under the auspices of the Church of England Zenana Mission, for women and children in Tank, the fame of which spread far and wide on both sides of the border. The Government in Peshawar was anxious about their safety and that of all Hindus and Sikhs whose lives were in danger. I was instructed to fly to Tank to report on the situation and to evacuate as many women and children as possible. I left Peshawar in a Dakota and, after landing in Tank, held a consultation with local officials and arranged for an evacuation, which included the wife of the Political Agent, who was expecting a baby. I then went round to see the missionaries. The hospital staff were very busy with wounded and injured women and children. From the town only a short distance away came a confused noise of shouting, punctuated by rifle shots, and there was a tense feeling everywhere like the front line of a battle. The three ladies took me for a brief moment into a cool inner room, protected from the glare of the sun by dark curtains. I said I had instructions to evacuate them if they wished to go and that a plane was ready to take them away to safety. They smiled and said of course they could not go: they were much too busy, but they were grateful to the Government for thinking about them. Then they added, "You must not think we are in any danger. We are in close touch with the tribal leaders through many of their womenfolk who have been to our hospital, and we got a message from them only a short time ago to say that they would, if necessary, send an armed tribal guard to protect us so we feel quite safe."

This story is a good illustration of the courage and devotion of Christian missionaries on the Frontier. The record of missionary work on this remote borderland, particularly in the medical and educational fields, is something of which every Christian can be proud. I felt particularly honoured when I was asked to preach the sermon at the Annual Commemoration Service in the Afghan Mission Hospital at Peshawar on the 31st March 1947.

As the date for the end of British rule (15th August 1947) drew nearer I was exercised in my mind as to whether I should offer my services to the new Pakistan Government for a short time after the transfer of power. All British officials were being pressed by the Government of India to consider this seriously. Personally, I had no desire to stay on after the end of British rule. My two boys were in England and being well looked after at Sherborne, but I was anxious to make a home for them as soon as possible. I had also planned to go to a theological college and enter the ministry of the Church of England. The sooner I could do this and settle down, the better. There was one purpose, however, for which I knew I could not refuse to stay if the Pakistan Government needed me, and that was to help in the execution of the Development Plan, particularly in tribal areas.

Although officially suppressed, the Plan was not dead. Like a child late for school, it had crept in just before the classroom door was closed. It was in time, by a hair's breadth, to be included in the British record on the Frontier, but too late for that administration to implement it. Would the new Pakistan government be interested? As long ago as November 1945, soon after my return to India from home leave, the contrast between warm public interest and intense local official hostility became alarming, and I tried to meet it by increased publicity in the form of an article on the tribal problem, intended for publication in the Journal of the United Service Institution of India. Before I could send it to the Editor, I had to obtain permission from my own Governor, and from the Government of India. Naturally, this was not easy to obtain, but the article was eventually published in July 1946, and attracted a good deal of attention. Its main theme was the pressing need for political stability in tribal areas, in order to provide an ordered basis for development of the whole area between the west bank of the Indus and the Durand Line. I argued that this could only be achieved by a reconstruction of the existing tribal system, preceded by a scientific investigation.

In December 1946, Ian Stephens,[1] then editor of the *Statesman* of New Delhi, paid a visit to the Frontier, the result of which was a series of six articles on various aspects of the situation, published during the first week of January 1947. By that time the Plan and my article on the tribal problem had been brought out and he was very interested in both, perhaps because they represented the only reasoned alternative to a solution by force;

> In the sixth and last of these articles occur the following words: "The contention that political organisation of the tribes must be the first concern of reformers because law and order must precede any economic or social uplift measures has received increasing recognition. Its latest exponent is Lt Colonel G.L. Mallam of the Reconstruction Department NWFP Government. He was the driving force behind the Province's recently published Five Year Plan." Then followed a reproduction of almost the whole of my article. Norval Mitchell, then Chief Secretary, noted on 9th February 1947, "The most interesting thing on the subject written for many years ... I hope it has made plenty of other people start thinking; as it has me."

Sir Malcolm Darling,[2] writing from New Delhi on 23rd April, said, "I am myself all in favour of maintaining indigenous institutions, not in sharp conflict with modern notions of right and wrong, and still capable of working effectively." He wished good luck to my endeavours.

On 29th January 1947, I broadcast from All India Radio Peshawar an appeal for wholehearted cooperation from all classes in the execution of the Plan, in

---

[1] Author of *Horned Moon, Pakistan*, etc.
[2] Retired Punjab civilian on special duty with Government of India War Department 1945–46.

order to obtain maximum benefit from it. Finally, on 1st March, while on tour in Dera Ismail Khan, I gave the Convocation Address at the Vedic Bharatri College, and dealt with development and other impending changes in India.

There was thus good reason to believe that the new Pakistan Government would be interested in implementing the Plan after the transfer of power. Accordingly, soon after Lieutenant-General Sir Rob Lockhart took over as Acting Governor (in succession to Sir Olaf Caroe) I went to see him to discuss my position. I took with me a copy of the Plan and of my article in the *USI Journal*, and asked him to have a look at them and give me his advice. He suggested I should see him a week later. When I did so, he said he felt strongly that it was my duty to offer my services to the Pakistan Government specifically to prepare the ground for the execution of the Plan in tribal areas.

Here at last, when I did not want it, was the official approval of my ideas on tribal policy, which I had been trying for years to obtain without success; and ironically the approval had come from a high-ranking military officer who was not a member of the Indian Political Service.

On 28th June I wrote a letter to the Governor offering my services to the new Government of Pakistan as an Adviser on Tribal Affairs for the special purpose of preparing a plan to form the basis of relations between the new government and the tribes.

For some weeks I lived in dread lest by some quirk of fate my offer with all its conditions should be accepted and I should be landed with an assignment which, the more I thought of it, appeared increasingly difficult. I had always advocated the establishment of a Bureau of Tribal Information and a scientific commission to study the indigenous tribal organisations, in order to provide the essential material upon which to base a plan for their political development. Now in desperation I had offered to do all this single-handed, under a new government which had not yet come into existence and at a time of great upheaval and uncertainty.

On 16th July I received from the Chief Secretary the copy of a telegram from Peshawar to New Delhi, which ran as follows:

"Mallam willing serve for six months. Provincial Government agree.
His special application forwarded to Foreign separately and transferred
to Partition Office."

I began to resign myself to the inevitable. There was no certainty that the Central Government or the Partition Office would accept the recommendation of the Provincial Government on a matter concerning the tribes, but that telegram pushed my offer a stage further towards acceptance. I was intrigued with the 'agreement' of the Provincial Government, which of course meant *Dr* Khan Sahib, and I began to realise how close his thoughts and mine were on the subject of the tribes. But forces much stronger than both of us were working to prevent any further association between us. The July referendum effectively terminated *Dr* Khan Sahib's power in the Province, and by 13th August I had received my own marching orders. On that day Sir George Cunningham returned unexpectedly to the Frontier.

When I met him I asked, "Do you want me to stay, sir?"

Quick and straight came the answer, "No thanks."

From that moment I was a free man and the relief was intense; but those two words sounded the death-knell of the Frontier Development Plan. Like a carcass in the jungle, it would now be fair game for any passing predator; it would be plundered and torn apart, and very soon cease to exist as a living entity. Its importance lies, less in its intrinsic value as a contribution to the cultural and ecological development of the Indus right bank, than in its existence as a British-Indian attempt at a solution of the Frontier tribal problem. It must be admitted (I think with shame) that the British failed to solve this problem, but it can no longer be said that no serious effort was made.

On the morning of 14th August, I summoned my office staff of almost fifty, handed over my duties as Revenue and Divisional Commissioner to my successor, a very able Muslim, and said goodbye to them all. They appeared stunned. I tried my best to cheer them up but I could not get a smile out of them. The next morning, the 15th at 9.00 a.m., I attended the ceremony at which the Pakistan national flag was hoisted for the first time, in the presence of the Governor, Muslim League leaders and a large crowd at Peshawar. *Dr* Khan Sahib and his Congress Ministry members, who were still nominally in office, stayed away to avoid a possible disturbance. I arrived a good half-hour before the ceremony was due to start and moved among the cluster of officials assembled close to the flagstaff. "This is a great day for you," I said, but they would not agree. All that they could say was, "There is a lot of trouble ahead for us." There was not a cheerful face among them. I felt sorry for them. The end of British rule and the transfer of power to the new states of India and Pakistan, which should have been a dignified and orderly process had been rushed and accelerated to the point of chaos. No one with a sense of responsibility could contemplate the immediate future without acute anxiety.

I was passing through the crowd towards my car after the ceremony when I was stopped by a Hindu journalist who I knew slightly. "Sir," he said, obviously under the stress of great emotion, "I am ready at this moment to accept Christ as my Saviour." His words astonished me. I did not think that anyone except the Governor knew of my intention to get ordained, so I asked him why he had said this. His reply was, "Only Christianity and the power of Christ can save Muslims and Hindus from flying at one another's throats now." He died, I believe, a few days later during the mass killings of Hindus and Sikhs in Peshawar.

As it would be some weeks before I could get a passage home, I went up to enjoy the cool air of Nathia Gali. The familiar little hill station was almost deserted and I wandered about peering through the windows of empty bungalows, haunted by the ghosts of the 'good old days'.

Dreadful stories began to reach me of wholesale murders and the wiping out of Muslim village populations in the Punjab by large bands of Sikh youths who had started a reign of terror. It was said that trains were constantly arriving in Lahore station, crammed with the dead bodies of men, women and children. A vast two-way migration by road had begun of Muslims from India and Hindus from Pakistan, but many of the unarmed refugees were attacked and slaughtered before they could reach safety. I felt helpless and angry that British rule in India should end in such disgraceful chaos. Then, on 7th September, news reached me that Afridi tribesmen had entered Peshawar and begun to murder Hindus and Sikhs as a reprisal for the killing of Muslims in the Punjab. Sir George and Lady Cunningham had returned from Nathia Gali to Peshawar that day. I had no longer any official position, but I knew that Robin would be glad of my assistance in organising Red Cross aid for wounded and refugees so I returned to Peshawar on the 8th and found plenty of work to do. The secretary of the Provincial Red Cross Committee, a Sikh, was among the surviving Sikhs and Hindus herded into the Fort for protection, so I took over his duties. The lady health visitor of one of the welfare centres, an Indian Christian, was wounded and in hospital. She was also badly shocked. Many Hindu women had flocked to her centre for protection, but as it was undefended, tribesmen had entered and slaughtered them all. She somehow managed to escape and took refuge with a Muslim family. I sat by her bedside and tried to comfort her. The Red Cross were now faced with two large refugee problems: first, Hindu-Sikh refugees in the Fort; secondly, Muslim refugees beginning to stream in from the Punjab. The two had to be kept strictly apart. I asked our Sikh Red Cross secretary to setup a temporary centre in the Fort and supplied him with medicines, materials and female staff for the women and children. The large Lady Cunningham Provincial Welfare Centre looked after all Muslims. It pleased me to see the institutions that Marie had planned stretched to the full. The need for a sizeable organisation, geared exclusively to the service of women and children was thus amply demonstrated, and I feel sure it was this that moved the members of the Muslim Ladies Purdah Club of Peshawar to invite me, less than twenty-four hours before I left, to talk to them on maternity and child welfare work.

I received the invitation in writing from the lady president of the Club. I could not refuse. We met in a room in the beautiful new Provincial Welfare Centre. The ladies came into the room wearing burqas, but threw them off immediately they got inside and faced me unveiled twenty or thirty of them. Some were old, some young and pretty. They were quite serious and businesslike. I had no time to prepare a set speech. I simply spoke to them about Marie and what she had tried to do. I ended by saying that I would always think of this centre as a meeting-place for the womenfolk of Peshawar. They might one day assemble here for a march through the streets, agitating for Women's Rights!

I found those last few weeks of voluntary work in Peshawar most rewarding. Robin Cunningham was tireless in her efforts to relieve the distress of all refugees, and long after I said goodbye to her at a little dinner party at Government House, she wrote to me in England regularly, giving me long descriptions of Red Cross activities.

I paid a last visit to my old friend, Mr K.A. Gai, Grocer and General merchant in the Sadar Bazaar. A Parsee of exceptional intelligence and enterprise, he had for some years supplied the British Legation in Kabul with all its general stores. He lived in a spacious house in Peshawar Cantonment, where he indulged his interest in books by converting a large room into a library. All round the walls shelves were built from floor to ceiling, and filled with volumes of the most exquisite binding.

Mr Gai was busy at the back of his shop when I arrived. As I stood waiting to see him, my eye was caught by the title of a book lying on his desk. It was a Commentary on St. Paul's Epistle to the Romans.

"I am surprised to see that book on your table," I said when he appeared.

"Oh I have several Commentaries on the Romans. By far the best is Professor Dudd's. Have you read it?"

I had to admit that I had not, and as I said goodbye, I made a mental note to acquire the book as soon as I got back to England. For some years, until his death, I received regular letters from him, and in October 1972, when in Pakistan again, I paid a visit to his daughters, who were still occupying the house.

I received instructions that a passage on a troopship leaving Karachi for Liverpool was reserved for me. I completed my packing, loaded all my worldly goods on to a lorry and jumped in myself. From that moment I too became a refugee. I said a silent goodbye to my faithful old bearer, Nasir Khan, who, like many of my other old friends, seemed so shocked by the sudden changes they were witnessing that they were unable to speak. I had bought a small shop for him in the Sadar Bazaar, vacated by fleeing Hindus, and hoped he would make a success of it; but he died about a year after I left.

I joined a tented camp at Rawalpindi, mainly for British women and children on their way home from hill stations in Kashmir and elsewhere, with only a sprinkling of men. I wore military uniform, with a crown and star on my shoulder for the first time for twenty-six years! I was given a rifle and fifty rounds of ammunition, and in due course boarded a train for Karachi, which we called 'The Paleface Special' because no servants or Pakistani passengers were allowed. We carried our own drinking water and food for four days. Slowly the train pulled out of Rawalpindi station, the long platform crowded with servants, among them my *khidmatgar*, Mohammad Din, waving a last farewell to their masters and mistresses in dead silence. It was a moving sight.

Our train passed slowly through several large stations without stopping, and we could see the platforms crowded with refugees who looked as if they had been camping there for days. Then we halted for a few minutes at one big station. I leaned out of the carriage window to see that the train was not being molested. Immediately, hundreds of refugees crowded up close, and asked me, "Where are you going?"

"To Karachi."

"Are you coming back?'

When I shook my head, "What is going to happen to us?" The utter despair in their faces was a comment on the end of British rule that I shall never forget.

CHAPTER XVIII

Country Vicar

The heir will inherit your keys,
And deep from the bins he'll fish up
The Madiera you thought to drink at your ease,
And port laid down for the Bishop.

The ship was full of serious and anxious faces. There were many women and children on board as well as troops. The female element both emphasised our plight as refugees and lifted us out of some of our depression. The voyage meant the start of a completely new life to most of the young officers and men, for whom the end of the war and the termination of British rule brought a farewell to arms and military uniform. There were a few Indians and Burmese among the young wives.

I could regard myself as fortunate in that I had visited England since the war and had a definite idea of my immediate future. I was destined to enter a theological college as soon as possible after the ship reached an English port.

The beautiful Dorset countryside seemed to welcome me as I hastened to Sherborne. David was already in the Preparatory School, with the intention of entering the big School at fourteen.

The Blenkinsops had kindly taken charge of both my sons. Marcus, then three years old, had been brought home from India a year previously by his Nanny, Violet Roach. Through these connections I got to know the School Chaplain, The Revd Tim Brooke, who passed me on to the Principal of Ridley Hall, Cambridge, and in an incredibly short time, I found myself nervously facing the prospect of entering a religious institution, catering mainly for young men half my age, all with university degrees. The outlook and attitude of the College were strongly evangelical. I have never regretted this experience, but, since retirement, have been called upon to take services in churches covering the whole range of Churchmanship. I have wondered whether it would not be better to give young ordinands some knowledge of approaches to Ministry and Sacrament different from that emphasised at any particular college.

The Principal of Ridley Hall, Allison,[1] was an outstanding man of great charm. He later became Bishop, first of Chelmsford and then of Winchester.

---

[1] The Rt Rev Sherard Falkner Allison, MA, DD, LLD.

Although younger than I, he behaved towards me like a father. For instance, the gates were closed every night at 10.30 p.m., and it was customary for any inmate returning late from some frivolity in the town to climb over the wall. Naturally, finding myself in the same predicament, I did likewise. The Principal somehow got to hear of this, and called me into his study.

"'The College wall is high," he said, rather sternly. "At your age (I was then fifty-three) you might easily break an ankle. Next time ring my front door bell, and I will let you through."

To my delight, one out of sixty-odd students at Ridley Hall was my vintage; Wilfred Pakenham Walsh had served in India in the ICS and had been a High Court Judge in Burma. Immediately we became great friends and shared rooms in the Hall. We were both barristers and soon began, rather impishly, to ask awkward legal questions during lectures. Wilfred was unhappy about the promises required at ordination. With the permission of the Principal, we obtained an interview with the legal Adviser to the Archbishop of Canterbury in London. The meeting was short, because we were all in agreement from the start.

"I accept your argument," said this legal luminarym, "but the difficulty is that to change the promises would require an Act of Parliament."

While I went through the formalities of ordination (with a few reservations), directly after leaving Ridley Hall, Wilfred, with his more meticulous mind, waited a year before he could bring himself to override his objections.

The pair of us were interested in everything that went on in Cambridge, whether connected with the University or not. Once we noticed advertisements of a public meeting at the Municipal Hall, at which the leading speaker was Harry Edwards; the well known spiritual healer, then nearing the height of his fame. We decided to attend.

On the way, we passed a stream of 'the maimed, the halt and the blind', some in bath chairs, some on crutches, some so lame that they needed the help of a friend or relative. The Hall was full to overflowing. There, on the dais, half-hidden by a pulpit-like lectern, upon which glowed a large cross in neon strip-lighting, stood the healer himself. He spoke briefly about the spiritual nature of his healing, and then got down to the treatment of his patients. One by one they struggled painfully onto the platform, then collapsed onto a seat. The healer spoke to each one personally, holding a wasted limb in his hands for a few seconds. Then, "Stand and walk." The patient made a superhuman effort to obey, thrusting one foot forward then the other, while the audience clapped enthusiastically.

Neither Wilfred nor I had ever been to one of these healing sessions before.

We did not quite know what to make of it. I have always been interested in psychic phenomena, and have for many years belonged to the Church's Fellowship for Psychic and Spiritual Studies, but I am practical enough to search for a scientific explanation, if one can reasonably be found. We would both have preferred to hear the comments of some medical authority on these 'cures', and, as the occasion was partly religious, the views of a Church dignitary (of which there were many in Cambridge). It seemed amazing that here, in the heart of a great centre of learning, a reputed healer could attract huge crowds with his miraculous cures, without a glimmer of interest from any section of the University.

After many years in the jungles of Burma (Wilfred), and the wilds (myself), the intellectual atmosphere of Cambridge was exhilarating. One day we saw a notice that there would be a series of lectures by Professor Herbert Butterfield on 'Christianity and History'.

Arriving for the first lecture in plenty of time, we found the building already packed out. It was decided to move there and then to the largest Examination Hall in the town. This was filled to overflowing once a week for the six lectures of the series. After two world wars, the mental climate was ripe for some interpretation of history, and Professor Butterfield's conclusions, which were confidently Christian, were greeted with tumultuous applause.

Among the students at Ridley there were a number of Africans and Asians. Because I knew something of his language and had lived in his country, I became friendly with Hassan Dehqani Tafti, who came from Iran. Being highly intelligent, he had studied deeply both Islam and Christianity, and was in a position to draw a comparison between them, particularly as he had been born and educated in a predominantly Muslim country. He used to say that intellectually Christianity was by far the more satisfying. After leaving Cambridge he had an interesting career. He married the daughter of Bishop Thompson of Iran, and eventually became Bishop himself. I have met him again in England, since his elevation, and keep in touch through the Iran Diocesan Magazine.

Soon after entering Ridley Hall, I went to London to receive the CSI (a parting gift from India) from King George VI at Buckingham Palace. Allison asked me to show him the insignia. There was no sign of interest from the students in such worldly matters. However, I was asked to give a talk about missionary work on the North West Frontier, and managed to make them all laugh with stories of Flora Davidson in Kohat.

Towards the end of the course, I went to Kidderminster, in the Worcester Diocese, to be interviewed by the Vicar of St. George's, who was in need of a deacon. On my return, I described to the Principal the conditions I found there.

"The Vicarage is dilapidated, wallpaper handing down in damp festoons, a pile of unanswered correspondence on the desk, and the Vicar himself unmarried."

"Oh, I don't think you ought to go there," said Allison, with some concern.

"I believe it is just the place for me," I replied. "The Vicar is a saint, a scholar, and one of the most charming men I have ever met."

I wanted experience of an industrial parish before I got too old, and the West Midlands was an obvious objective. I was ordained Deacon in Worcester Cathedral on Trinity Sunday, 1949. Parish work, including intensive house to house visiting, is a wonderful cure for loneliness or depression. I missed Marie and our children terribly, but had no time to brood over my misfortunes and the days were filled with other peoples' troubles. I had lived abroad for so long and had lost touch with the thoughts and feelings of English men and women. In the centre of a large industrial town, I was introduced to a host of new experiences, and met with real friendliness almost everywhere. It was soon obvious that any mention of India raised a barrier, the old prejudice against Imperialism, so I kept quiet about my past, only mentioning it occasionally in sermons designed to compare Christianity with other religions. My rooms in Chester Road South were comfortable, but far from luxurious. The landlady was strict and strait-laced. I had to be in by 10.30 p.m. or give an explanation, and the bath water was limited to three or four inches!

These rather spartan conditions attracted the attention of the daughter of Canon W.H. Cory, Vicar of Wilden near Stourport, with whom I became friendly. Sophronia Cory and I began to see a good deal of one another. Soon we became engaged. We were married in Wilden Church on 6th July 1950 with her father officiating. However, it was another eighteen months before we were able to collect the whole family under one roof. The curacy of St. George's was followed by Priest-in-charge of Broadwaters, a new parish on the northern boundary of Kidderminster, consisting almost entirely of a recently built housing estate. This was an interesting experience in what might be described as pioneering pastoral work, with few ready made resources.

Our base was a largish all-purpose building, housing Church, Parish Hall, and a Dance Hall which was well patronised by a young community, particularly on Saturday nights. I forgave a certain amount of rowdiness provided the services on Sunday were well attended. I became the first Vicar of Broadwaters, but left after only a short while to take over a country parish at Eckington, near Pershore, in the southern part of the Diocese of Worcester. Here, a large rambling vicarage, with an extensive garden, provided an ideal home for our children, now three in number, a daughter, Anne, having been

born on 14th August 1951. Our eldest boy David, had graduated to the big
school at Sherborne, earning a minor award (being eligible for the following
three exhibitions: as the son of a WWI soldier, of a Barrister, and of a Priest!).
Marcus entered the Dragon School at Oxford, being also destined for
Sherborne School, where he later won a scholarship.

Phro and I look back on the thirteen-and-a-half years spent at Eckington
with the greatest pleasure. On the face of it, the job was a sinecure: a small country
parish with only one Church, set plumb in the middle of a village, easily accessible
to all the inhabitants, and adorned with a beautiful Norman arcade, to which
we added a stone altar in the South aisle, according to the style of that period.

A single church, with a population of under one thousand is a luxury
unknown to clergy in the mid-seventies, when no incumbent has less than two
and often more churches to serve, with populations running to many
thousands, sometimes scattered over large areas of countryside.

The changes that have taken place, however, since I retired from Eckington
in 1965, at the age of seventy, have not necessarily meant more work for the
clergy; what they have meant is less pastoral service for the people, and this, to
my mind, is a tragedy.

Regularly every Sunday at Eckington Church I took three services, Holy
Communion, Matins and Evensong and frequently, in addition, a Children's
Service in the afternoon. During the week there was always a Parish Meeting
and a Choir Practice; any spare time was fully occupied in intensive house-to-
house visiting.

Soon Phro and I knew each individual of every family in the village. One
day I opened the front door in answer to the bell.

"I am correspondent of the *Birmingham Post*," announced the gentleman
on the doorstep.

"What can I do for you?" I asked in some surprise.

"I have come for more information about this alarm clock business," he
replied quite seriously.

After racking my brains for a few seconds, I remembered a recent heading in
a local newspaper entitled, 'Vicar calls on his parishioners with an alarm clock.'

"As you have travelled all the way from Birmingham for this story, you
must come in and hear it," I told him, shaking with laughter:

Comfortably ensconced in my study, I recounted the true tale.

Recently my wristwatch had stopped, and was under repair. One evening, as
I was about to leave the Vicarage to hold a Confirmation Class in the Vestry, I
looked round for a portable timepiece to take with me. I had an understanding

with the young people in the class that if they turned up punctually at 7 p.m., I would not keep them longer than three quarters of an hour. They had kept loyally to their side of the bargain. I wanted to make sure that I kept mine. An alarm clock just happened to be handy, so I picked it up, and went off to the vestry. When the class was over, I decided to call on a parishioner who lived close to the Church. He invited me into his house.

"Do you mind if I leave this clock on your hall table?" I asked.

"By all means," he replied, as we went into a room to talk. I was just saying goodbye, when, to my horror, the alarm went off.

Now, that story went round the village, and some bright person thought the local newspaper might be interested. "Lo and behold," I said to my guest, "it has brought you all the way from Birmingham."

Parsons, particularly country ones, are often credited with queer idiosyncrasies. Sometimes we wondered what the villagers thought of us. There was no central heating in the vicarage, and the rooms were large with high ceilings. In very cold weather it was impossible to warm them, so I wore a Chitrali *chogha* inside the house, sometimes Tibetan boots and a woollen Moroccan cap as well. I must have looked more like a Muslim Mullah than a Christian Vicar!

For the last half of our stay, I was District Commissioner for Boy Scouts in the Pershore area, and Phro was Divisional Commissioner for Girl Guides for the Evesham Division.

Almost every evening there was a meeting of some kind in the Vicarage. In addition, we had a large garden with extensive lawns to keep tidy for the annual Church Fete. It would be unfair to give the impression that a country parson's life in the fifties and sixties was easy. There was a perpetual strain of maintaining a good attendance on Sunday. Many were apt to believe that the duty of 'hauling' people into church rested exclusively on the shoulders of the Vicar. There was the evergreen argument that parsons can easily cause offence by the way they take the service, or by some remark in the sermon (although in the old days, priests were apt to speak their minds and even name names from the pulpit), so why should they not accept responsibility for attracting new worshippers? I was always racking my brains for new ideas to brighten up the services. In Eckington, I was fortunate in having (apart from excellent Church Wardens) a good choir with a strong musical tradition and a loyal and reliable organist, but the old levers, 'hell' and 'damnation', were gone. The villagers were rapidly emerging from the poverty of an isolated rural community, and many had given up their time-honoured pursuits to commute to Cheltenham,

Worcester and Birmingham. Some held responsible jobs in Dowty's, Metal Box and Leyland.

The village was going ahead fast, and the Vicar had to get 'with it'. Towards the end of my time, I decided to do just that, and risk scandalising the old faithfuls by staging a Pop Service. The young people now had their own guitar group, which became very popular for local dances. Talking to the group, I found them enthusiastic; we worked out the skeleton of a service and they rehearsed really hard.

The result, on an Easter Sunday afternoon, was loud and vigorous, but surprisingly reverent. Towards the end of the service, the west door opened and into the packed church came a lady, who stood spellbound just inside. A few minutes later she almost embraced me, though I had never seen her before. She told me that while passing the church in a car she had heard the sound of guitars which intrigued her so much she had to stop and look in. She was brought up in Eckington as a child, but had spent most of her life in America. She was thrilled to find the old church so full, and echoing to the sound of young voices.

One other Service sticks in my memory: we named it 'The Bengal Lancer Service', because the preacher was my old friend John Harris. As related before, we were both in the 2nd Bengal Lancers. John, known to everyone as 'the Brigadier', possesses a commanding (though very lovable) personality, and was for some years Vicar of Burbage, near Marlborough. No one seemed to think it strange that, while he was there, most of the boys of the village joined the Army!

In comparison with other possible avenues of employment open to a retired Government servant in his early fifties, the Ministry of the Church of England offered a number of advantages, the most important of which was independence. The Vicar of a country parish was, to a large extent, his own master as the Bishop was far away, the Rural Dean too busy with his own parish to interfere much in any others. Theoretically, complaints against the Vicar by his own parishioners could at any time be lodged with higher authority by a Churchwarden, and once a year at an Archdeacon's Visitation, these elected representatives were asked to make, verbally, a confidential report on their Minister. I remember one occasion on which a pistol was pointed at my head by an irate mother who threatened to report me to the Bishop unless I appointed her daughter a Sunday School teacher!

The Deanery Clergy met once a month at a 'Chapter' presided over by the Rural Dean. I soon discovered it was necessary to clarify my position in my own mind in regard to Church affairs and policy, outside the parish. Entering the Ministry at fifty-five, you can't expect to take charge; it was a case of lending a hand. This meant that relations with fellow clergy were easy and uncomplicated. My background was very different from theirs they were the professionals. I spoke my mind on occasions, but did not press a point that was likely to upset the apple cart. This attitude could be at times a bit of a strain. Curiously, no serious climax came until my eightieth year, when I found myself at the centre of a controversy in the Deanery Synod over changes in the ruble of the Ministry, consequent upon a drastic reduction in the number of clergy in the Diocese. Some of the younger priests seemed to favour removing all incumbents from their parishes and grouping them in threes or fours at central points in the Deanery somewhat like a Medical Practice where they could supervise lay work.

"A supervisory Ministry is a remote Ministry, and a remote Ministry is no Ministry at all," I said at a crowded meeting of the Synod. "It would be like turning all the clergy into bishops, or into Dukes of Plaza Toro; who lead their regiments from behind! The place for the clergy (however few on the ground) is in the front line."

These remarks seemed to upset my younger and more militant brothers, so, rather than embarrass them in their task of adjusting the ministry to the changing times, I resigned. I do not regret the remarks or the resignation. It was time for me to go.

I claimed to speak with authority, however, in the field of 'Comparative Religion'. I had personal experience of Hinduism, Islam and Buddhism, and since retirement have made a study of the Indo-European migration (about 1500 BC) which links ancient Greece and Rome with Iran and India, with a corresponding link between European languages and Sanskrit.

In September 1965, at the age of seventy, I retired finally and went to live in Pershore, only three-and-a-half miles from my old parish at Eckington.

Some dread retirement, wondering what they will do with their spare time. Others look forward to it eagerly, picturing themselves (rather as we used to do in India) living a life of ease in a cottage on the Cotswolds, with their feet up on the mantlepiece, or strolling along to the local for a pint of beer and a bit of company. In practice, the problem boils down to the simple question of finding something interesting to do.

Often this will necessitate a complete break with past habits and timetables, and starting afresh with new interests, new tools, new hours of work, and the exercise of different muscles! A retired parson does not need to change his habits or his timetable. He can continue to take services on a Sunday; local clergy are usually glad to know of a priest to turn to, when they are ill or on holiday. The Diocese, also, relies on a certain number of retired clergy to do duty for longer periods during a temporary vacancy, before the appointment of a permanent incumbent.

As this kind of work involves no parochial responsibility (beyond hatching, matching and dispatching!) it is not a heavy strain. I have officiated in all the country churches round Pershore, some twenty-six of them, rejoicing in such names as Upton Snodsbury, Wick, Churchill, Defford, Croome D'Abitot and Elmley Castle, each with its little circle of devoted followers who supported it and cared for it with unswerving loyalty. How beautiful these secluded places of worship are, many of them dating back to Norman times, and all benefitting from the considerable wealth that has invaded rural parts of England in recent years. There is a peculiar intimacy and reverence about an act of worship taken before a small, but intelligent congregation in a lovingly tended sanctuary in the quiet of the country.

I inevitably came face to face with the changes in the Communion Service, represented by Series 1, 2 and 3. One Sunday I might take a '1662' at 8 a.m. in one church, to be followed by a Series 3 at 9.30 a mile away. The next Sunday morning a Series 2 Service would be thrown in, all of course different versions of the same Office. The reforming zeal of modernist clergy, intent on changing the Prayer Book Services at all cost, took little account of the feelings of older members of the Church, priest or lay, to whom the traditional forms and language meant so much.[2] This sacrifice of the familiar and beautiful would be readily given in return for the allegiance of many more young people to the Christian faith. The number of people who (as I write) attend Sunday Communions, though encouraging, is only a fraction of the total youth population. The age of pleasure-seeking, and unabashed materialism, is still with us, although inflation is making it all look a bit shaky.

On moving to Pershore, I was asked to become Chaplain to the local branch of the Royal British Legion. The town was full of ex-service men and their dependants. There was a clear need for someone to visit them regularly in their homes, in the Cottage Hospital, and in institutes for the elderly.

Beginning with one or two tentative calls, I worked up to about twenty-five visits a month. It was easy to become absorbed in the joys and sorrows of my little flock, reporting any problems to the monthly meetings of the Branch Service Committee.

Mr T. was gassed in the First World War. He had led as far as possible a

---

[2] 'Brigadier' John Harris, ex-Bengal Lancer, always said: "If you want me to take a Communion Service, it's 1662 or nothing!"

normal life, in spite of periodic attacks of bronchitis, until eventually his lungs gave way, and he 'existed' for the last ten years. When I first met him, he was confined to his home, struggling for breath, with a large oxygen cylinder by his chair. He could not lie down at night, and had to sleep prepped up in a sitting position. But he was blessed with an indomitable spirit, a wonderful wife and a loyal family. We became great friends he was always cheerful, loved to talk politics and, until near the end, never failed to struggle to his feet to shake hands, when I entered the room. I had the privilege of conducting his funeral service in Pershore Abbey.

'No Legs T' was another outstanding personality. As the result of a war wound, one leg was amputated, and in due course the other as well. I went to see him in hospital when he was recovering from the second operation. One might have thought that the loss of both legs would have damped the courage of the bravest man. Not so with 'No Legs T'. He kept the morale of the men's ward (usually containing some pretty depressing cases) as high as I have ever seen it. Without being a nuisance to the other patients, he amused them by his sheer determination to treat pain and physical setbacks as a joke.

There followed a long drawn-out agony over the fitting of artificial limbs. As one stump was longer than the other, the pressure was excessive first on the right, then on the left. It became impossible, even after many visits to Selly Oak, Birmingham, to hit a comfortable balance. Finally, he gave up all hope of walking, and remained in a wheelchair. His wife sacrificed a lucrative job to look after him at home, but there were long delays before an electric hoist could be supplied, and in the meanwhile she strained herself badly trying to lift him from place to place. When the precious hoist at last arrived, and 'No Legs' triumphantly pulled the cord to lift himself into the bath, there was a loud crack: the seat, made of some plastic material, split open at the back, and the old man began to fall. Fortunately, his tall, muscular son, who was looking on, caught him before he hit the side and a new hoist was ultimately supplied. By that time his wife was as much an invalid as 'No Legs' himself, but the two of them laugh at their misfortunes; a truly marvellous couple!

Many of my visits are to widows of ex-servicemen, living alone. Most of these old ladies are housebound with blindness or arthritis, but they are fascinating to talk to. They employ all sorts of dodges to keep me in the room, changing the conversation rapidly from one subject to another. It is extraordinary how strong these personal attachments can become.

In recent years the position of Remembrance Sunday as a national institution has become uncertain. As the men and women who participated in the wars die off, the original object of Remembrance disappears. There is increasing interest in the idea that on one Sunday in the year we should recognise the debt we owe to the past to all those known or unknown, who throughout the world and in all history, have gone down into the depths of suffering for the sake of future generations.

As one gets older, it is easy to be saddened by the decline of the old country from the proud status of a world power to the insignificant position of a small problem island off the west coast of Europe. There are elements in our present situation which may exasperate many: the lack of positive leadership; the necessity to bow to the dictates of powerful trade unions, committed to furthering sectional interests; the feeling of being swept along by a few trendy intellectuals, lacking a knowledge of human nature; of being uprooted from the healthy soil of tradition, and cast upon a slag heap of uncertainty.

Our world in the late seventies seems to have lost its values. Religion has been undermined by materialism, morals by laxity, education by lowered standards, excellence by dull uniformity, prosperity by borrowed wealth, the beauty of nature by pollution, individual responsibility by bureaucratic power, the rule of law by thuggery.

As a parson I am interested in the cure. If the root cause of our present ills is spiritual, no amount of surface change will be effective. I am suspicious of the revolutionary; his motives are too often personal ambition, greed, hate, jealousy or pure destruction. In the areas of our national life, of which I have experience: religion, law and democracy, I am convinced that we rest on a sound foundation. What is needed is a deeper, more general concern for the strength and stability of these three pillars of our wellbeing.

The British brand of democracy is, I am sure, the freest, the fairest, the most humane social and political system the world has ever seen. Its very excellence exposes it to attack by unscrupulous marauders; it can also be destroyed from within. It has spiritual roots, which need constant care and nourishment. Because these roots are invisible and can be ignored, they are in danger of withering away.

The preservation of democracy is an art, not easy to learn. Possibly, the only specialists in this particular field, with experience extending over many centuries, are the Pathan tribes of the old North West Frontier (where else in the world will you find a living indigenous democracy?) They can be said to have won the struggle with British Imperialism. They emerged from a hundred years of bloody confrontation, with their democratic machinery severely damaged, but their spirit unbroken.

They would say: "Good leaders are invaluable, particularly in times of crisis; but, as soon as any individual, or group, within the body politic begins to get powerful, knock him down hard!"

They based their lives on three fundamental principles: firstly, that no one can be trusted with power for long. They were acutely aware that power corrupts. No Pathan would willingly bend the knee to a dictator.

Secondly, they knew instinctively the need for constant alertness to preserve their way of life. They would understand Edmund Burke's famous aphorism: "All that is necessary for the triumph of evil is that good men do nothing."

Thirdly, they acknowledged, universally and deliberately, the predominance of religion in tribal affairs, although this meant entrusting the Mullah with a good deal of secular power. The submission was both spiritual and severely practical. It involved an unquestioning belief in God as Creator and Governor of the Universe, and a stern Judge of men. It involved fear of the consequence of wrongdoing. The reality of this fear is well illustrated in the story of Molly Ellis, rescued from the clutches of Afridi tribesmen, with the help of Mullah Mahmoud Akhunzada, who inspired holy terror in the minds of the murderers.

Fear of God's ability and intention to bring every man, woman and child to judgement, whether in this world or the next, helped to raise the moral standard of this free community; I have already mentioned its power to preserve the sanctity of the oath.

Nowadays Christianity plays down this element in religious belief. Compassion and unselfishness are more positive things than fear. At the same time fear remains, becoming acute in times of hardship and distress: fear of the power and the majesty of God, fear of the unknown, fear of our enemies, fear of pain and death, fear of all the mystery and blind cruelty of nature, and the conscience-stricken fear of exposure and punishment. These fears are a real part of our experience.

It may be that when we are passing through a period of extreme materialism, of violence and contempt for the feelings of others, a wholesome fear becomes necessary to the survival of religion and freedom. The conviction that our world is based ultimately on truth and justice turns us all into sinners. Yet some are much bigger sinners than others, and there must be atonement for man's inhumanity to man.

Beatus vir qui timet Dominum.

The Great Frontiersmen

Well before the end of the war, it was obvious to most Englishmen serving in India that a term had been set to the life of the Empire, though no one could anticipate the sudden clipping of the end by the Mountbatten guillotine. There were two ways of looking at this situation:

You could either cease to initiate any new schemes or policies, keep the routine of Government ticking over, and just wait for the end, perhaps pruning here and there, to make it look as tidy as possible.

Or, you could go all out to make a last resounding contribution to the welfare of India, so as to enable the departing rulers to leave behind a good impression. Try as one might, some of the darker patches of the British record could not be obliterated, but one could at least strive to close a chapter of history in an atmosphere of goodwill.

The Government of India chose the latter alternative. As soon as the end of the war was in sight, they initiated comprehensive schemes of cultural and economic development throughout India, unprecedented in the whole history of British rule. Every Province was required to prepare a Five Year Plan for implementation as soon as the war was over. The Central Departments in Delhi were strengthened with experts on every conceivable subject to scrutinize these plans, before they were passed for implementation, and huge sums, drawn mainly from Post War Credits in England, were made available to finance them. In response, India made a valiant effort to become development-minded. As those responsible for the preparation of the plans were soon to discover, the whole idea ran counter to the deeply ingrained fatalism of Hindus and Muslims alike. Scientific development of all the resources of a great subcontinent and the objective of universal prosperity, was a new religion that had to be preached patiently and persistently to an incredulous public, inured for generations to unrelieved poverty. Once a start had been made, it attracted an immediate and enthusiastic response from all the Provincial Ministries, as well as from the small, educated section of the public.

The Frontier Ministry was no exception. Once the idea of developing the Province and the tribal areas as a single economic unit as far as the Durand Line (thus eliminating the administrative border) took hold, Congress and Muslim League Ministers alike welcomed it wholeheartedly.

The picture was very different when it came to the Governor and to some

Senior British Politicals and Heads of Departments. To them the Frontier was no place for development, and the very idea of including the Tribal areas was ludicrous. "All the tribesman understands is war, and raiding the comparatively rich towns and homesteads in the plains." One or two Politicals who had entered the service via Oxford or Cambridge and the ICS, would add, "I don't believe in development initiated by Government. If it comes at all, it must come from below by private enterprise."

In the strange intransigence of the last two Governors, Cunningham and Caroe, may lie the answer to the question so often asked by historians of this period, "Why did the British fail to solve the tribal problem?" All through the war, when Caroe was Foreign Secretary in Delhi, and Cunningham was in Peshawar, these two men were closely associated, and to understand their post war attitude one must look behind them to the legend of the "Great Frontiersmen".

The North West was not of course the only frontier of India, yet it gripped the imagination of the British all over the world in a unique kind of way. Quite apart from the old threat of a Russian invasion of India through Afghanistan, there was a romance about the idea of a lone Englishman holding a bastion of civilisation against barbarians, while British and Indian solders fought bloody battles over steep and rugged mountains near the roof of the world against a cunning and ruthless enemy. Adding a sparkle and vivacity to the whole picture was the warlike figure of the barbarian himself: a clear-eyed, bearded Pathan of magnificent physique, almost European in features and colouring, his head swathed in a floppy *pagri*, his shirt outside his baggy trousers, bare toes showing through leather chaplis, over his sheepskin waistcoat a bandolier studded with cartridges, and in his hand a modern rifle apart from his illiteracy, the equal of any man on earth. The aggressive independence of the Pathan was a challenge to British Imperialism. His virility provoked in some Englishmen the baser and more primitive instincts of human nature. It was inevitable that the Frontier should throw up a dynamic type of British administrator. The Great Frontiersmen were all men of action, brave, stern, tough – at times as ruthless as the Pathan. Remoteness and insecurity gave them powers that would not be exercised in other parts of India. They became larger than life. Their names resounded throughout the Empire, and found immortality in history books: John Nicholson, Herbert Edwardes, Mackeson, Deane, Roos-Keppel. These were what Philip Woodruff calls "The Founders" they were of the calibre that carves out new dominions; they were autocrats, paternalistic, reactionary, men who lived fox their own times, who gloried in the danger that gave them prominence, and scorned the very idea of peace and progress. Among these men there was a sneaking respect for Pathan democracy, but most could see in it only lawlessness, anarchy, chaos; they dismissed it as unworthy of civilised recognition and never took the trouble to study it and understand it thoroughly. On the other hand, they posed as experts on everything connected with the tribes; they guarded the Frontier as their own particular preserve; they were supremely confident of their own ability to handle tribesmen without any detailed knowledge of the internal working of the tribe   and they had more than an element of truth on their side. Men like 'Griffy',[1] 'Bunch'[2] Parsons and George Cunningham knew instinctively what went on in the tribal mind. They were superb at handling a large jirga of well over a hundred rough-looking characters shepherded like sheep into a level shaded plot in the open air; and asked to sit down on the ground. The Political Officer addressing them knew all the tricks, the phrases, the jokes, the old Pushtoo proverbs, the poking of innocent fun at the British, which could keep rows of turbaned squatting figures swaying with mirth. But these displays of histrionic skill did not necessarily mean that the British were the masters. The Pathan was no fool. Time and again the greatest of the Frontiersmen had to acknowledge failure to achieve submission to the demands of government, without the use of force. The presence of the army and later the RAF as well preserved the tradition.

Cunningham and Caroe belonged to this tradition; but by 1940 it was beginning to lose its 'raunaq' (shine). Eight years previously in 1932, the great man in Peshawar had been deprived of half of his autocratic powers by the elevation of the Frontier Province to the same status as all other Provinces in India. The old Chief Commissioner had become a 'Governor', a constitutional head, the real power being vested in Ministers responsible to a democratically elected legislature. The Great Frontiersman was not however wholly extinguished by this conversion. He still retained autocratic powers over the independent tribesmen who lived between the administrative border and the Durand Line. His task as Governor now became complicated. He was required to do a balancing act to be diplomatic with his right hand, and autocratic with his left. He had to be strictly constitutional in his attitude to the Provincial Ministry, although allowed a free hand in dealing with the tribes. Cunningham was masterly in this dual role. He combined an air of authority with an irresistible charm of manner. He had a detachment and sense of humour that saved him from commitment to any single party in the legislature, and he

---

[1] Sir Ralph Griffith.

[2] Sir Arthur Parsons.

could effortlessly descend to the level of the ordinary tribesman. Under his wing, succeeding Ministries gained experience and power, and by 1940 had begun to take an interest in the problem of the tribal areas. The tribes were after all their own kith and kin, and responsible Ministers began to resent more and more the invisible line (the so called administrative border) that separated them. Sir George had no difficulty in keeping such ideas under control during the war; but he became alarmed as soon as plans were formulated for large-scale development of the Province and tribal areas as a single unit.

Although the antipathy of Cunningham and Caroe is not easy to explain, it was in keeping with the tradition of the Great Frontiersmen, all of which equated with weakness the slightest diminution of the autocratic power of the Governor over the tribes. It will be recalled that the only agency available for the implementation of the Frontier Plan in tribal areas were the Provincial departments under the control of the Ministers, who, through these departments would inevitably share some of the Governor's power.

Could it be argued then by the Governor or by the military that development in tribal areas presented a threat to the safety of India? In reply it could be said that the Frontier reputation for insecurity was largely British manufactured.

After the Third Afghan War of 1919 the threat of the invasion of India through Afghanistan, which had for years been rapidly fading, almost entirely disappeared. The problem facing the British was much less a Frontier, than a purely tribal one. If the British could reach an understanding with their own tribes east of the Durand Line, based on mutual confidence and respect, the fabled insecurity would vanish overnight. Pathans were intelligent enough to react to a threat against any part of the Muslim world, but in general it could be said that they seldom 'caused trouble', unless provoked, when they instinctively turned to arms. And they were provoked, specifically both in the Province and in Waziristan.

The decision of the Home Government to deny the Province the benefits of the Government of India Act of 1919 downgraded the Pathan in the eyes of the rest of India. Consider the enormity of this provocation to a race whose forbears had once been rulers of the sub-continent. The whole of Hindu India, comprising hundreds of millions of human beings, were imprisoned within one of the most vicious social systems the world has ever seen caste. Created by the Aryan founders of Hindusim, in order to perpetuate the enslavement of India's dark skinned aboriginal inhabitants, known as Dravidians, caste (under the guise of religion) split the population into five original divisions, within which a man was condemned by his birth to live, work, marry and die.

The highest caste, who believed themselves to have issued from the mouth of Brahma the Creator, were the Brahmans, the priestly class; next came the Kshatriyas, warriors and rulers who were said to have sprung from his biceps; below them Vaishyas, traders and businessmen, from his thighs; next, Sudras, artisans and craftsmen, from his feet; and finally, the Untouchables, the outcasts who could claim no divine origin at all. Within the system were thousands of occupational sub-castes each as rigid as the original five, spreading like a cancer through the whole body of society. It would be hard to find a greater contrast anywhere in the world between the cramped, intolerant, bigoted, pitiless existence within the four walls of Hinduism, and the simple freedom and equality of every human being in the Pathan democracy, within which was enshrined the very essence of Islam. Imagine then the contempt with which the Pathan and indeed all Muslims regarded the Hindu.

However, the British decreed that Hindus were worthy of self-government, but Pathans were not, and the man above all responsible for this decision, Sir George Roos-Keppel, was recognised as a 'Great Frontiersman'. From 1919 to 1930, the Pathans remained restive and unhappy, chafing at the indignity which had been imposed upon them, until with the support of the Hindu Congress Party, and under the able leadership of Abdul Ghaffar Khan they broke out into the revolt which ended the career of a Chief Commissioner and almost brought the British to their knees. Under pressure from more conventional Pathan leaders, such as Nawab Sahibzada Sir Abdul Qayyum, the Home Government at last saw the light, removed the injustice of 1919, and elevated the Province in 1932 to its rightful position with elections, Ministry and Legislature in line with the rest of India. Thenceforth there was peace in the Province.

And now Waziristan. After the end of the Third Afghan War, the misbehaviour of the Mahsud and Wazir tribesmen who inhabit this arid mountain tract at the southern extremity of the Frontier, could well have merited severe punishment. But the military occupation of salient points and the construction of a network of roads and fortified government posts within the tribal area was a break with the traditional policy of non-interference (apart from punitive expeditions). So long as the occupation lasted, development in this area would probably have to be ruled out altogether. Here, more than anywhere else, it could be said that the insecurity (which sometimes involved an army of 30,000 men) was British manufactured. The permanent presence of government forces, and their constant movement along winding mountainous roads, passing over numerous bridges and culverts were a threat, an irritation and an overpowering temptation to a people to whom independence meant everything. From the start of the military occupation in 1922 until the very end, when troops were withdrawn in December 1947, there was war, whether the tribes were 'quiet', or whether they were openly hostile. This does not mean to say that Mahsuds and Wazirs would not be interested in development. As soon as all troops were withdrawn, after the transfer of power, the tribesmen from this area took an immediate interest in education, and in all kinds of commercial and industrial activity inside the Province.

What stands out in the record of the Great Frontiersmen (in particular the last two) is the absence of any sense of obligation towards the tribal communities, not only in Waziristan, but all along the border. The occupation of Waziristan was justified in the interests of the inhabitants of the settled districts, who, because they were revenue payers, deserved to be protected from the predatory attention of tribal raiders. The tribes themselves (Wazirs and Mahsuds) responsible for the raids deserved no consideration, firstly because they were the guilty party, secondly because they paid no revenue, and thirdly because they lived on the far side of the Provincial border. They were beyond the pale, because they were unadministered. No single one of the Great Frontiersmen ever considered seriously the removal of the border and the inclusion of the tribes within the embrace of the British Indian administration. Either they regarded this as impossible without a genocidal war of subjugation, or they thought it much simpler and less trouble to leave things as they were. The tribes were in a cage where they could be controlled with a minimum of effort why not leave them there? Both Cunningham and Caroe clung desperately to this so-called 'solution' of the tribal problem, throughout their period of office; but long before the end of British rule, it became thoroughly discredited. Obviously no radical change in Frontier policy was feasible during the war, but as time went on public opinion in the Province, in the Ministry and in the Legislature began to assert itself in favour of removing this unnatural line, which became an offence to all self-respecting Pathans. As soon as the Frontier Development Plan took shape, it was obvious that every district was dependent economically, socially and politically on the tribal area adjoining it, and vice versa. The Province simply could not afford to leave the tribes any longer without a constructive programme of political and economic development, so as to bring them in to line with the standards set for India in general. The whole stretch of country between the Indus and Afghanistan could only be developed as a single unit; there was only one true border, the international one, known as the Durand Line, and the Government of India had a legal and moral responsibility for the welfare of all the inhabitants (whether tribal or other) up to that line.

Our last two Great Frontiersmen, of course, never saw things that way. But what of the Viceroy and the Government of India? What was their attitude? The short answer is that as soon as they saw the Frontier Development Plan, in the spring of 1947, they sanctioned it; no questions were asked. But in his book *The Indian Political Service* (pages 186–188) Sir Terence Cohen describes how, unknown to me, Frontier policy was reviewed by the Viceroy (Lord Linlithgow) in Delhi, just before the outbreak of hostilities in 1939. All his expert advisers (including presumably Cunningham and Caroe) impressed upon the Viceroy that the policy in Waziristan adopted in 1922 of military occupation and road making (referred to euphemistically as 'peaceful penetration') was sound and should continue, and that the other tribal areas were "in good shape". Linlithgow agreed reluctantly, with the important exception of welfare. "In the improvement of the welfare of the tribes, and the extension of civilisation among them, I cannot resist the conclusion that we have failed or failed at any rate in a material degree." And then, as if conscious that he was being driven into an equivocal position, he quoted the following important pronouncement of 1936, which had been communicated officially to the Afghan Government:

> "The policy of the Government of India in regard to their tribal territory is to preserve the peace of the border, foster good relations with the tribes, and gradually to introduce standards of civilisation and order into the tribal area together with the improvement of their economic conditions. Moreover, it is their policy to pursue these ends by peaceful means and in agreement with the tribes, and not to resort to military action except where it is necessary to do so."

The divergence between the official policy of the Government of India and that actually in force on the Frontier was so wide that one can only assume that the Great Frontiersmen in Peshawar (possibly backed by the military) had got into the habit of snapping their fingers at the Viceroy.

The Viceroy's words make it clear that ever since 1936, in the view of the British rulers of India (as opposed to the Great Frontiersmen), the safety of the inhabitants of the settled districts could best be achieved by a close and friendly understanding with the tribes, rather than by holding them at arms' length, or by continuous confrontation. Now supposing for a moment that Cunningham and Caroe had followed the lead of the Viceroy and identified themselves from the start with the whole concept of developing the Province and tribal areas as a single economic unit, the Frontier Development Plan would have seen the light of day very much earlier than the spring of 1947; implementation would have started well before the actual transfer of power, and an entirely different slant would have been given to the history of the British connection with the North West Frontier. It would still have been necessary to relate the wars, the disturbance and the blood-letting; but before the end a new spirit would have appeared, a spirit of understanding and mutual confidence, born out of a readiness by the British to welcome these unique indigenous democracies, reconstructed where necessary, into the modern world of India.

Our last two Great Frontiersmen would claim that they were realists, facing the unpleasant truth that the tribesmen were brutal savages, whose independent spirit would have to be broken, before they could be accepted as equals in a civilised world. Such a conclusion takes no account of the past glories of these remarkable people. No race with a history as proud as the Pathans could justly be denied the benefits of Western civilisation.

Would the tribes themselves have rejected all efforts to link them with the Province, all advances into their mountain strongholds by representatives of the Provincial departments in furtherance of a development plan? Everything would depend on the initial approach, and on the success or failure of efforts to convince the tribesmen that the British Government's change of heart was genuine. Here the co-operation and advice of the Ministers, legislature and leading personalities in the Province would have been indispensible. Yes, but once you let the Ministers into the tribal areas, the Great British Frontiersman is dead!

APPENDIX II

Notes on a visit to Pakistan and the North West Frontier
October 1972

Under the shock of defeat in war with India and the loss of the East wing to Bangladesh, the Pakistan Government under President Bhutto has split up the one unit of West Pakistan and recreated the Frontier Province. Pathans are once more autonomous and free to express their National consciousness. Whether they are any happier is doubtful. Their immediate political choice is apparently a puritanical Islamic dictatorship under a Mullah, as Chief Minister.

While we were in Peshawar, the fast in the month of Ramadzan was enforced by stringent penalties under the law, and we watched a mob of University students smash up the leading hotels, including the well-known Dean's Hotel, on suspicion that they were serving meals to Muslims. The Police were there but did not interfere.

This kind of behaviour is apt to exasperate the more progressive Punjabi, who is anxious to develop Peshawar as the most popular and attractive Centre for tourism in the whole of Pakistan, and by this and other practical means to make the Frontier more self-supporting financially.

A puritanical Islamic rule also threatens progress in other directions. It enforces purdah more severely than ever, and by lowering the status of women impedes the social advancement of the whole community. Organisations for the welfare of women and children, such as those founded and planned by the British, are still in existence, but starved of money and support. There are schools for girls and colleges for women but very few female students are visible in the streets. There is something sinister about the sight of an exclusively male population on the roads and pathways of Peshawar Cantonment, particularly as several of them are armed; and there is a subtle cruelty about a system that educates girls up to the degree standard and then forces them to pine away in their homes, unable to follow any career except marriage, excluded from the outside world by high purdah walls.

All this is of course a domestic problem for the Governments and people of Pakistan and the Frontier. Has it anything to do with the old British Empire dead for twenty-five years? Apart from the bond of affection between British and Pathan, which is as strong, if not stronger, than ever, and which will always constrain old 'Frontiersmen' like myself to be concerned for the welfare and happiness of Pathans, the answer must surely be "No" except for one thing. I suspect that the present situation, which is in danger of causing friction between Pathans and the rest of Pakistan, is due to pressure from the tribal areas. This same pressure has swept away the rulers of the three Frontier States, the Mehtar of Chitral, the Nawab of Dir, and the Wali of Swat (the 'blue-eyed boy' of the British), and threatened the landed aristocracy in the Province. Pathans are a proud people, and when allowed to assert their separate racial identity, will naturally fall back for strength and inspiration on the tribe from which they sprang. The Welsh do it, the Scots do it, the Irish do it, the Ugandans do it. Confirmation of this in a small but significant way occurred while we were in Peshawar. All Deputy Commissioners and Political Agents on the Frontier were ordered to wear Pathan dress. Some apologised to us for their appearance! Moreover, in the tribal set-up a Mullah often occupies a position of great authority. If this theory is correct, and if the present behaviour of Pathans in the Province is influenced by the attitude and mentality of the tribe, then we must look to the latter for an explanation and recognise that if social and political reforms are needed, it is here that they must start. You cannot expect the Pathan to step into the modern world and play his full part, unless you bring the tribe with him. It could be said that the British failure to recognise this vital truth during the hundred years in which they ruled the Frontier is in part responsible for the present situation.

It is instructive to note that in the last two chapters of his book *The Pathans*, Sir Olaf Caroe visualises, indeed records, a Pathan Renascence, independent of the tribe. It is hard to resist the suspicion that the author's object was to divert attention from the awkward subject of the unsolved tribal problem.

To ignore this problem, to treat it as if it did not exist or as if it would in some way solve itself is completely unrealistic; but it is in keeping with the British Frontier tradition stubbornly maintained unbroken to the end.

As I sat in the garden of Dean's Hotel in October 1972, my Pakistani friend, who knew the Frontier well, complained, "Our Political Officers do not possess the experience of the world you British have."

Is it reasonable to expect Pakistan, to be able to find an easy solution to the tribal problem, merely on the ground that they are a Muslim Government? This undoubted advantage that they possess over their British predecessors encourages one to believe that the problem will receive more sympathetic attention than it did in the past. During the last twenty-five years, when great progress has been made in providing education, and a certain measure of economic development in tribal areas, there appears to have been little, if any, social and political development within the tribe. Without this, the tribe cannot grow, and may actually impede the progress of the whole area West of the Indus, giving rise to tensions between the Pathans who inhabit this area, and the Central Government that has direct responsibilities there.

Glossary of Abbreviations

AC	Assistant Commissioner
ADC	Aide de Camp (a personal officer assigned to Generals)
ASP	Assistant Superintendent of Police
Baba log	Children
Babu	Clerk, including those within the ICS
Bannias	Market sellers
Burra Saheb	Senior 'Sir'
CB	Companion of the Order of the Bath
CBE	Commander of the Order of the British Empire
CC	Chief Commissioner
Chota peg	A Drink (eg before supper)
CID	Criminal Investigation Officer (in a police force)
CIE	Companion of the Order of the Indian Empire (awarded for meritorious service
CMS	C? Medical Service
CO	Commanding Officer (usually of the rank of Lieutenant Colonel)
CP	Central Provinces
CSI	Companian of the Order of the Star of India
DC	Deputy Commissioner
Dak	Government rest house for officials and with staff
DIK	Dera Ismail Khan (a tribal district of the NWFP0
EAC	Extra Acting Commissioner
Faqir	Moslem holy man or religious dignitary
F and P	The Foreign and Political Department
FD	Finance Department
GOI	Government of India
HQ	Headquarters
IC	Indian Cavalry
ICS	Indian Civil Service
IMS	Indian Medical Service
Jirgars	Tribal elders
Jirghahall	Committee Room
Khidmatgar	deputy head of staff in a house

Khud-side	The steep slope in the mountains
Memsaheb	Wife of Head of House (feminine of 'Sir')
MES	M? Electrical Services
MO	Medical Officer
Mullah	Moslem priest or religious dignitary head of village
Munshi	Arabic language teacher
Murghi	Chicken
NCO	Non-Commissioned Officer
Nullah	River bed
NWFP	North West Frontier Province
OC	Officer Commanding (usually of the rank of Major)
PA	Political Agent
PHD	Public Health Department
Piffer	Punjab Frontier Force Rifles
PO	Petty Officer
Qazi	Moslem judge for Sharia
Riwaj	code – standards of right and wrong
SAACU	South Asian Archives Cambridge University0
Shikari	Hunting guide
Sharia	Moslem sacred law
SMCU	???
SNO	Senior Naval Officer

Index